BLACK AMERICA SERIES

HALL COUNTY
GEORGIA

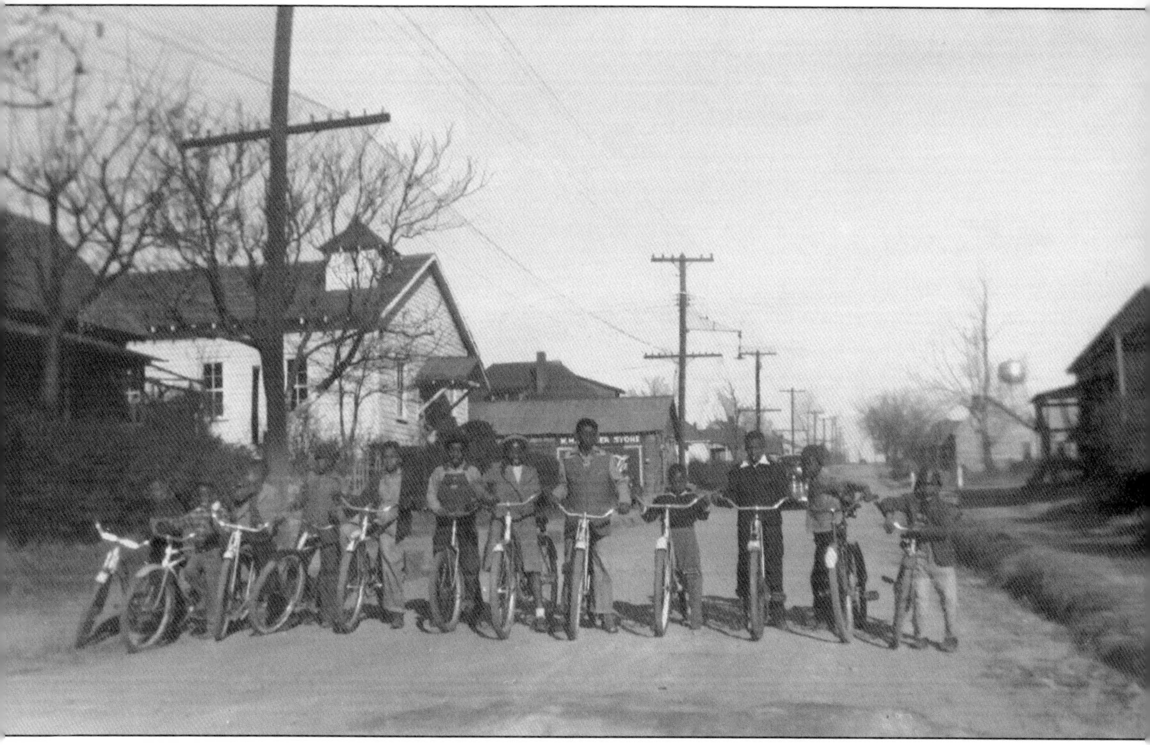

These youngsters are shown riding their bikes on College Avenue in Gainesville in the mid-1940s. The Gethsemane Holiness Church and Rev. A.J. Butler's store can be seen in the background on the left. The Fair Street water standpipe is pictured on the right in the extreme-rear background. (Courtesy of Linda R. Hutchens.)

(on the front cover) Members of Pacolet Manufacturing Company's New Holland Mill Workers' Savings Club posed for this picture in the 1930s. Pictured from left to right are (front row) Leadus Wilburn, Mance Thompson, unidentified, Marlow Byrd, unidentified, and Frank Moorehead; (back row) James Hargrove, George "Buck" Moon, Milton Hargrove, Artice Hale, Louie Chapman, and Howard Rucker. (Courtesy of Mrs. Jennie Harris.)

(on the back cover) This picture of the St. Paul Methodist Church Sunday School was taken on the steps of the church in 1927. Members pictured from left to right are (first row) Dorothy Barnett, Gertrude Kinner, Jenny Porter, Alberta Bradley, Elease Fields, Helen MaGee, Nell Cleveland, Walter Lee Brown, Ernestine Whelchel, and Elvella Whelchel; (second row) Soloamie Lipscomb, Georgia Bell Quillian, Eulalia Morrow, Hattie McHaffey, Lucy Merritt, Helen Haywood, Charlie Bell Brown, William Barnett, and Austin Brown; (third row) Bessie Strickland, Cornelia Hutchens, Ruth Owens, Carrie Kinner, unidentified, Sammie MaGee, and Gertrude Morrow; (fourth row) Robert Cantrell, William Johnson, Herman Johnson, Edward Johnson, Oscar Brown, Dupree Barnett Jr., Rev. Jacob Walter Moore (church pastor), and Lamar Kinney. (Courtesy of Mrs. Gladystine Green.)

BLACK AMERICA SERIES

HALL COUNTY
GEORGIA

Linda Rucker Hutchens and Ella J. Wilmont Smith

ARCADIA
PUBLISHING

ISBN 978-0-7385-1639-4

Published by Arcadia Publishing
Charleston, South Carolina

Printed in the United States of America

Library of Congress Catalog Card Number: 2004101190

For all general information contact Arcadia Publishing at:
Telephone 843-853-2070
Fax 843-853-0044
E-mail sales@arcadiapublishing.com
For customer service and orders:
Toll-Free 1-888-313-2665

Visit us on the Internet at www.arcadiapublishing.com

This book is dedicated to the late John W. Morrow Jr., Gainesville, Georgia's first African-American mayor; the late Willie Frances Jenkins Meadows, Hall County's first African-American commissioner; the late Patricia Brown Hudson, past historian of the Fair Street/Butler Alumni Association; and to all of the past, present, and future pioneering citizens of Hall County, Georgia.

CONTENTS

Acknowledgments

We owe a huge debt of gratitude to Mrs. Tena Dumestre of the Hall County Library, who provided us with the essential technical assistance and advice for this publication. We are grateful to library director Susan Stewart, assistant director Adrian Mixon, and reference librarian Ronda Sanders for their assistance. We are deeply grateful to all of the individuals who contributed photographs for this book. We thank our respective spouses George Hutchens and Walter L. Smith for their unfaltering support. A special thanks goes to Hall County Black History Society member James (Jimmy) Brooks, who was always willing to give an extra hand in whatever capacity needed. We thank Mr. Charles R. Morrow, our seventh-grade American History teacher, whose classes motivated us to want to learn more about our history. We would also like to thank the following individuals, organizations, and members of the Hall County Black History Society for their assistance in compiling this publication: Wilbur and Dixie Ramsey, Gainesville City Councilwoman Myrtle Figueras, Gainesville City Councilman George Wangemann, Gainesville City Housing Director Frances L. Williams, the Hall County Library staff, *The Times,* The Fair Street/Butler Alumni Association, the Men's Progressive Club, Mary Render Acree, Gary and Bobbie Jean Cox, Gladystine Burt Green, Walter J. Rucker, Nathaniel Shelton, Linda Cheeks Carruth, Doris Williams Evans, Samuel B. Evans, Una W. Fortson, Jennie Porter Harris, Berlinda Turner Lipscomb, William H. Maxey, Major Nelson, Donna Stringer, Walter and Doris Thomas, and James and Alphia Wills.

INTRODUCTION

Hall County, Georgia is a pictorial history depicting the daily lives of African-American citizens residing in Hall County. Established in 1818, Hall County is in Northeast Georgia, amidst the foothills of the Blue Ridge Mountains. The vast majority of the early African-American inhabitants of Hall County were slaves. The 1820 census compiled shortly after Hall County's inception reported 399 slaves and 6 free African Americans. By 1850, the slave population had increased to 1,336 individuals. Comparatively, the number of free African Americans only rose to seven.

In the aftermath of the Civil War, African-American citizens of Hall County struggled to survive the harsh living conditions; however, despite many obstructions, they somehow managed to achieve a small degree of success. Between 1880 and 1900, African Americans in Hall County organized a number of churches, benevolent lodges, and other organizations. In 1883, the Northwestern Baptist Association began making plans to establish a private school (Northwestern School) in Hall County. Although public schools were established in 1872, records show that only one school existed for African Americans in 1875. There were 353 African-American children in Hall County at this time. The establishment of a public school system in Gainesville, the seat of Hall County in 1892, resulted in African-American city students being housed in the Methodist church. In the fall of 1892, 120 African-American students registered for classes.

The early 1900s found African Americans in Hall County progressing in other areas. The Messenger Company was organized to produce an African-American newspaper, *The Gainesville Messenger*, which published local news. It reportedly consisted of four pages with six columns of print. Rev. J.D. Lovejoy, a community leader, served as the head of this newspaper. Prof. C.E. Williams, principal of Summer Hill School, served as the editor and Mr. J.B. Neal was the general agent.

By the mid-1900s, African-American entrepreneurs had begun to develop businesses along the corridor of Athens Street in Gainesville. In ensuing years, Athens Street evolved into a virtual "Mecca" and became a main thoroughfare for African Americans in Hall County. Here, one could have most of one's needs met in one's neighborhood without having to chance an unpleasant or undignified encounter while venturing downtown. Athens Street hosted a black theater, a drugstore, two funeral parlors, several restaurants and cafes, a tourist home, taxi stands, a shoe shop, pool halls, a record store, dry cleaners, and barber shops with shower facilities.

Many of the photographs displayed in this publication came from treasured family collections. A significant source for a large number of them was the Fair Street/Butler Alumni Association. Fair Street/Butler Alumni Association's past historian, the late Mrs. Patricia Brown Hudson, diligently collected and preserved school and community history and memorabilia for over a decade. Other pictures were collected from the private collection of Mr. and Mrs. Wilbur (Dixie) Ramsey, the Hall County Library System, the City of Gainesville, and the local newspaper, *The Times.*

This saga of pioneering African Americans in Hall County is long overdue. The Hall County Black History Society, Inc. is proud to present this previously untold story. The readers of this pictorial history will be able to reflect upon the countenances of some of Hall County's most outstanding pioneering citizens in the areas of education (Mrs. Beulah Rucker Oliver, Prof. E. Thompson, Mr. G.S. Moon, and Prof. W.H. Harper), community leadership (Rev. Green Hunter, Dr. E.E. Butler, Mrs. Roberta Cifors Morgan, and Miss Mattie Moon), entrepreneurs (Mr. George Stephens, Mrs. Rena Bush Harrison, Mr. Walter Chamblee, and Mr. Dock Harrison), and many others who helped to shape and mold Hall County. It is our sincere hope that this pictorial history will fill a historical void that, until now, has been sadly neglected. "To God be the Glory" for the great things He inspired and enabled these African-American trailblazers to achieve.

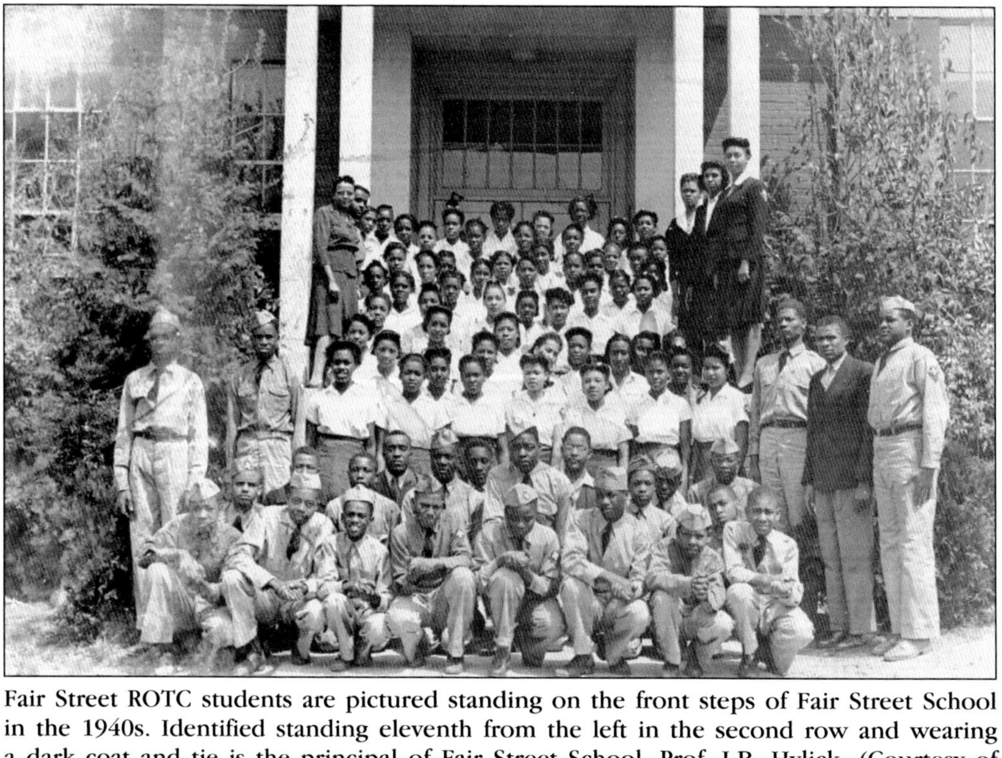

Fair Street ROTC students are pictured standing on the front steps of Fair Street School in the 1940s. Identified standing eleventh from the left in the second row and wearing a dark coat and tie is the principal of Fair Street School, Prof. J.B. Hylick. (Courtesy of James Brooks.)

One

Making A Joyful Noise
Churches

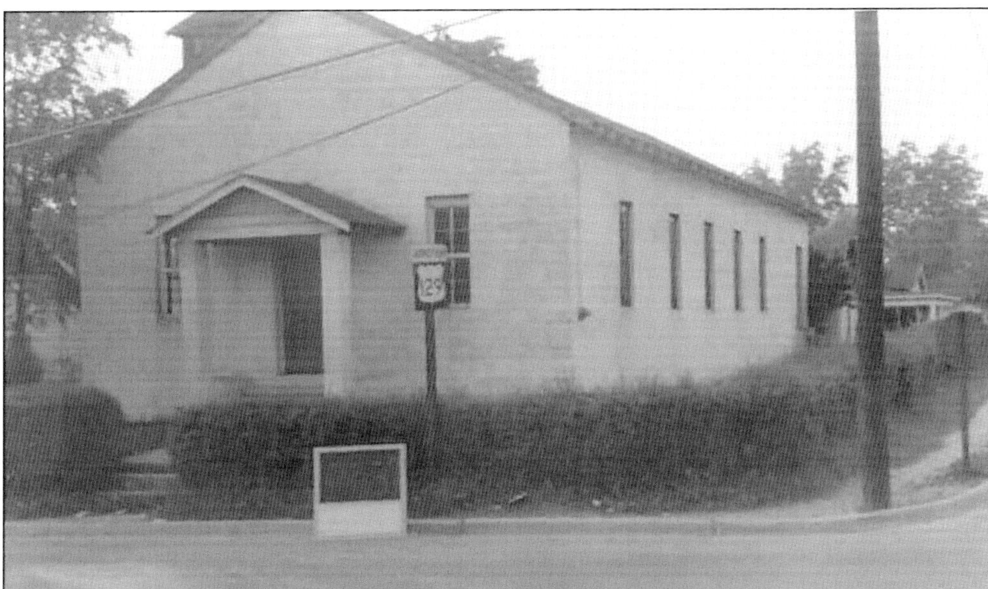

Originally located on College Avenue in Gainesville, Georgia, the Gethsemane Fire Baptized Holiness Church was founded in 1907 by Mother Nan Stanley and a few other Christians. Bishop W.E. Fuller Sr., the founder of FBH Church of God of the America, served as the church's first pastor. The church is now located on Old Athens Highway in Gainesville. (Courtesy of the City of Gainesville.)

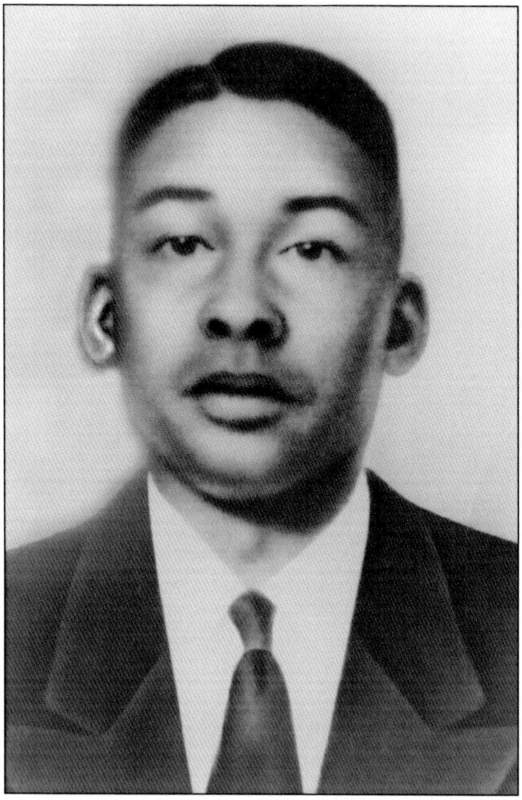

Rev. John W. Evans Sr. was called into the ministry in 1931. He founded the Antioch Baptist Church on Mill Street in Gainesville in 1941. Reverend Evans served as the pastor of Antioch Baptist Church for 25 years until his untimely death on July 21, 1966. (Courtesy of Brenda Evans Hughey.)

Antioch Baptist Church is located at 1010 Mill Street in Gainesville, Georgia. This church was once located at 634 Mill Street in the building which presently serves as Bethel AME Church. Antioch Baptist Church completed a 1.2 million dollar renovation and expansion project in March, 2004.This project resulted in an enlarged sanctuary, a new kitchen and fellowship hall, eleven new classrooms, additional restrooms, a bridal room, an upstairs video room, and a library. (Courtesy of Brenda Evans Hughey)

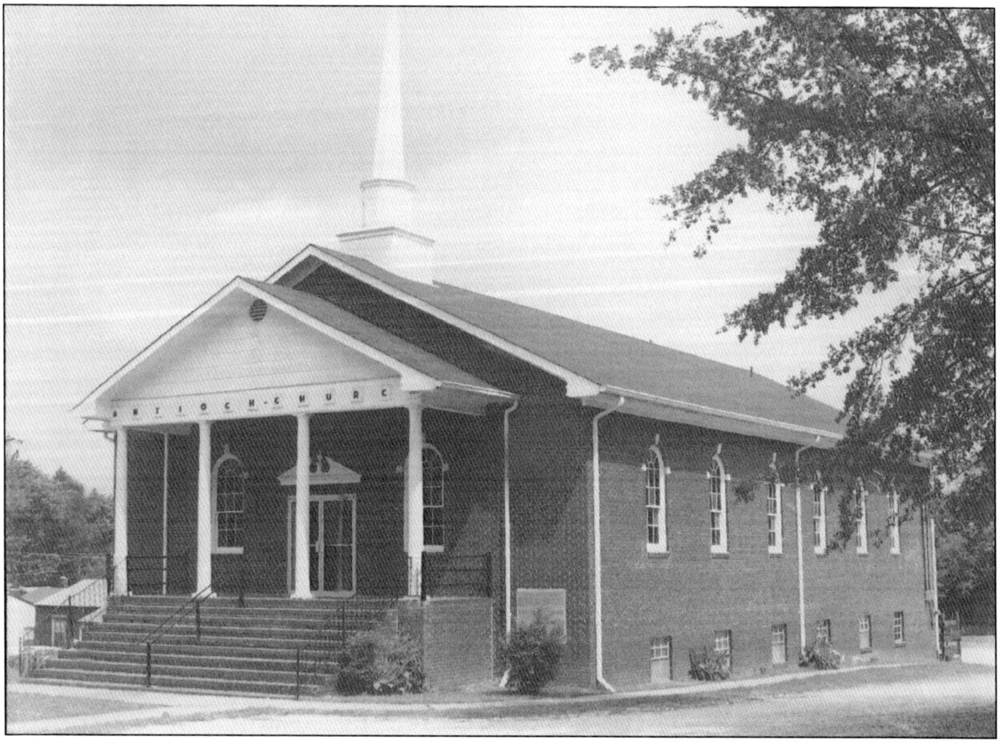

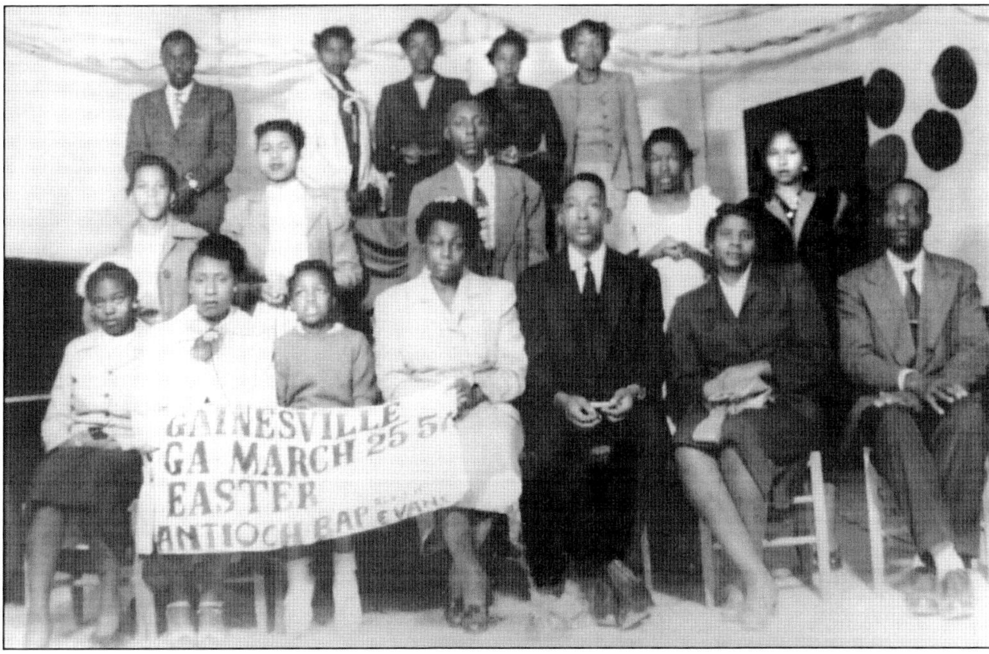

Antioch Baptist Church's congregation posed for this picture on Easter Sunday, March 25, 1954. Pictured from left to right are (front row) Lily Mae Sadler, Lucy Mae Stephens, Beatrice Evans Stephens, Trummie Evans, Rev. John W. Evans Sr., Mary Nell Lott, and Anderson Stephens; (middle row) Hazel Hopkins Buffington, Genieve Thompson, Horace Stephens, Ruby Nell Evans, and Inez Randolph; (back row) Rev. Ike Stephens, Corrine Hall, Lois Evans, Mary Jo Cantrell, and Frances Stephens. (Courtesy of Brenda Evans Hughey.)

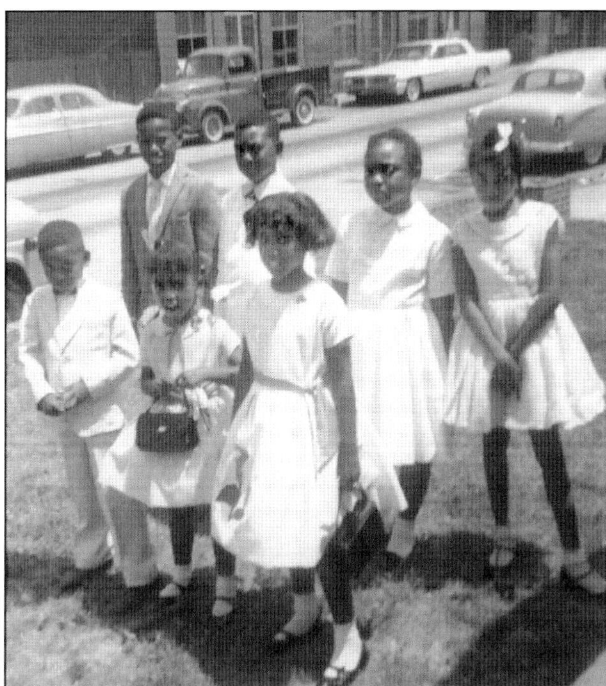

These children posed for this photograph on the front lawn of Mount Calvary Church of God in Gainesville, Georgia in July, 1962. Mount Calvary is located on Athens Street (E.E. Butler Parkway). The Oddfellow Building, which housed several African-American businesses, can be seen in the background. (Courtesy of Margaret Osborne)

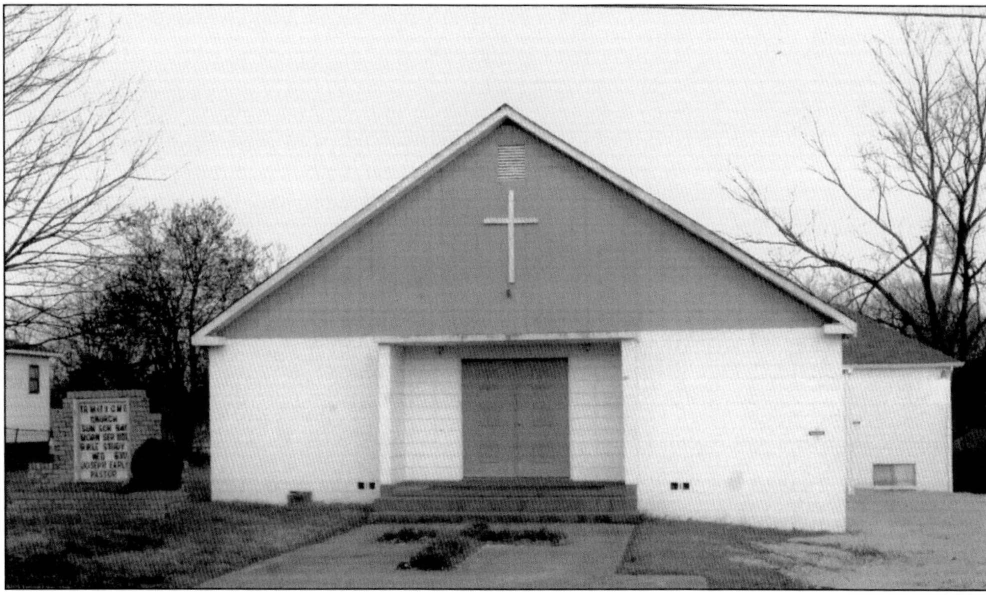

Trinity CME Church was established in 1876. The church was originally located on East Summitt Street in Gainesville. It was destroyed by the tornado of 1936, but was rebuilt in the same location after the storm. In the early 1960s, the property was rezoned and the church had to be relocated. Worship services were held in Dr. Nelson McGhee's office until property was secured on Black's Drive in Gainesville to build a new church. The present edifice was constructed in 1963 under the leadership of Rev. Alton Jones. (Courtesy of Audrey Glenn)

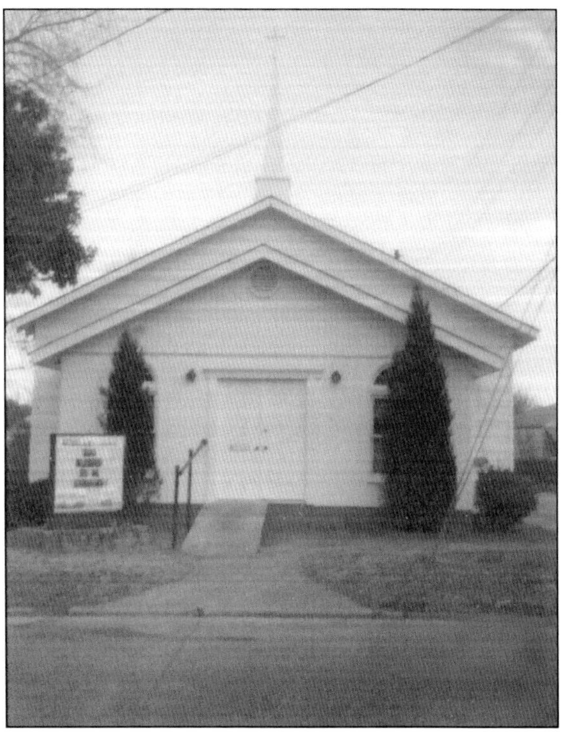

Bethel African Methodist Episcopal Church was organized and dedicated in 1901 under the direction of Bishop M. Turner, Elder C.A.Wingfield, Reverend Phillips, and a few other devoted Christians. The early church was located in Lula,Georgia. According to church records, Bethel's address changed five times between 1901 and 1915. In 1915, the congregation moved to Palmour Street. The church was destroyed by the 1936 tornado but was quickly rebuilt. Bethel remained at the Palmour Street location until 1974, when it relocated to its current site on Mill Street in Gainesville. (Courtesy of Cornelia Martin.)

The Bethel AME Church Sunday School class is shown standing in front of the church in 1945. (Courtesy of Cornelia Martin.)

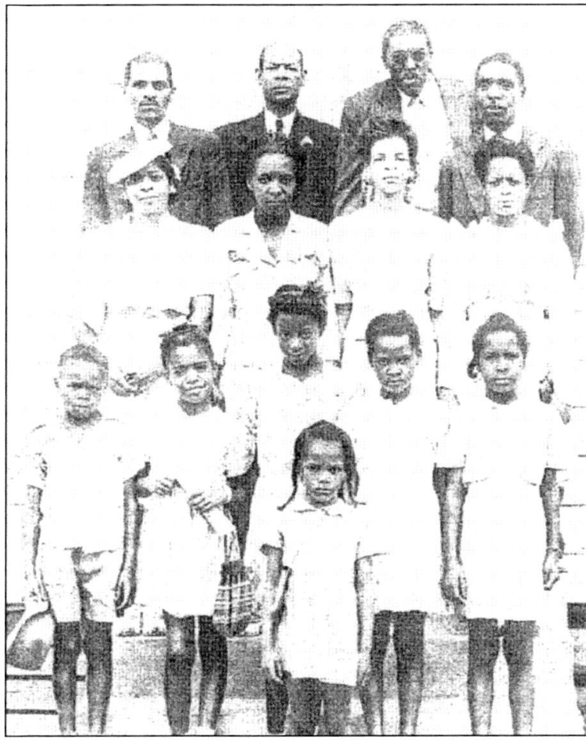

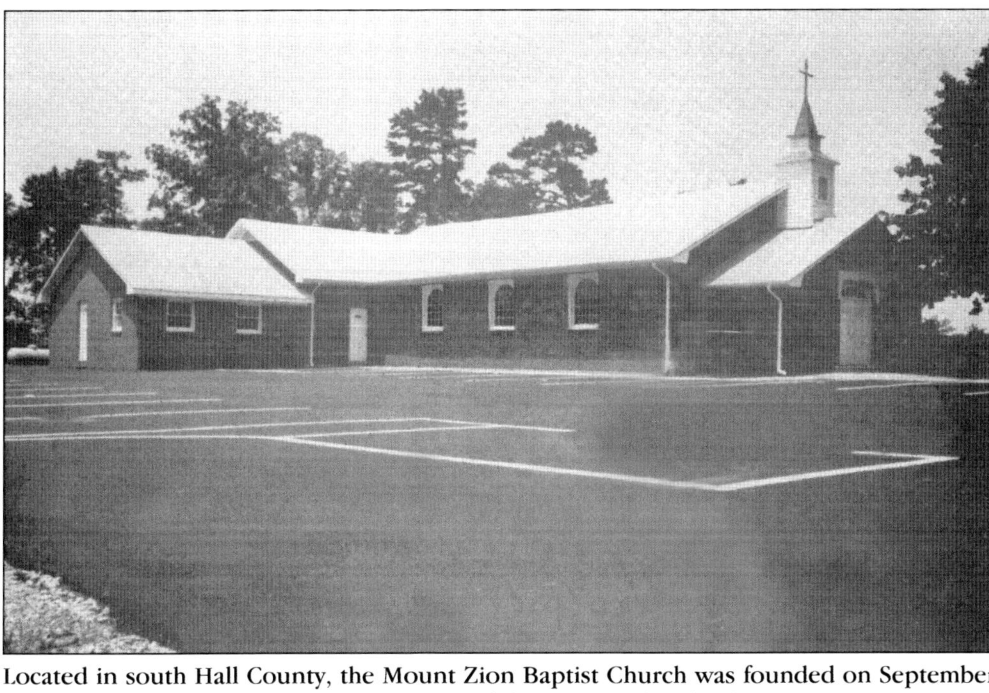

Located in south Hall County, the Mount Zion Baptist Church was founded on September 24, 1889, under a brush arbor near the site of the present church. The present structure was built in 1962 under the pastorate of Rev. W.A. Bowens. The senior deacons were Marshall Stringer, Fletcher Williams, Roy Stringer, and Dan Cowart. (Courtesy of Doris Evans.)

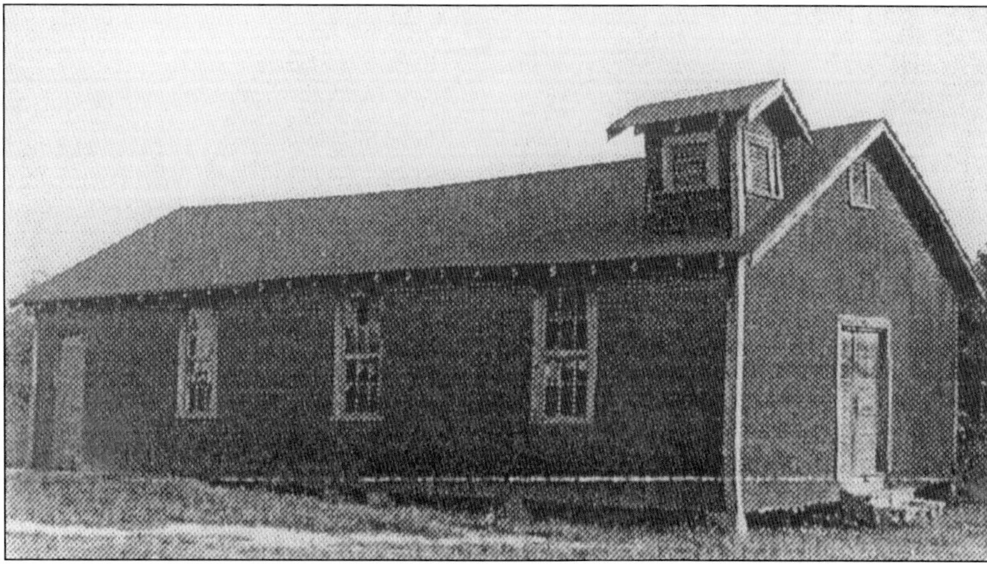

The Sanders Chapel Baptist Church, located on High Street, Gainesville, was the forerunner of the Rucker Memorial Baptist Church. Sanders Chapel became dilapidated and eventually discontinued its services and closed its doors. Beulah Rucker Oliver and Deacon Hamp Ware are credited with the preservation and rebuilding of this church. (Courtesy of the Fair Street/Butler Alumni Association.)

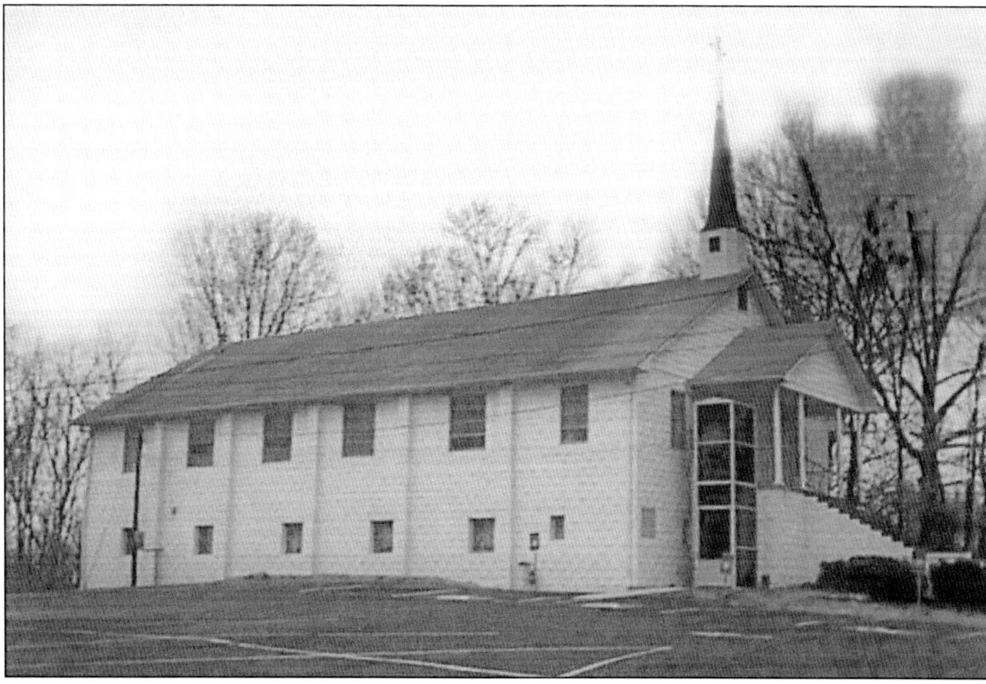

Rucker Memorial Church, located on Floyd Road in Gainesville, was named in honor of Mrs. Beulah Rucker Oliver following her death in 1963. This church's original name was Sanders Chapel. Beulah Rucker Oliver helped reorganize this church. She also donated the land for the construction of the present building. (Courtesy of Walter Lee Smith.)

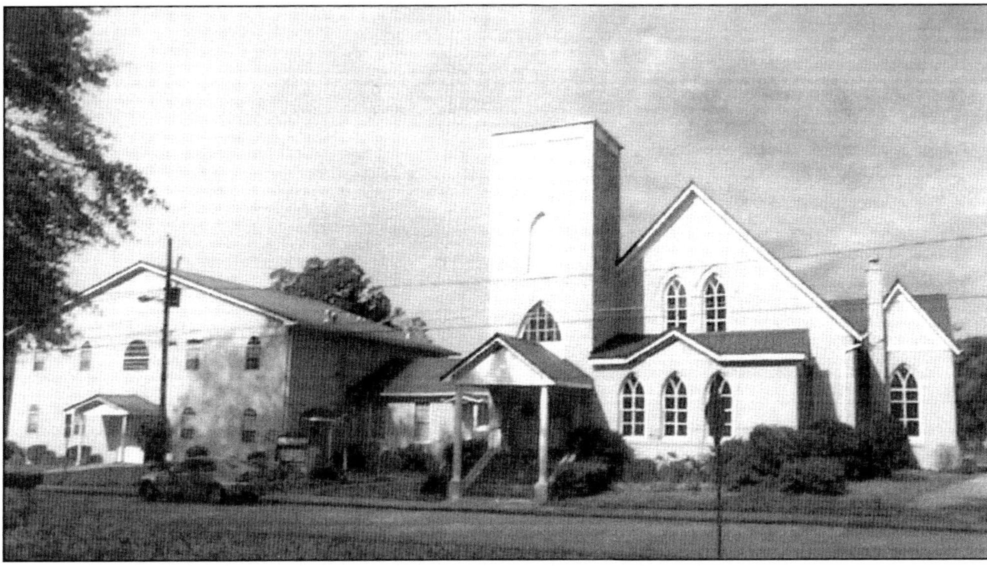

The Northern Methodist Church, which became known as St. Paul Methodist Church, was founded on February 26, 1876. The first structure was located on Rice Hill (Bradford Street) in Gainesville. St. Paul was relocated to Summitt Street after one of its members, Mr. Nelson Jackson, donated property to the church. The current structure was built during the pastorate of Rev. J.D. Lovejoy in 1905, following the tornado of 1903. This picture of St. Paul was taken during the 1990s. The church's educational wing was added in 1988. (Courtesy of Gladystine Green.)

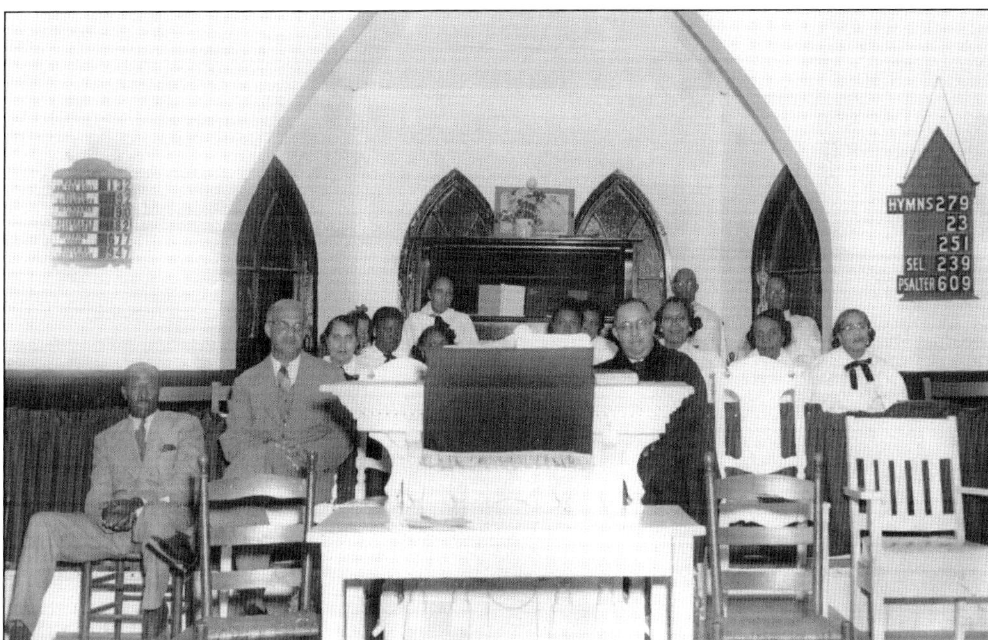

Seated in the pulpit of the sanctuary of St. Paul Methodist Church in the 1950s, from left to right, are Rev. A.J. Butler, Rev. H.H. Fortson, and Rev. F.J. Hunter, pastor of St. Paul Methodist Church. (Courtesy of Jennie Harris.)

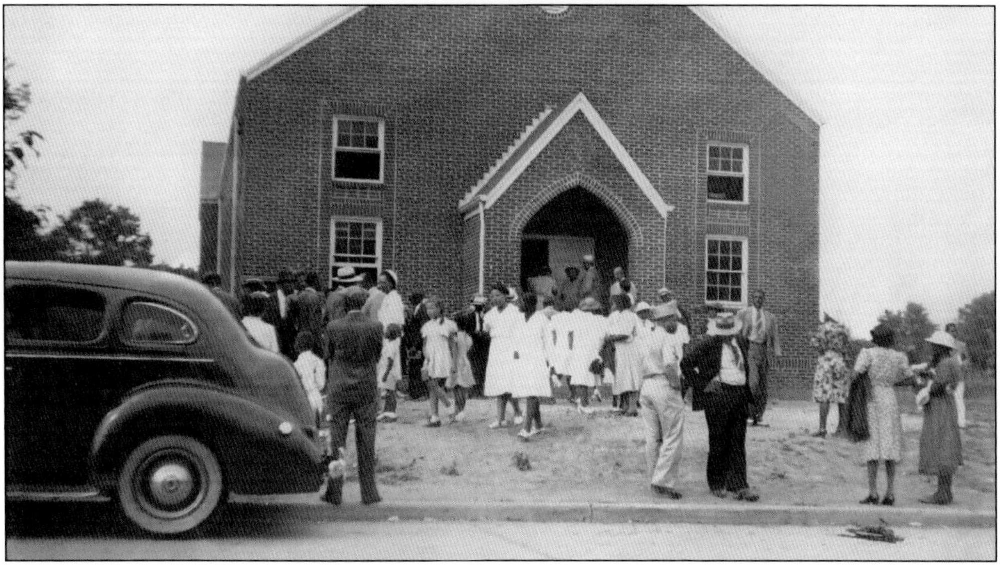

St. John Baptist Church is located at 741 E.E. Butler Parkway in Gainesville. The current edifice was constructed under the pastorate of Rev. Hosea H. Fortson in 1941. This photograph of St. John Baptist Church was taken on its dedication day. (Courtesy of Cathy McCrary Kimbro.)

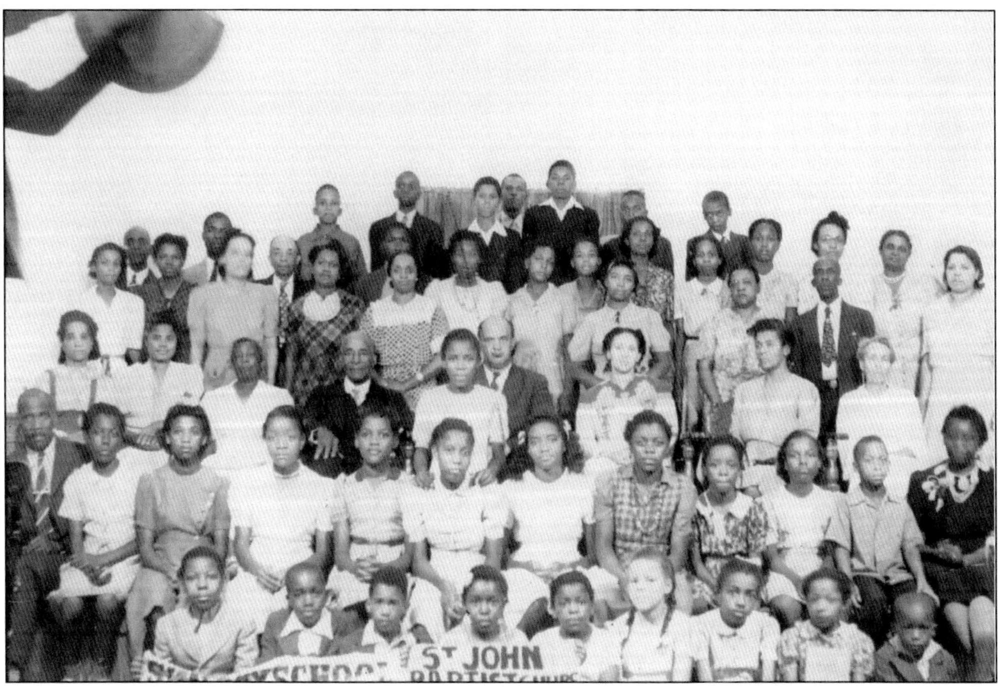

The St. John Baptist Church Sunday School assembled for this photograph on Easter Sunday morning in 1942. Identified sixth and seventh respectively from left to right in the third row are Rev. and Mrs. Hosea H. (Nannell) Fortson. Reverend Fortson served as the pastor of St. John Baptist Church for 19 years. His pastorate ended upon his death on August 27, 1956. (Courtesy of Fair Street Butler Alumni Association)

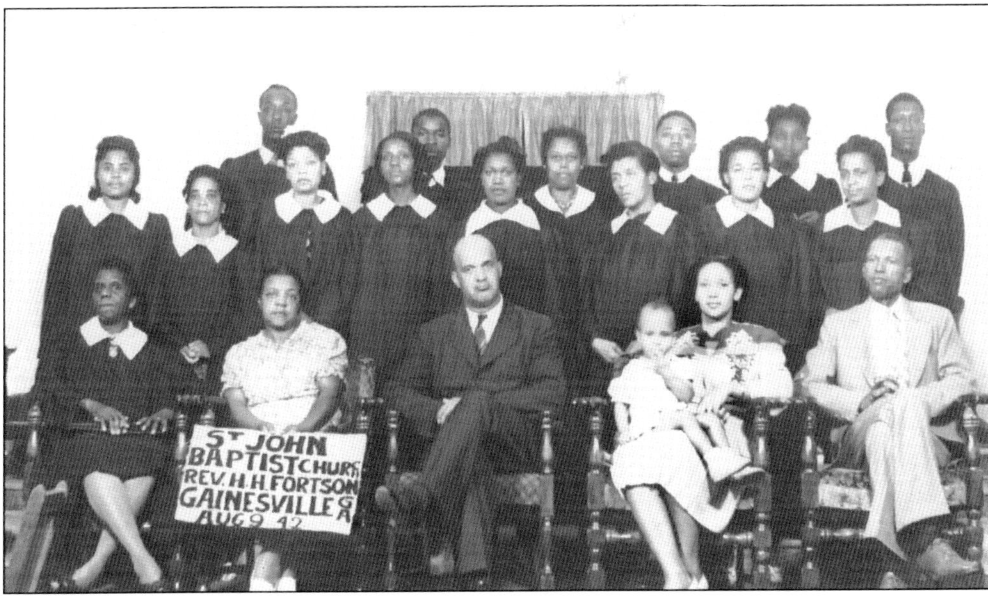

The St. John Baptist Church choir posed for this photograph on August 9, 1942. Choir members are from left to right (front row) Junior Roberts, Ella Rucker (musician), Rev. Hosea H. Fortson, Nannell Fortson with daughter, Hosenell, and L.H. Rucker Sr.; (middle row) Helen Caudle, Polly Robinson, Elise Morrow, Clara Bell McCrary, Hazel Meadows, Sallie Glover, Nettie Cook, Mildred Merritt, and Geneva Bray; (back row) Sam Thomas, Claude Norfleet, J.Wesley Merritt, Eva Colbert, and John Harris. (Courtesy of Annette Cantrell.)

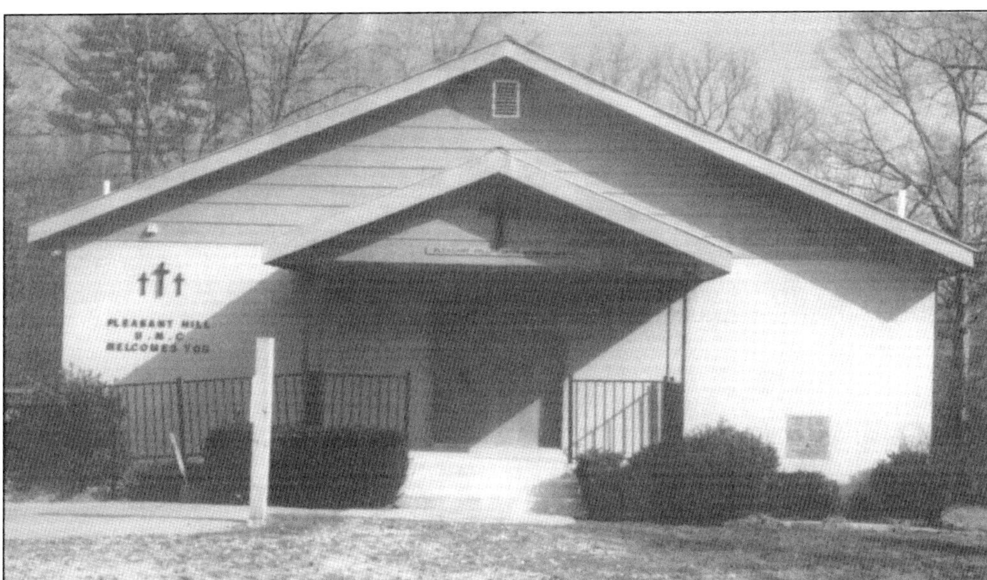
The Pleasant Hill Methodist Church was established under a brush arbor in 1872. The original arbor, one of three in the state of Georgia, still exists today. The current church building is one of three to have been constructed. Two earlier buildings were casualties of fire. (Courtesy of Rev. and Mrs. William [Shirley] Lipscomb.)

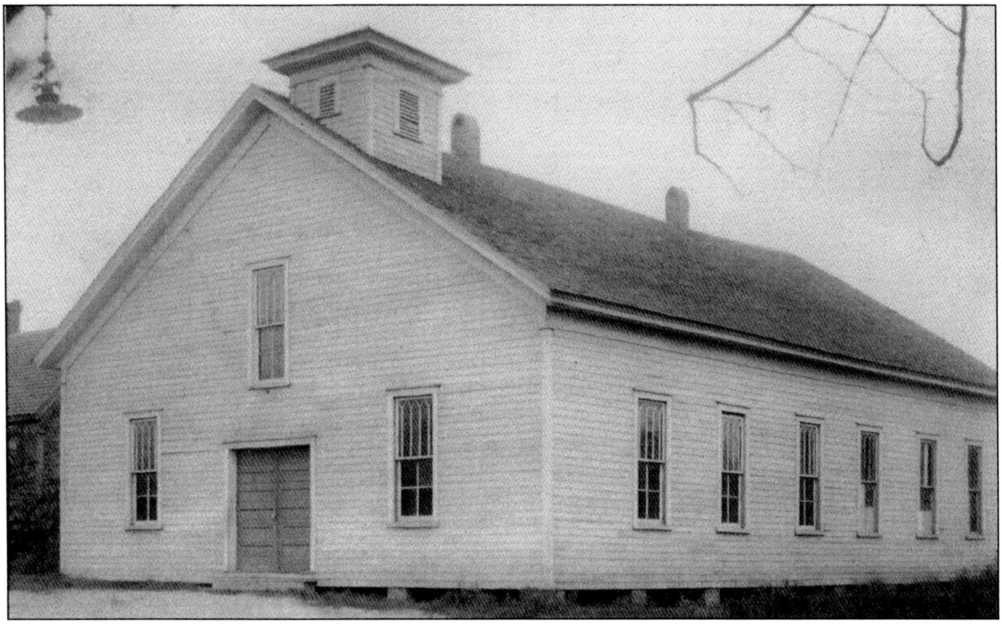

The First Baptist Church, located on Martin Luther King Drive in Gainesville, is one of the oldest churches in the Hall County area. First Baptist Church was organized in 1838. The original church building was located at the intersection of High Street and Pine Street. The current sanctuary was built in 1923 under the pastorate of Rev. William Dorsey. First Baptist is pictured here in the 1930s. (Courtesy of Mattie Lowe.)

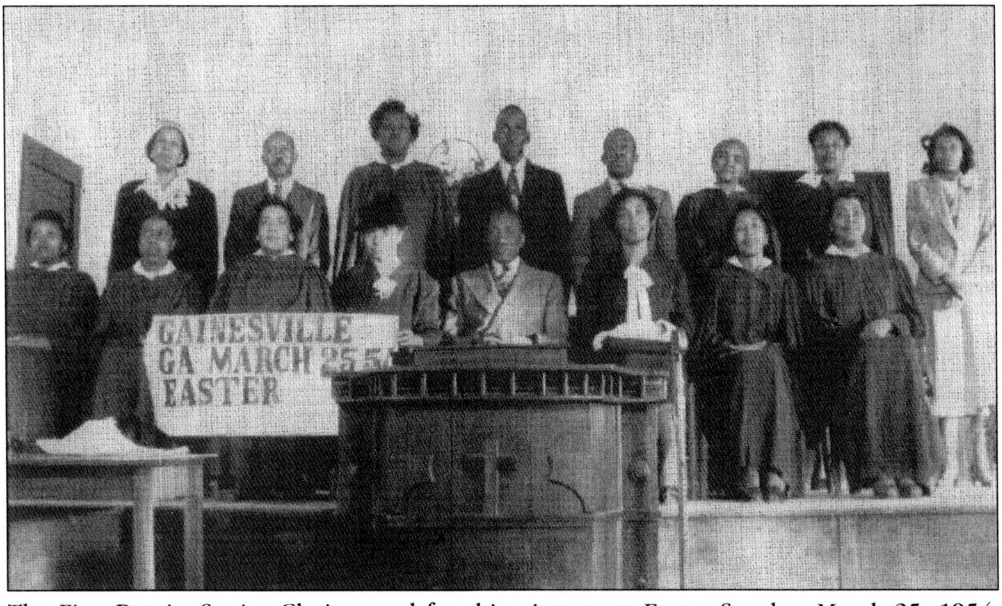

The First Baptist Senior Choir posed for this picture on Easter Sunday, March 25, 1954. Pictured left to right are (front row) Ludella Walker, Nell Randolph, Emma Thompson, Florence Thompson, L.G. Greenlee, Willie Maude Bond, Mattie Haynes, and Amanda Haynes; (back row) Pearl Moon, George Couch, Lola Mae Gatherwright, Amos Riley, Jodie Thompson, Olivia Brown, Willie Mae Bell, and Amanda Keith. (Courtesy of Mattie Lowe.)

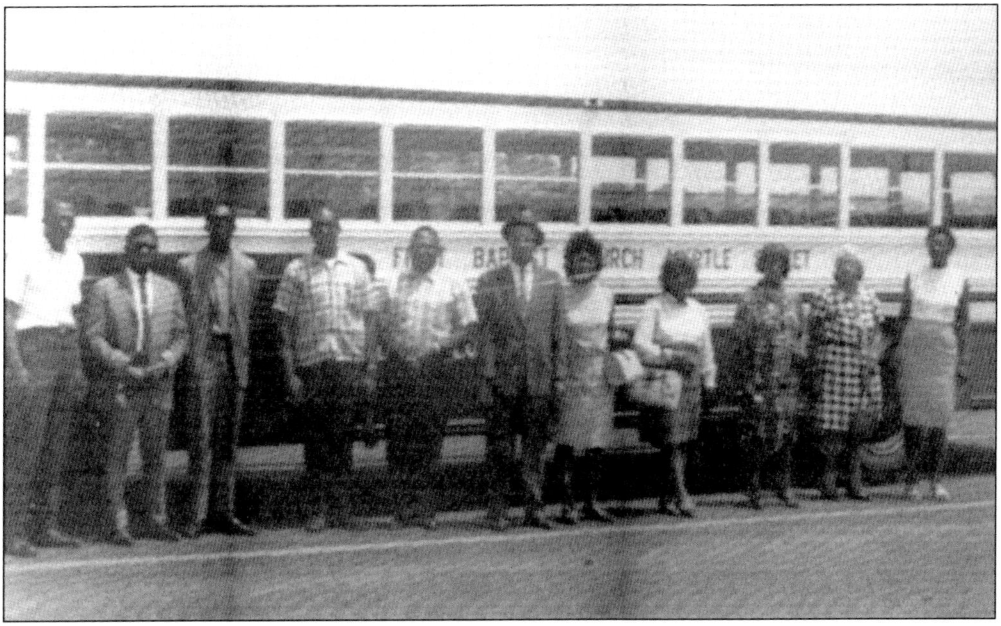

In 1969, First Baptist Church purchased a 63-passenger Blue Bird Ford bus of that year. The church paid $10,000 in cash for the bus. Rev. Calvin Williams, a native Hall Countian, was the pastor in 1969. The bus committee is seen standing in front of the new vehicle. (Courtesy of Miss Mattie Lowe.)

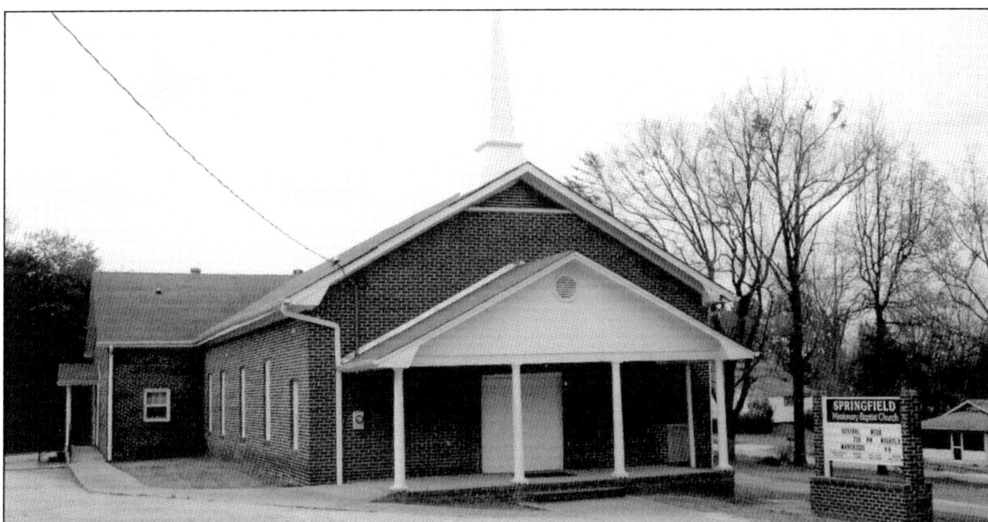

Springfield Baptist Church was organized *c.* 1875 in Belton (Lula), Georgia. Services were first held at the home of Mr. Lee Bryson, one of the church founders. Later services were held in a cotton gin until land was purchased and an edifice erected near the corner of Hammett Street and Belton Bridge Road. Springfield's current location was obtained during the pastorate of Rev. H.T. Healey. The church purchased an old school building located on property at Hammett and Sixth Street. Reverend Healey was a carpenter and some of the men of the church renovated this building to use as a sanctuary. (Courtesy of Linda R. Hutchens.)

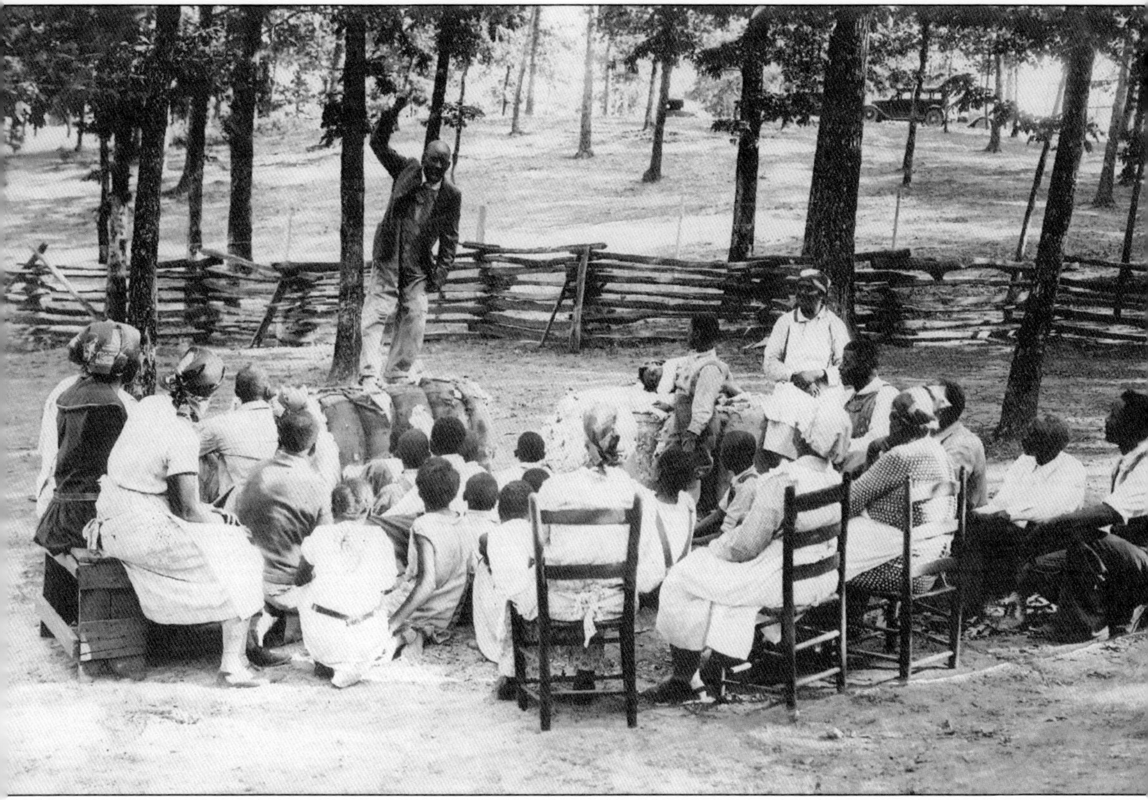

The congregation of the Springfield Baptist Church of Lula, Georgia, listens as a local minister delivers a sermon during an outdoor service. (Courtesy of Sarah Kidd.)

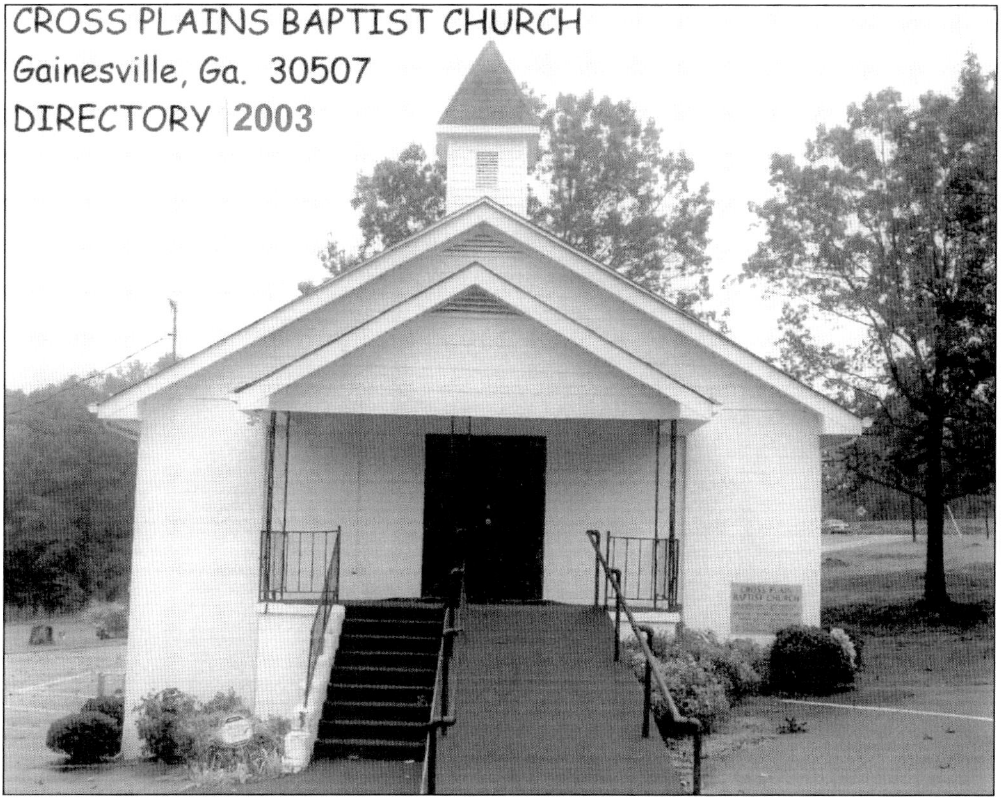

Under the guidance of Rev. Green Hunter, the Cross Plain Missionary Baptist Church was established under a brush arbor on March 18, 1879. Cross Plain Church is located off of Candler Highway in Gainesville, Georgia. (Courtesy of Judy Williams.)

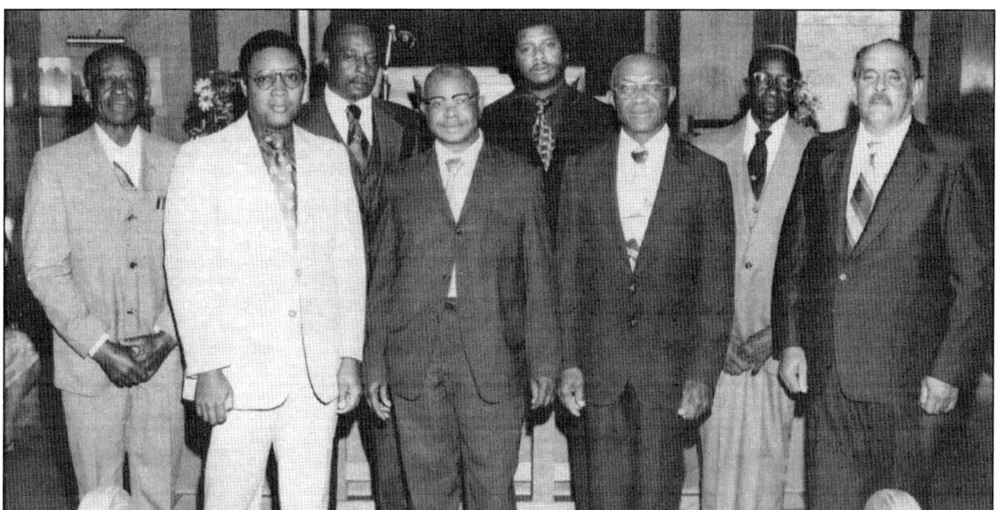

The deacons of Cross Plain Baptist Church are seen in 1979. From left to right are (front row) L.V. Young, Cedric Goudelock, Curtis Young, unidentified, and Edward Cheeks; (back row) Albert Williams, John Millsap, and unidentified. (Courtesy of Judy Williams.)

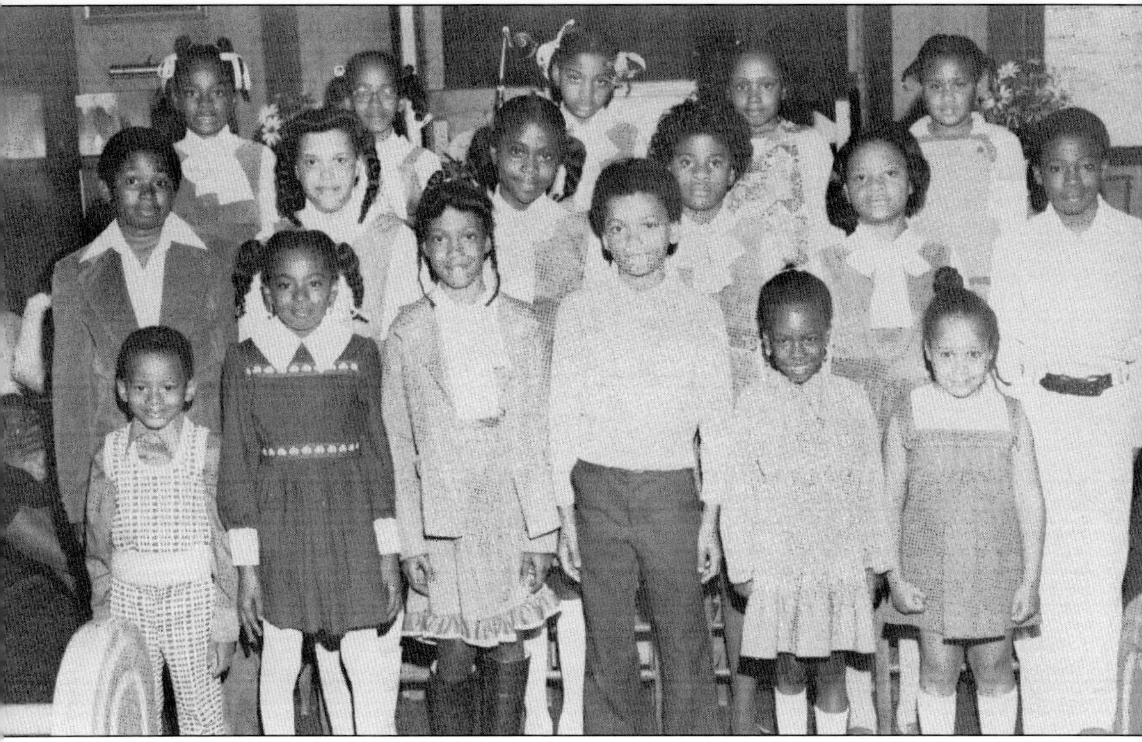

The Cross Plain Junior Ushers in 1979 are, from left to right, (front row) Jason Stringer, Rebecca "Betsy" Stringer, unidentified, Keldin Randolph, Consuela Randolph, and unidentified; (middle row) Patrick Stringer, Brandy Hester, Matavia Smith, Misty Randolph, Kim Randolph, and Stacy Randolph; (back row) Sequoia Randolph, Lequitta Stephens, Susie Randolph, and two unidentified junior ushers. (Courtesy of Judy Williams.)

Two

IT HAPPENED HERE
Landmarks

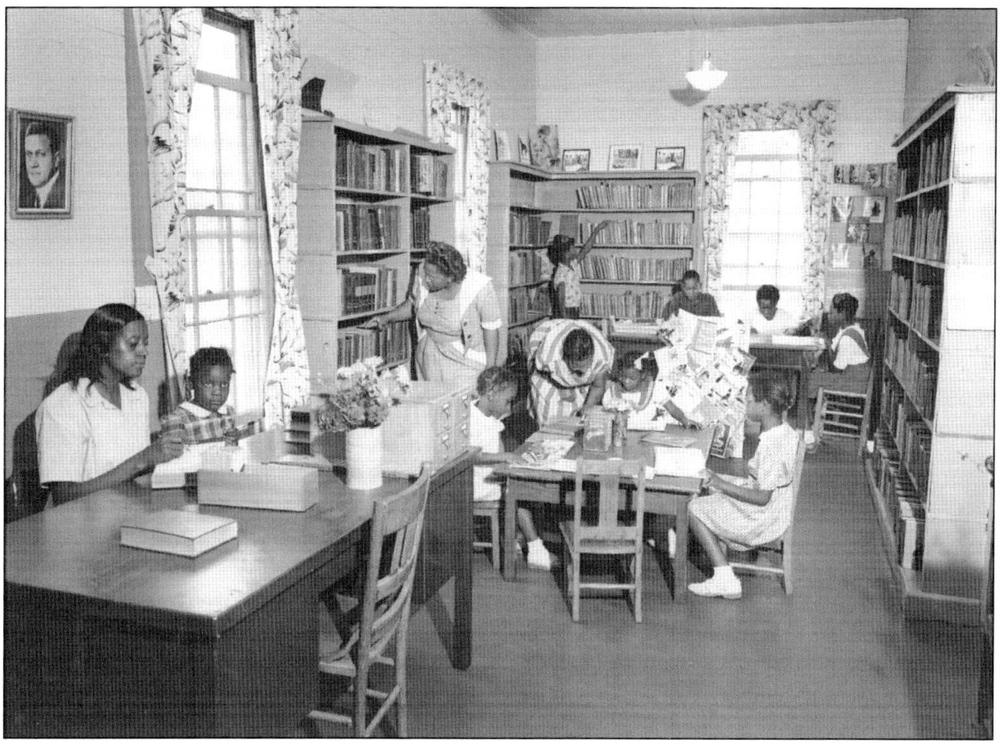

This branch of the Hall County Library was established in 1948 and was originally housed in a classroom of the old Northwestern School. It moved to the old Summer Hill School building on the corner of School and Fair Street in December 1949. In 1957, the library was renamed in honor of Miss Clara B. McCrary, who is pictured here seated at the desk with an unidentified student. Miss Geneva Bray, a teacher, examines the books on the shelves while Mrs. Ella Rucker, an assistant librarian, helps students at a front table. (Courtesy of Cathy McCrary Kimbro.)

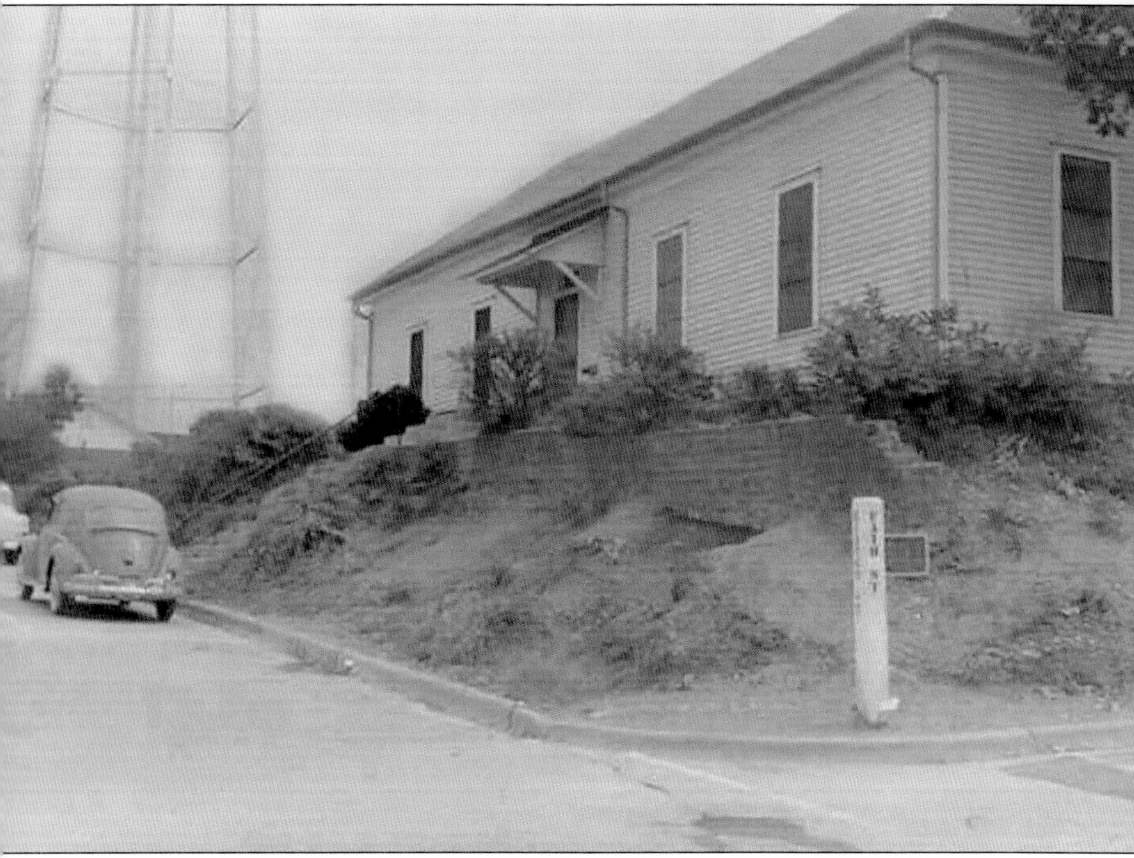

The building pictured was located at the corner of School and Fair Streets. It once served as a school lunchroom for Fair Street and Northwestern School students. Later, it housed the McCrary Branch of the Hall County Library. (Courtesy of Cathy McCrary Kimbro.)

Roger Wilmont of the Gainesville Eagles baseball team stands on the Dock Harrison ball field off the Old Athens Highway in Gainesville. This ball field was owned by Dock Harrison. Today, this is the location of Harrison Square Apartments. (Courtesy of James Brooks.)

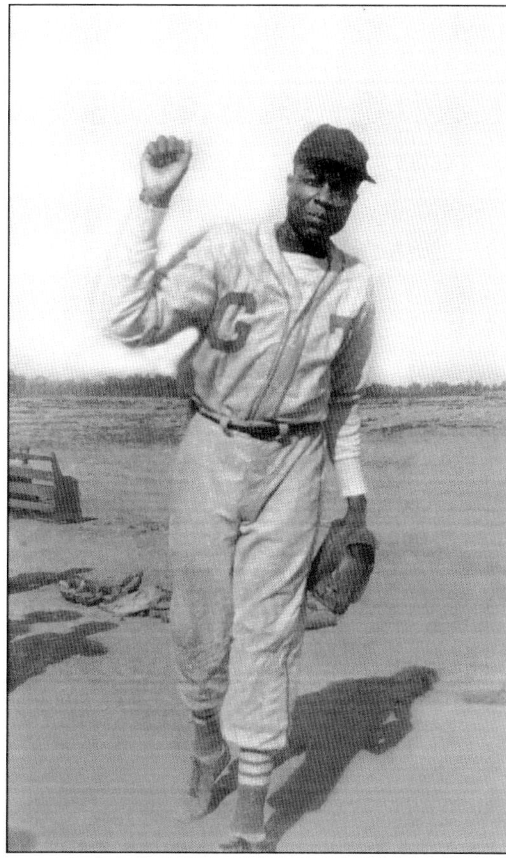

Dock Harrison Lake, a popular recreational spot in the 1950s and 1960s, is located off of Old Athens Highway in Gainesville. It was owned by Dock Harrison. (Courtesy of James Brooks.)

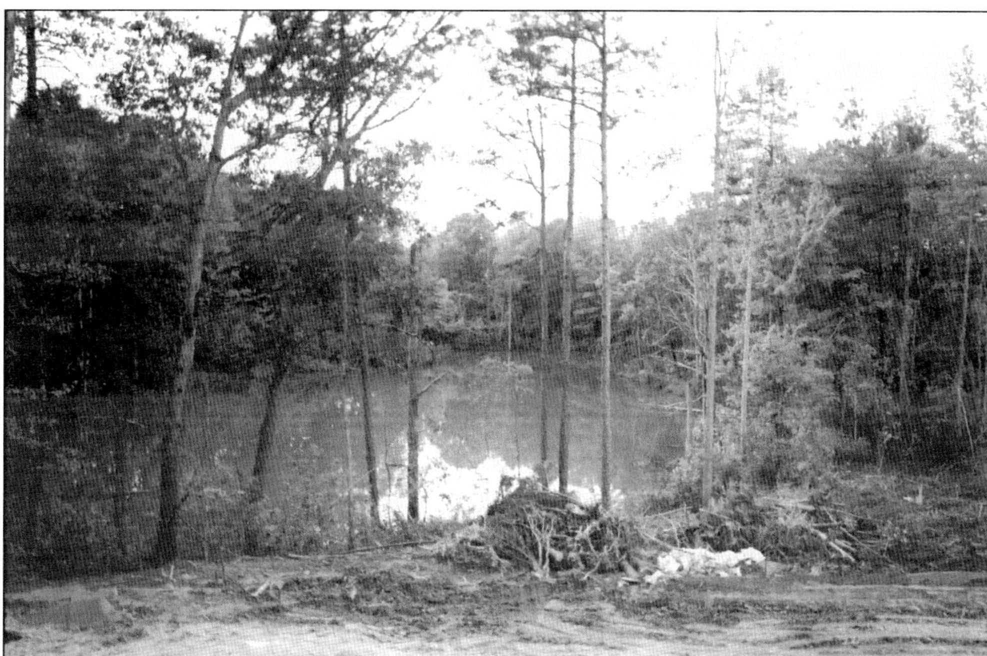

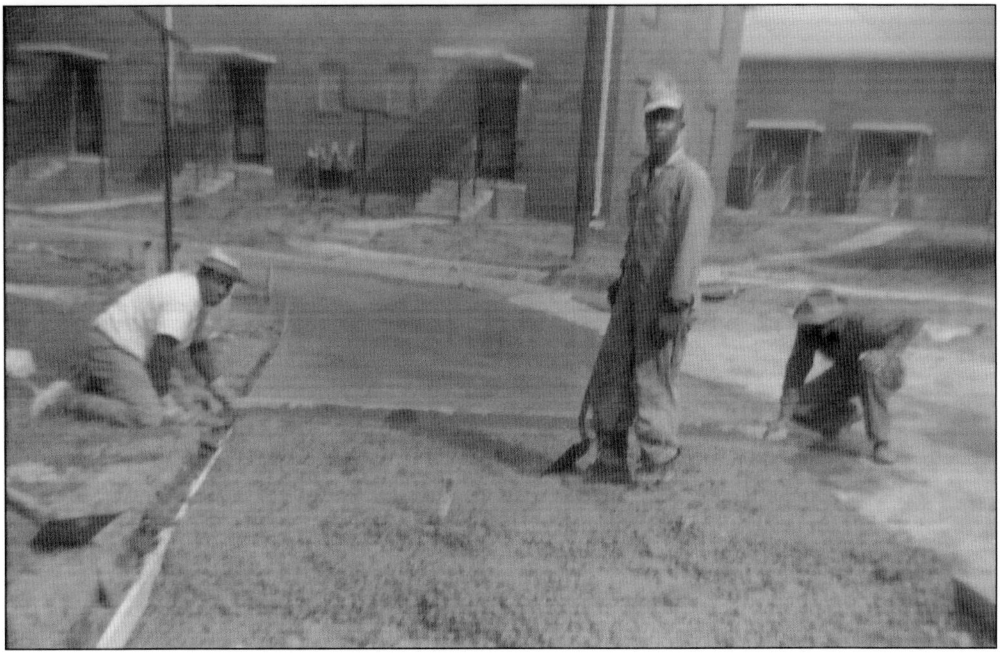

This photograph depicts the construction of Green Hunter Homes, or the Atlanta Street projects, *c.* 1951. The housing projects were named in honor of Rev. Green Hunter, a pioneer minister in Hall County. Included in these projects was a community building, which served as a daycare center from 1952 to 1978. The daycare facility was sponsored by the Gainesville Junior Service League. (Courtesy of Jennie Harris.)

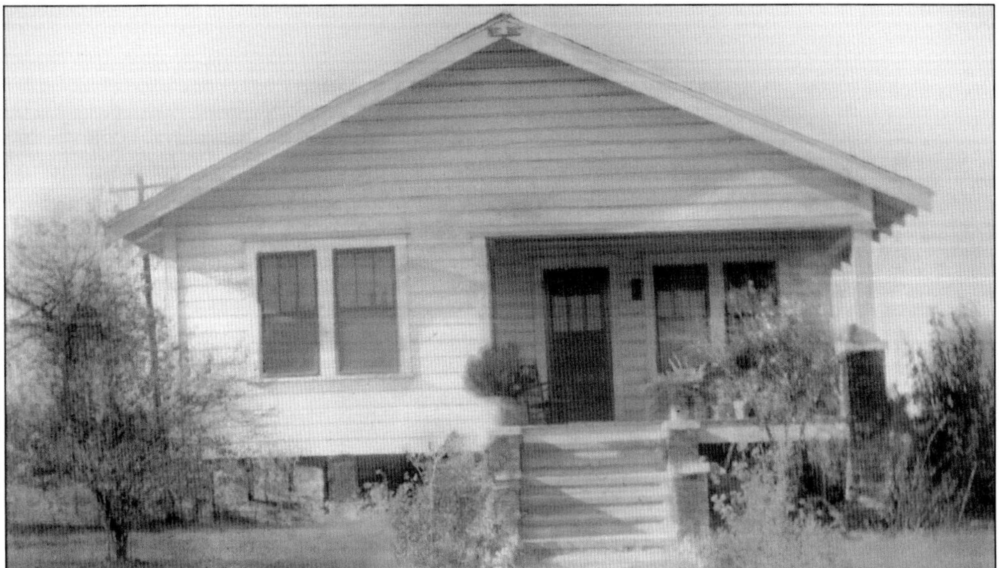

This home, which was owned by George and Pearl Neal, is reportedly one of a very few homes on College Avenue to escape the fury of the 1936 tornado. This deadly storm caused 162 deaths (8 persons remain missing), 950 injuries, and destroyed or damaged 992 structures in Gainesville. (Courtesy of Annette Cantrell.)

The home of former Summer Hill and Fair Street School principal W.H. Harper is seen here. This picturesque home is located on Athens Street in Gainesville. (Courtesy of James Brooks.)

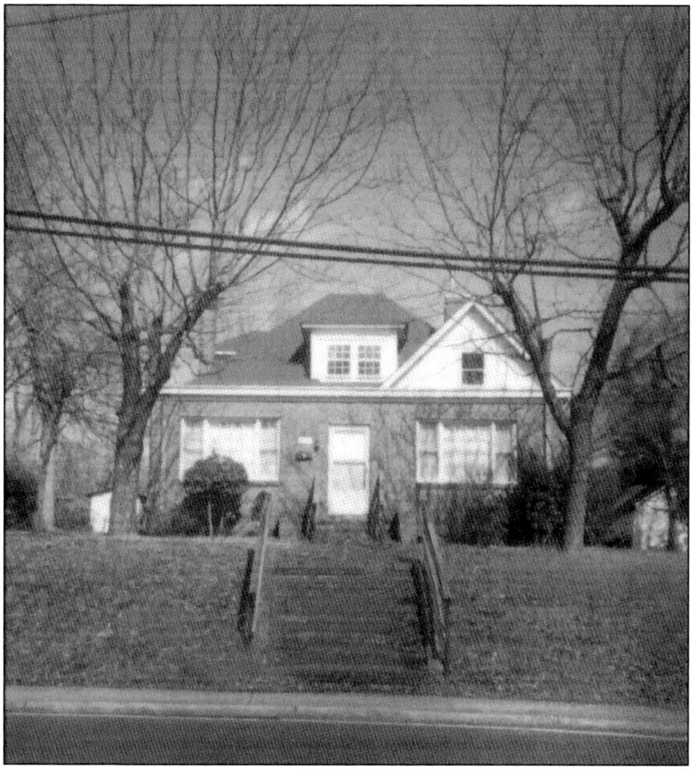

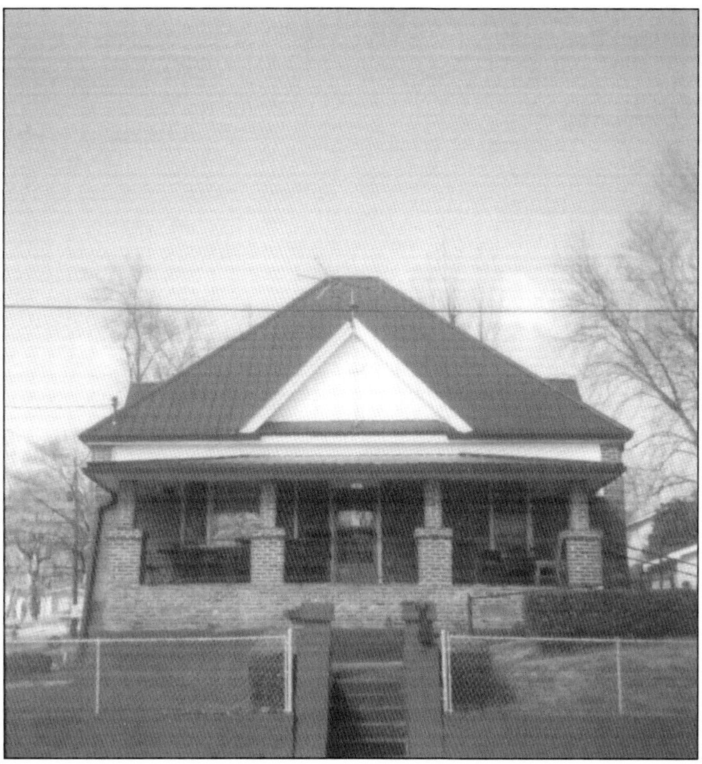

This stately home, located on Martin Luther King Drive in Gainesville, was originally owned by Martha Rucker. It was later purchased and renovated by Grady Young. (Courtesy of James Brooks.)

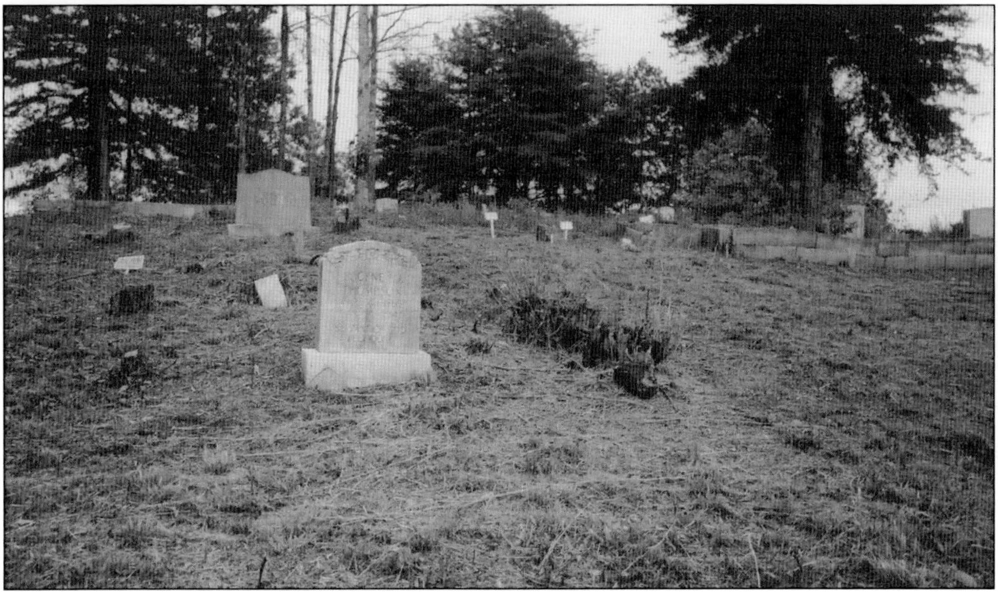

Eureka East View Cemetery was established in the early 1940s by Levi G. Greenlee. Greenlee purchased the property for Eureka for the sole purpose of providing a cemetery for African-American residents of Gainesville and surrounding areas. All of the grave sites were personally sold by him. In 2002, the Restoration and Preservation Committee of Hall County, led by Anderson Flen, spearheaded an effort to clean up and restore this cemetery. (Courtesy of James Brooks)

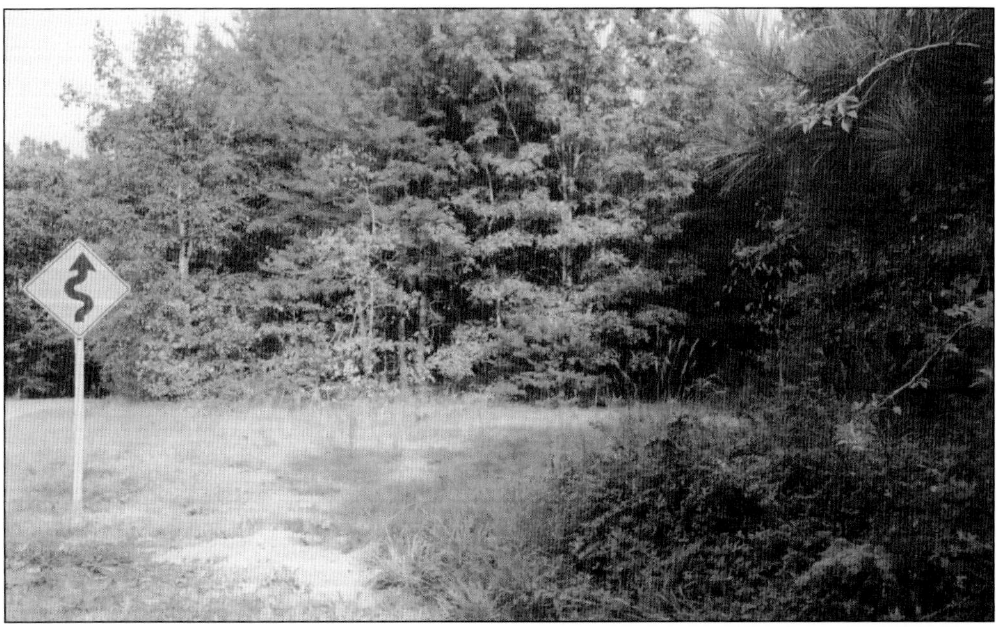

The entrance to Wahoo Cemetery, which is located off Thompson Bridge Road in Gainesville, is pictured here. The property for the Wahoo Church and cemetery was donated by the Dunlap Family of Gainesville. Although the church is no longer in existence, the cemetery remains and is scheduled to be restored soon. (Courtesy of James Brooks.)

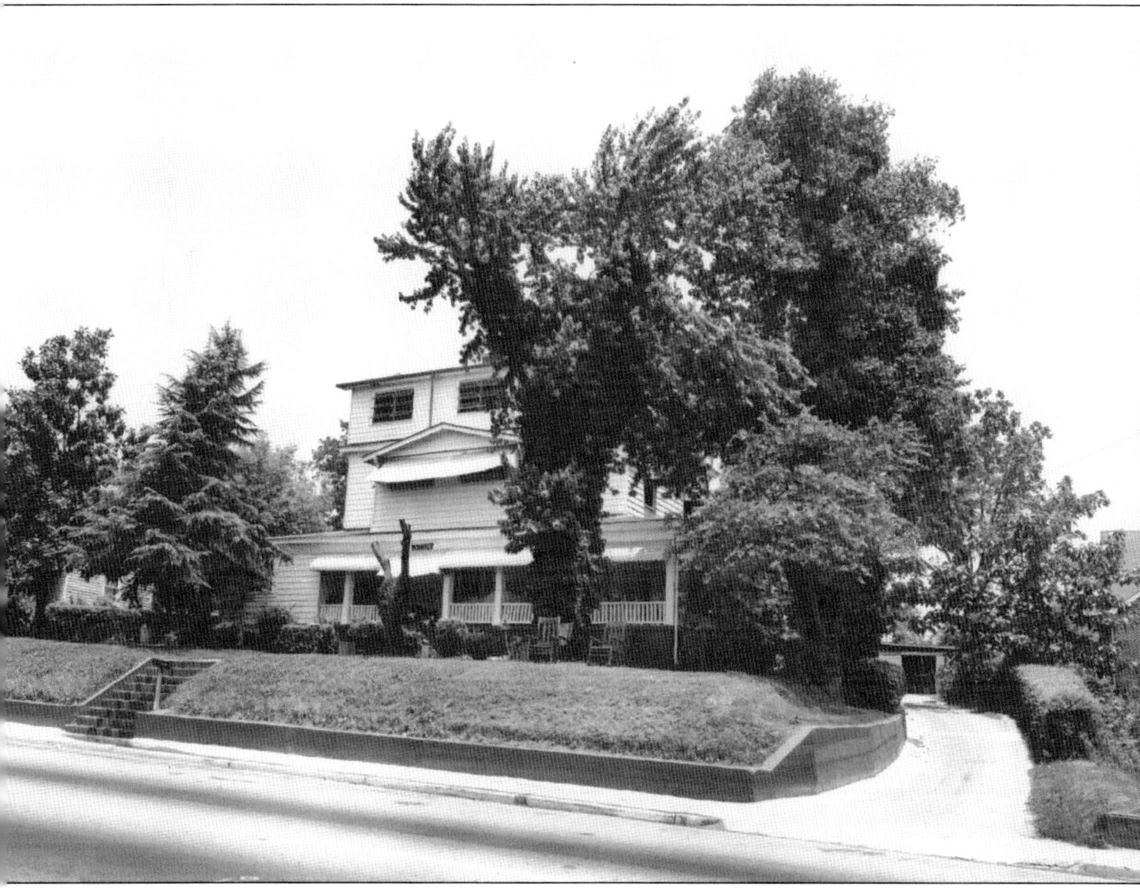

Mr. and Mrs. Adam J. Bryant Sr. were the proprietors of this tourist home for African Americans, located at 825 Athens Street in Gainesville. (Courtesy of Hall County Library.)

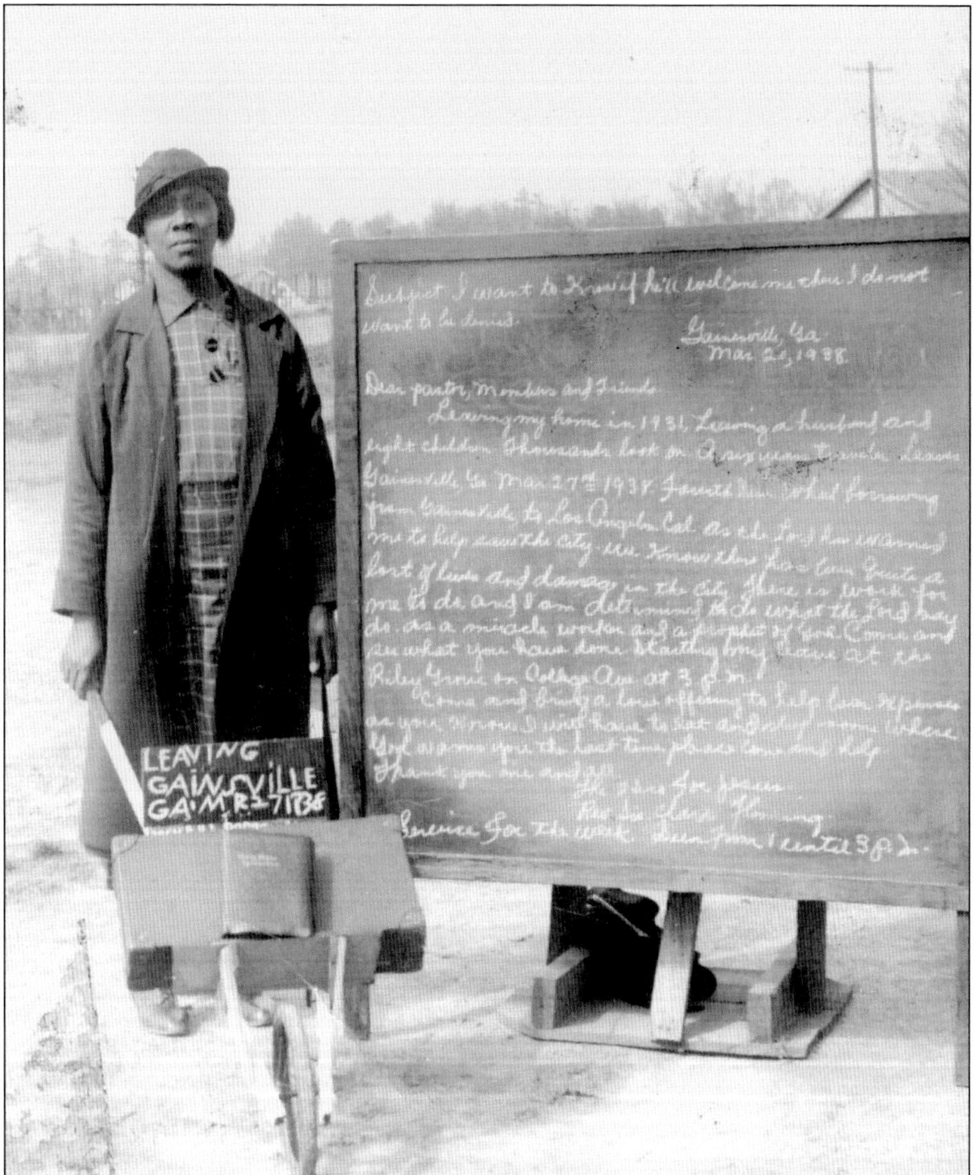

Reverend Sister Clara Fleming stands in Riley's Grove making an appeal to Gainesvillians for financial aid. Sister Fleming, a self-professed prophet and miracle worker, is leaving for Los Angeles, California, on March 27, 1938 to minister to the people there. She states in the written message on the board that she left a husband and eight children in 1931. Sister Fleming is asking the people of Gainesville to help bear her expenses for the California trip. Riley's Grove was located near College Avenue in Gainesville. (Courtesy of James Brooks.)

Three

Getting It Together
Organizations

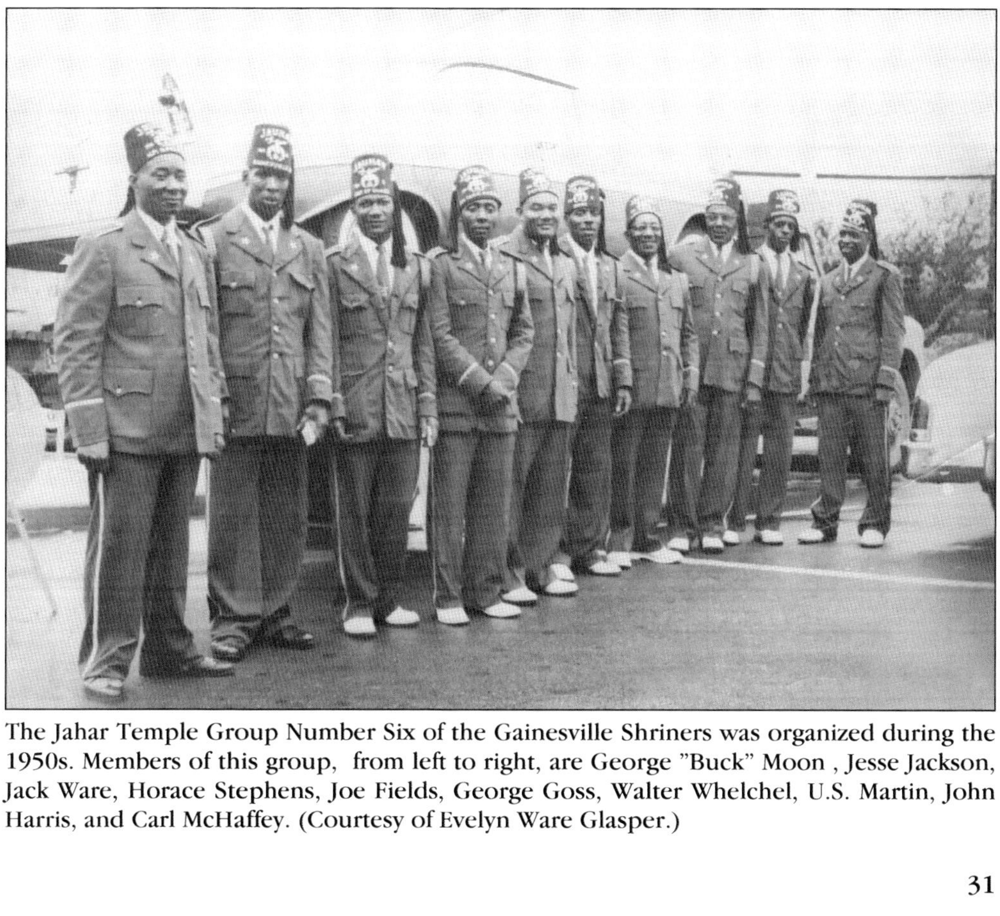

The Jahar Temple Group Number Six of the Gainesville Shriners was organized during the 1950s. Members of this group, from left to right, are George "Buck" Moon , Jesse Jackson, Jack Ware, Horace Stephens, Joe Fields, George Goss, Walter Whelchel, U.S. Martin, John Harris, and Carl McHaffey. (Courtesy of Evelyn Ware Glasper.)

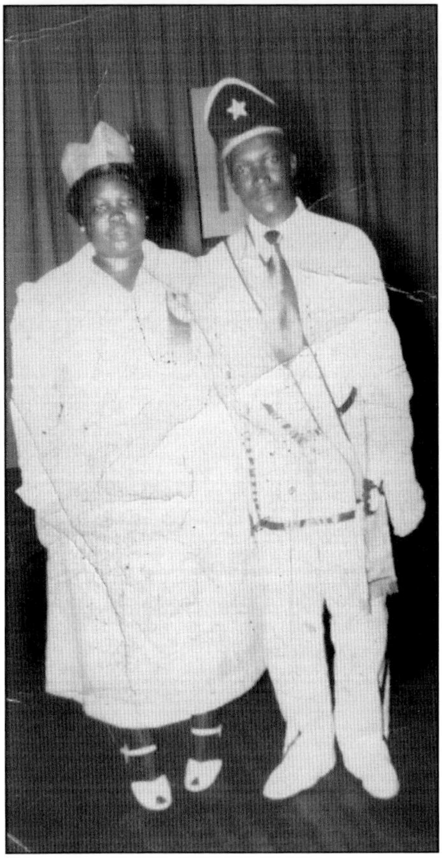

Mr. and Mrs. Jack (Annie) Ware are shown here at a Shriners' Ball. Mr. and Mrs. Ware were crowned King and Queen of the ball. (Courtesy of Evelyn Ware Glasper.)

The Widow's Son Lodge Number 66 of the Free and Accepted Masons was organized on October 9, 1948 at Trinity Methodist Church in Gainesville, Georgia. Identified seated in the front row, fourth from the left, is the Worshipful Master Brother Edgar A. Byrd. Identified in the second row, standing second and third respectively from the left, are Senior Deacon Esco Riley and Brother D.S. Lowe. (Courtesy of Esco Riley Jr.)

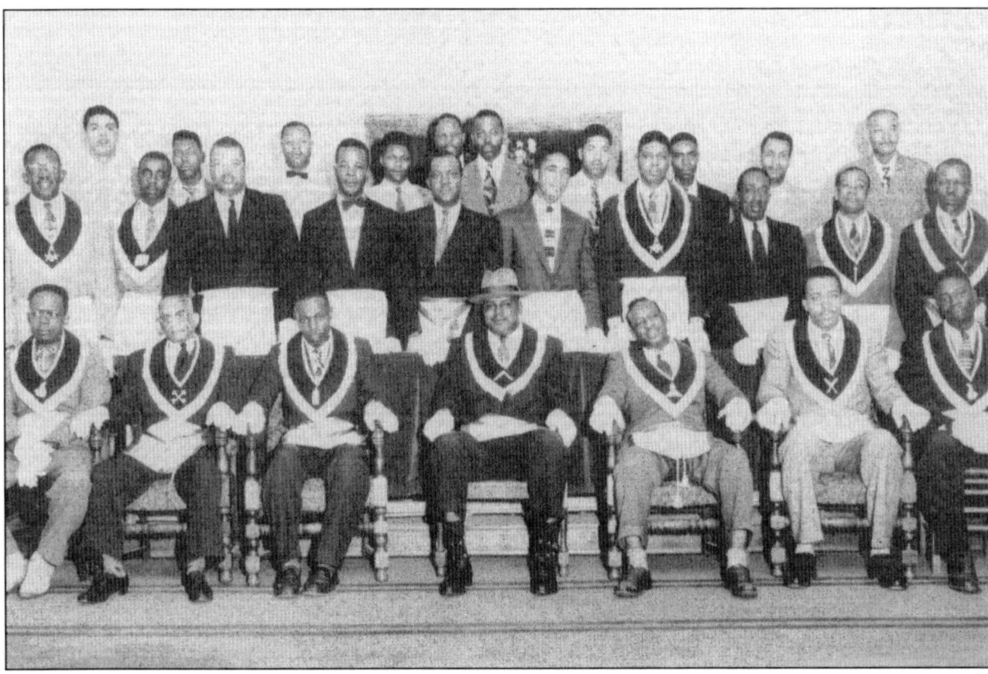

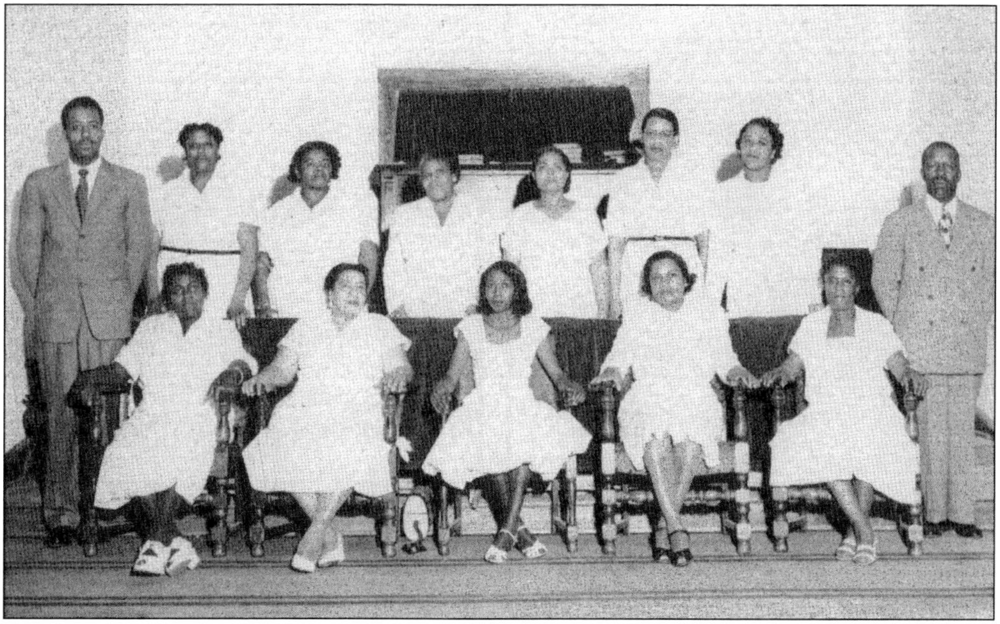

Members of the Eastern Star Lodge, seated from left to right, are unidentified, Sister Emma Lee Thompson, Sister Martha Camp, Sister Alvonia Blake, and Sister Jennie Harris. (Courtesy of Esco Riley Jr.)

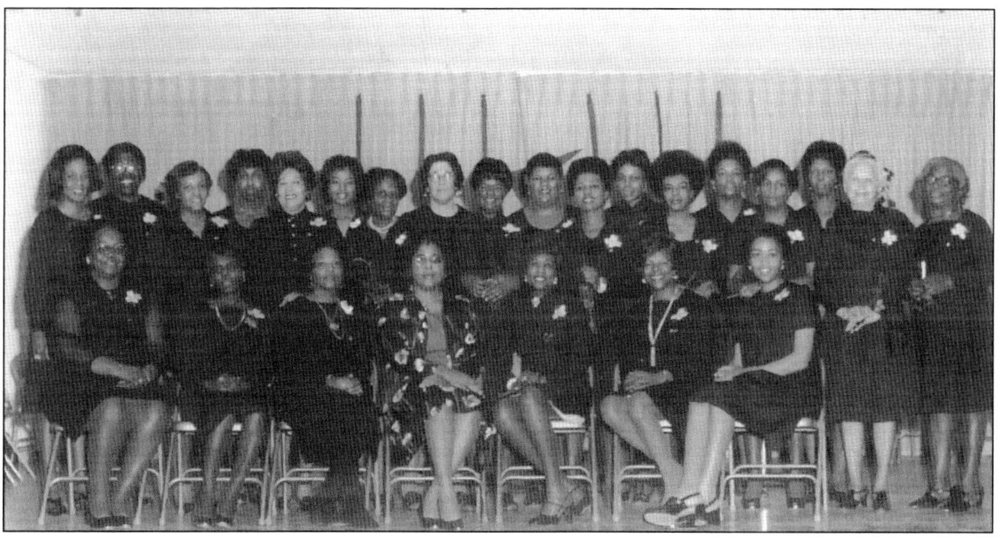

The Lambda Iota Omega Chapter of Alpha Kappa Alpha Sorority was chartered in Gainesville on December 11, 1976 at Brenau College. Sorors from the Kappa Omega Chapter of Atlanta and Soror Norma S. White, the South Atlantic Regional Director and later A.K.A. Supreme Basileus (seated fourth from the left, front row), conducted the ceremony. Members of the newly chartered Gainesville Chapter are from left to right (second row) Janie Shelton, Dorothy Rucker, Alphia Wills, Lila Bell, Nannell Fortson, Shirley Childers, Jennie Harris, Clara Poole, Joyce Rucker, Sally Jenkins, Pauline Pope, Linda Hutchens, Melissa Bell, Janice McGruder, Joane Ramsey, Gloria Anderson, Mattie Moon, and Josie Billingsley. (Courtesy of Alphia Wills.)

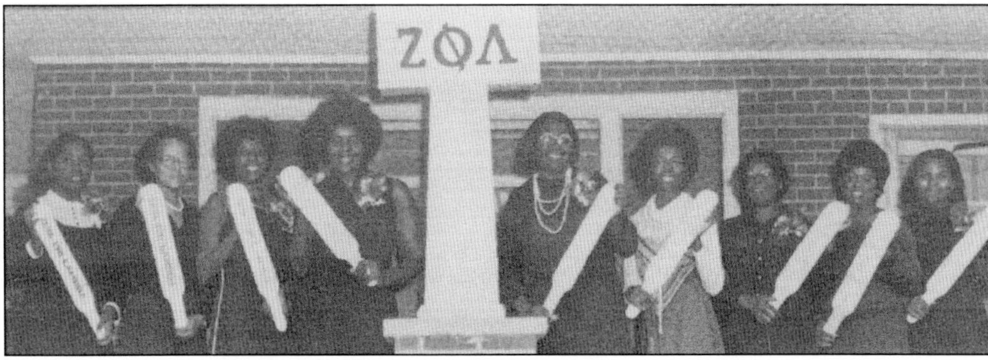

The Gamma Rho Mu Chapter of the Zeta Phi Lambda Sorority for Christian Women, Inc. was chartered on September 16, 1977 in Gainesville. This sorority was the first of its type to be organized in Georgia. Members of the sorority (from left to right) are Reelah V. Rucker, Dora L. Bell, Carree N. Bailey, Hazel Thompson, Dorothy O. Rucker, Vanessa Wells, Annie L. Hughey, Naomi Stephens, and Cheryle Akers. Not shown is Amy Ingram. (Courtesy of the Fair Street/Butler Alumni Association.)

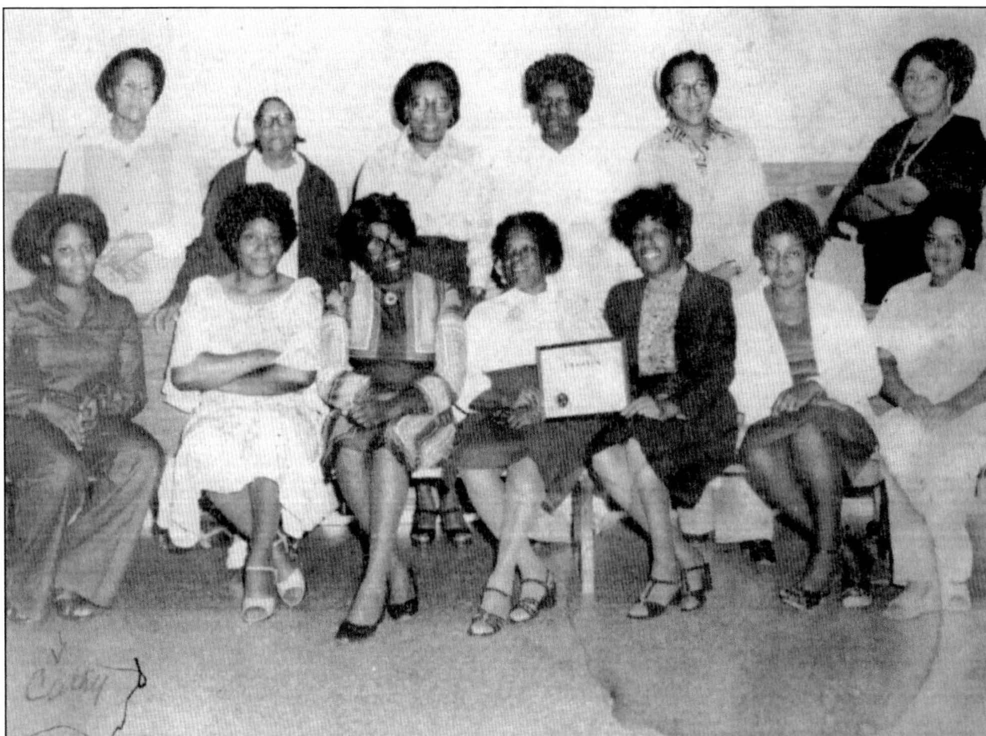

The Housewives' League of Gainesville-Hall County was chartered on September 10, 1978. The league's purpose is to raise the economic status of minorities through an educational program, which promotes wise budgeting in the buying and selection of consumer goods. Members of the Housewives' League, from left to right, are (front row) Cathy McCrary, Lois Lytle, Dorothy Rucker, Annie Lou Hughey, Carree Bailey, Anne Bailey, and Jackie Champion; (back row) Dora Lee Bell, Callie Morrison, Edna Young, Annie R. Martin, Marion Christian, and Bertha D. Hamilton. (Courtesy of Eddie Dabney.)

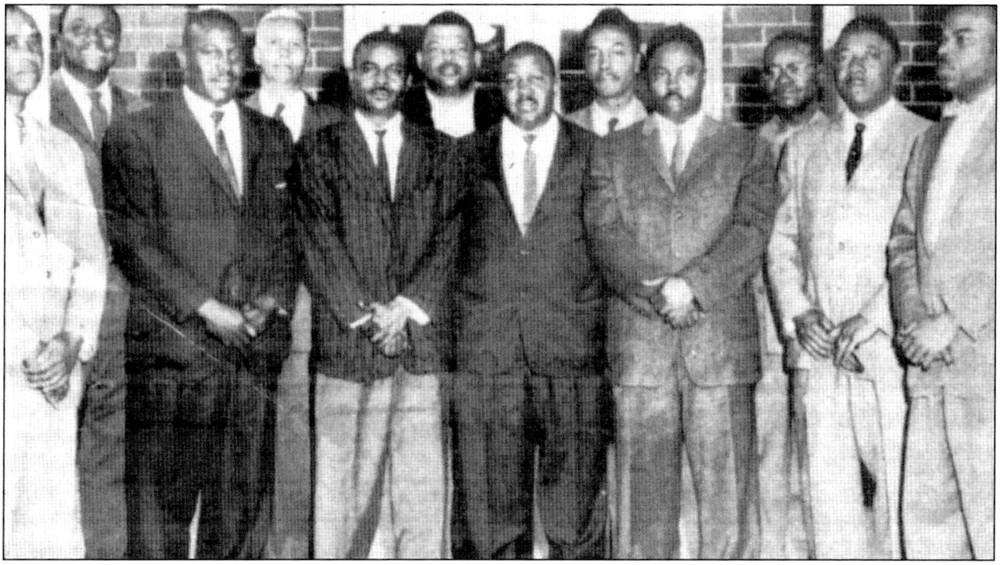

The Athletic Association was organized by the members of the Men's Progressive Club in 1950 in Gainesville. Members of the association, from left to right, are (front row) Willie T. Robinson, Maynard Brown Sr., L.C. Baylor, E.L. Cabbell, Nelson McGhee M.D., J. Wesley Merritt, and Ulysses Byas; (back row) W.S. Dinkins, William Merritt, D.S. Lowe, John Morrow, and Austin Brown. (Courtesy of *The Times*.)

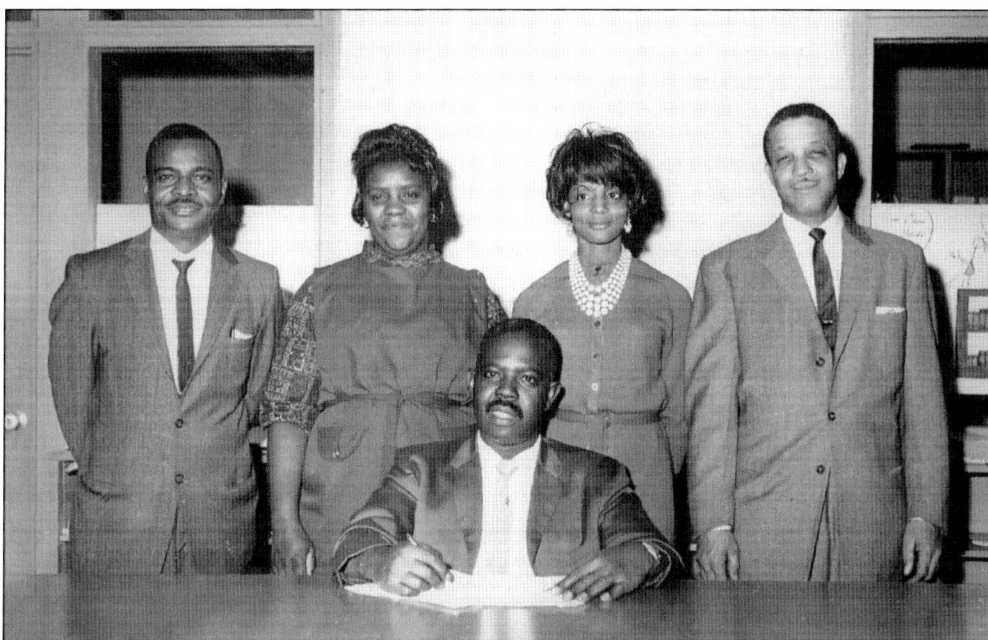

The 1964–1965 Fair Street Elementary School PTA officers were, from left to right, (seated) President Rev. W.B. Hawks; (standing) Principal L.C. Baylor, Vice President Jeanette Blake, Secretary Blondine Summerour, and Treasurer Doyce Hughey. (Courtesy of Cathy McCrary.)

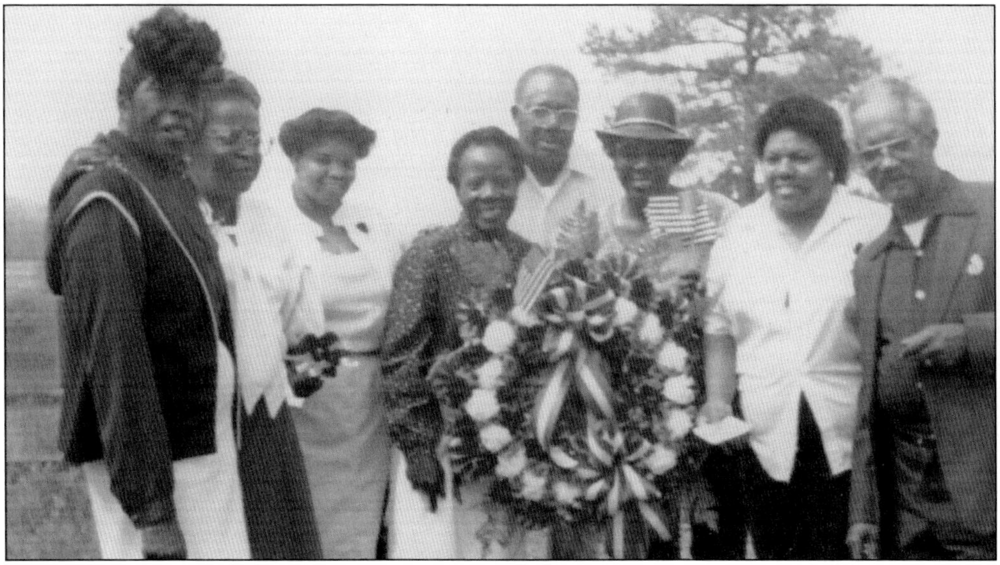

Members of the Eugene Brown Post #521 of the American Legion are pictured as they place a wreath on the grave of Eugene Brown. From left to right are Carree Bailey, Patricia Hudson, Louvenia Richardson, Katherine Goudelock, Grady Richardson, Mary Powell, Sherry Richardson, and Frank Law. (Courtesy of Katherine Goudelock.)

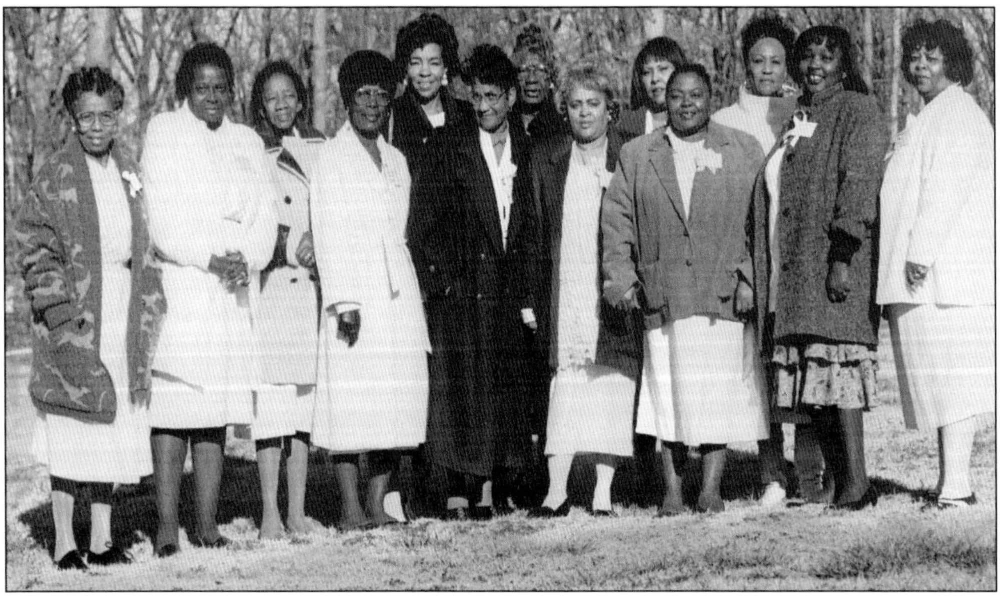

The Newtown Florist Club is a community and environmental activist organization established in Gainesville in the late 1950s to provide support and limited financial assistance to neighborhood families during times of bereavement; however, the club gradually shifted its focus to other community issues and concerns as various needs arose over the years. Members pictured from left to right are Eloise Price, Florence Tanner, Geraldine Collins, Mae Catherine Wilmont, Sarah Nash, Faye Bush, Mozetta Whelchel, Annette Westbrook, Jackie Mize, Coretta Young King, Dorothy Kea, Pauletta Wilkins, and Peggy Brown. (Courtesy of Faye Bush and the Newtown Florist Club.)

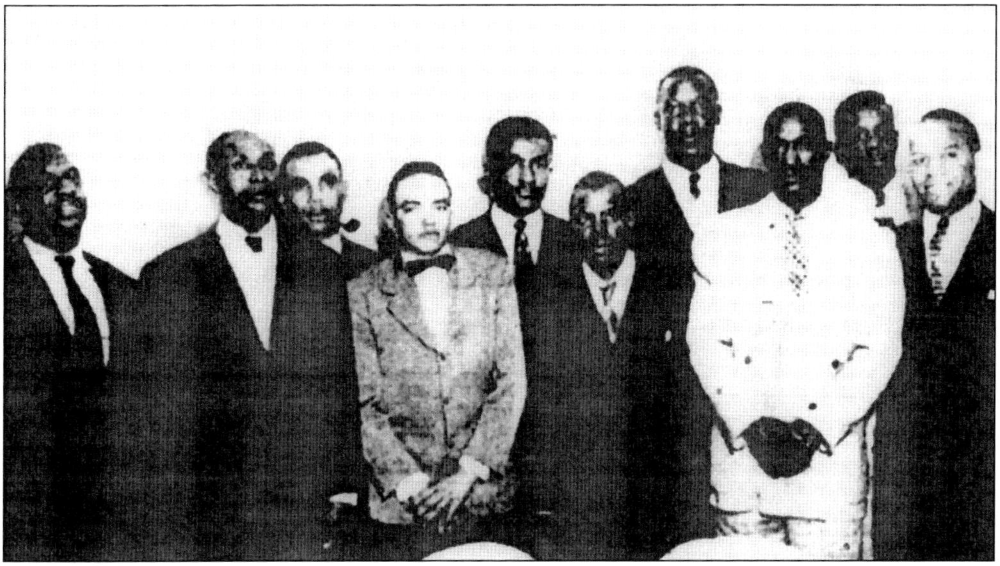

Members of the Southside Chamber of Commerce met in November 1956 to discuss and plan a fund-raising project. Pictured from left to right are (front row) Henry Christian, Grady Young, Grady Cheek, Leroy Stringer, Dr. George L. Burgess, and Edgar D. Billingslea; (back row) Juluis Griffin, Paul Brawner, Rev. Boyd B. Cantrell, and Fred R. Morton. Not pictured are Charles Moorehead, William H. Maxey, and Walter Chamblee Sr. (Courtesy of *The Times.*)

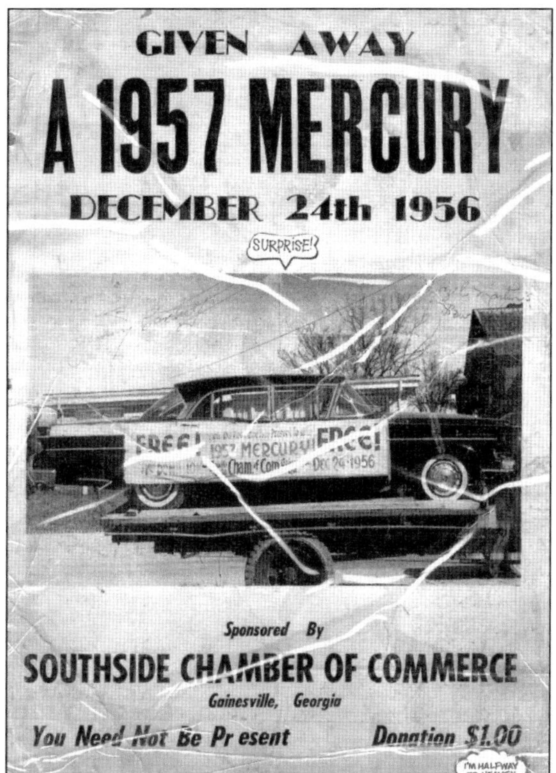

The Southside Chamber of Commerce sponsored this drawing in December 1956 as a fund-raiser. Jimmy Cantrell of Gainesville won the car. (Courtesy of the Fair Street/Butler Alumni Association.)

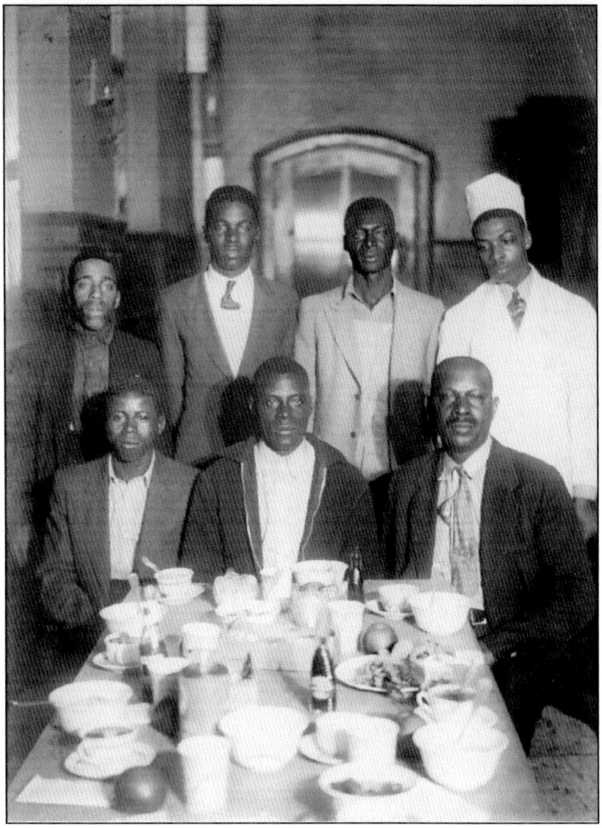

The men pictured in this photograph were employees of the Gainesville Elks Club. From left to right are (front row) Alvin Wells, Leadus Wilborn, Mance Thompson; (back row) A.D.Williams, John Doyle Thompson Sr., unidentified, and Kyle Moorehead Jr. (Courtesy of Wilbur and Dixie Ramsey.)

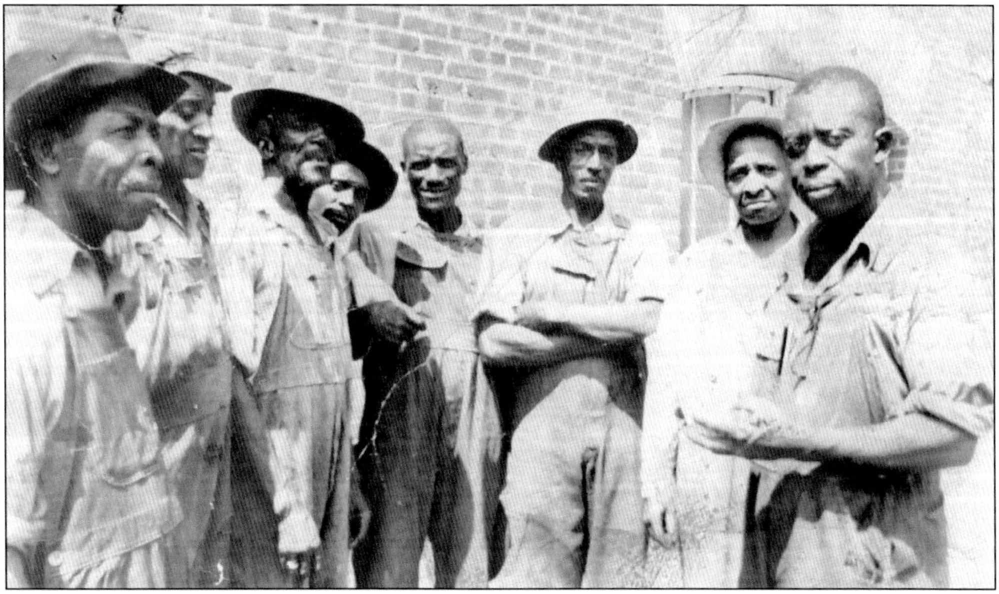

Pacolet Manufacturing Company's Gainesville Mill workers posed for this picture. From left to right are unidentified, Emanuel Goss, Parchal Chatman, Cliff Thompson, unidentified, Joe Force, John Barnett, and Almon Castleberry. (Courtesy of Eldon Goss.)

Mr. and Mrs. Dock (Christina) Lowe posed for this picture as they were being presented at a Men's Progressive Club ball. The Men's Progressive Club was organized in 1950 to promote community progress. Mr. Dock Lowe Jr. was president of the club in 1954. (Courtesy of Mattie Lowe.)

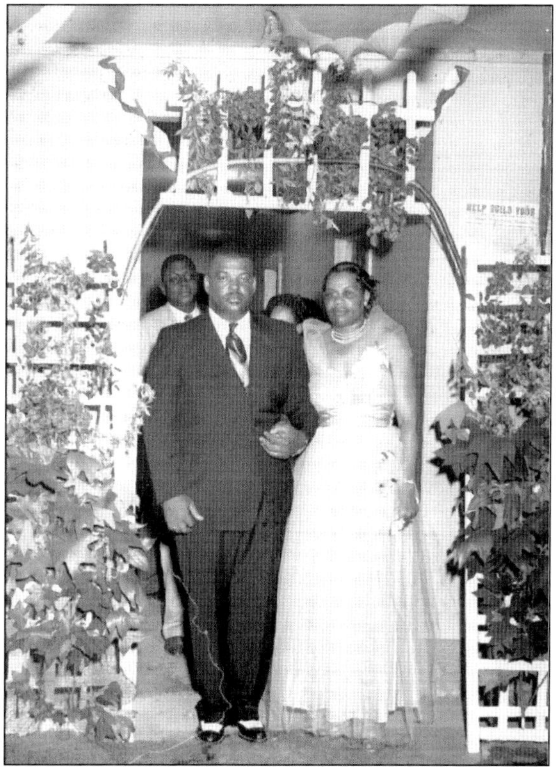

Posing for the camera and wearing dark glasses at this social function in September 1967 is Cosmopolitan "Cosmo" Club member, Ray Stovall. The Cosmo Club was a Gainesville social club. (Courtesy of Mattie Lowe.)

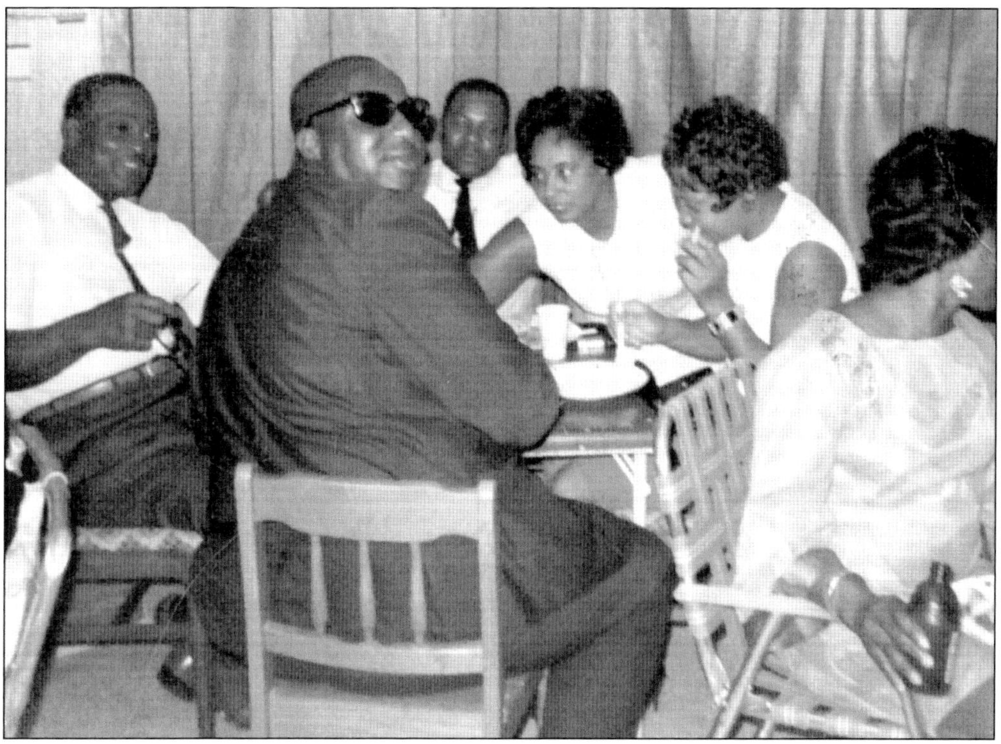

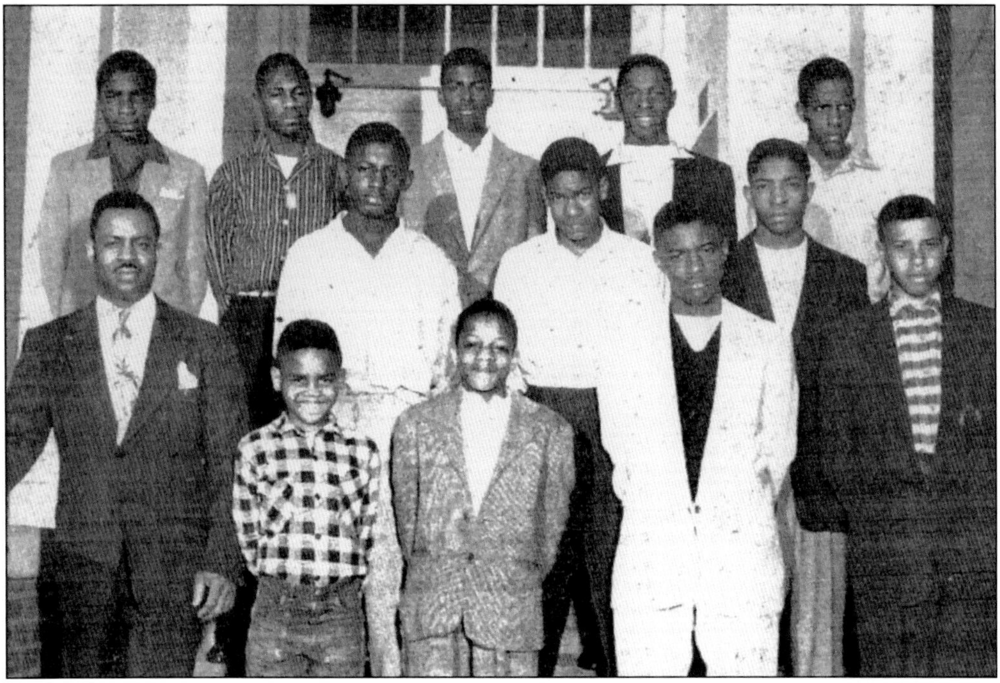

Members of the Gainesville Colored Boy's Club are shown here. This club was organized by Rev. Thomas H. Carter, who was the assistant pastor of Mount Calvary Church of God in February 1956, to promote, inspire, and entertain the youth of the community. From left to right are (front row) Rev. Thomas H. Carter, Willie James Christian, Isaiah Carter, Alton Mattox, and Joe Nathan Jackson; (middle row) L.C. Brown, Fletcher Johnson, and Marshall Carter; (back row) Thomas Lawrence (assistant secretary), Jack Johnson (vice president), Adale Ivory (secretary), Thomas Carter Jr. (treasurer), and Jimmy Worsham (president). (Courtesy of *The Times* and Eddie Dabney.)

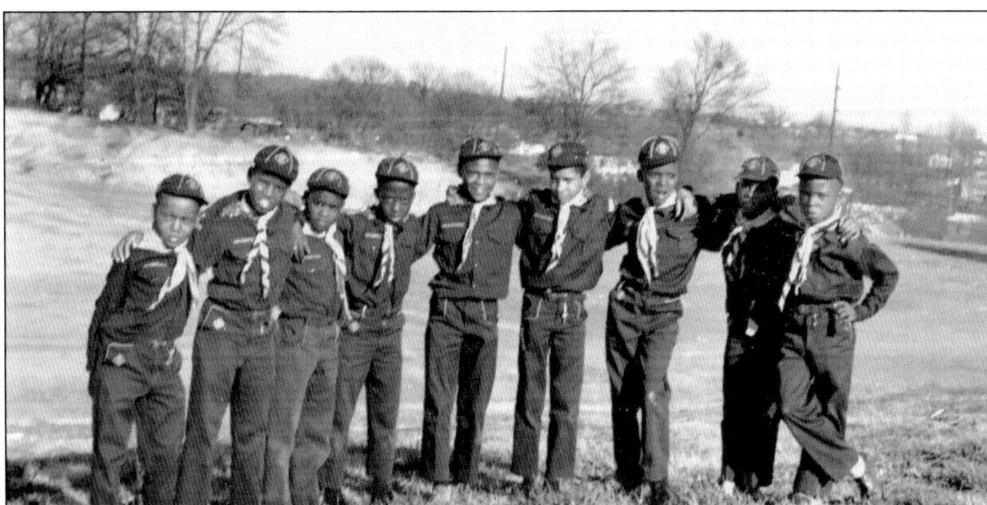

The Fair Street Elementary School PTA sponsored Cub Scout Troop Pack 45 in 1968. Mr. George Pryor was the Cubmaster. (Courtesy of Cathy McCrary Kimbro.)

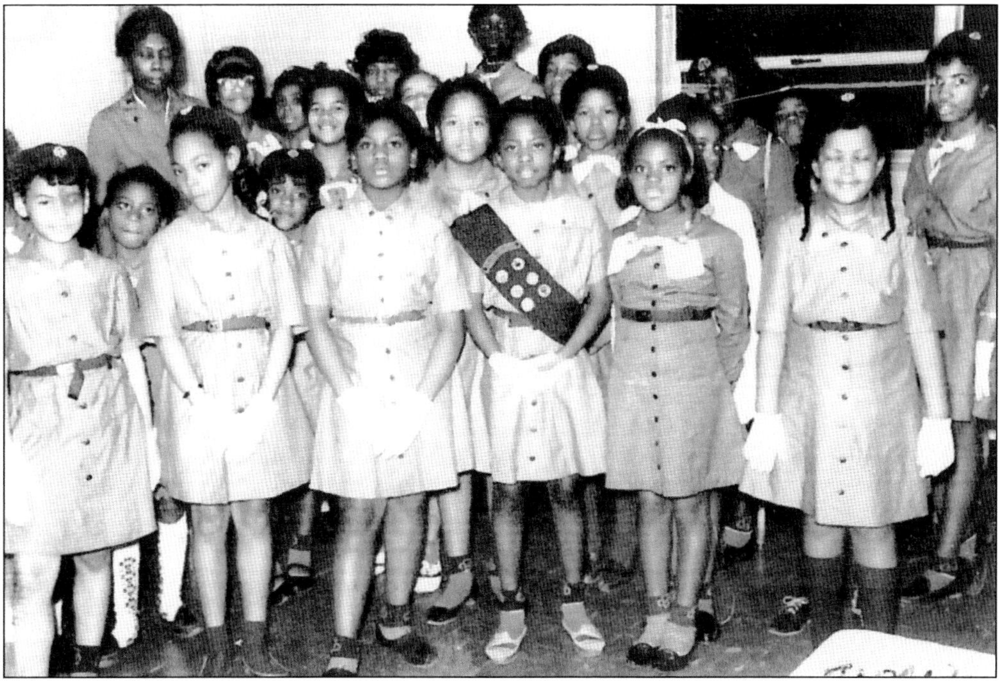

Girl Scout Troop #24 of Gainesville is pictured here. Mattie Lowe was the troop's leader for many years. She received a pin of merit for her leadership of Troop #24. (Courtesy of Mattie Lowe.)

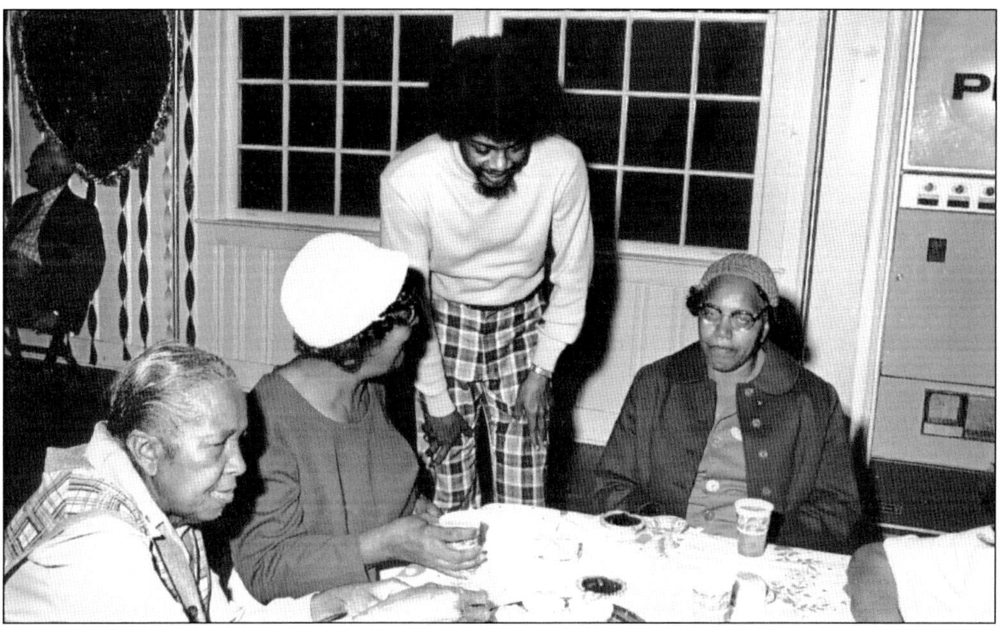

The Esquire Club hosted a dinner for senior citizens in 1973. The Esquire Club was a civic and social organization for young men. It was organized at E.E. Butler High School in November 1966. Harold Goss was the club's founder and first president and Dr. Marcellus Barksdale was the club's advisor. (Courtesy of the Fair Street/Butler Alumni Association.)

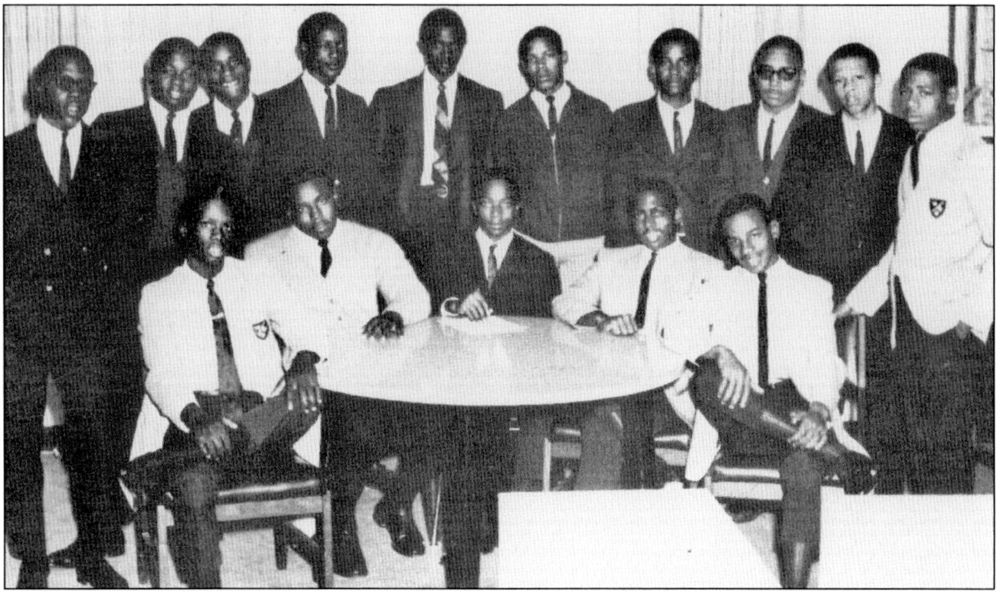

The Gents Club was organized at E.E. Butler High School during the 1967–1968 school year. Nathaniel Shelton became the club's advisor. Members pictured from left to right are (seated) Charles Watson, Terry Marshall, Kenneth Brown, Esco Riley, and John Thompson; (standing) Cornell Lawhorn, Emertus Young, Jackie Littlejohn, Rosco Morris, Larry Johnson, Graham Montague, Gregory Mize, Thomas Marshall, Lonnie Moore, and Emmett Moorehead. (Courtesy of the Fair Street/Butler Alumni Association.)

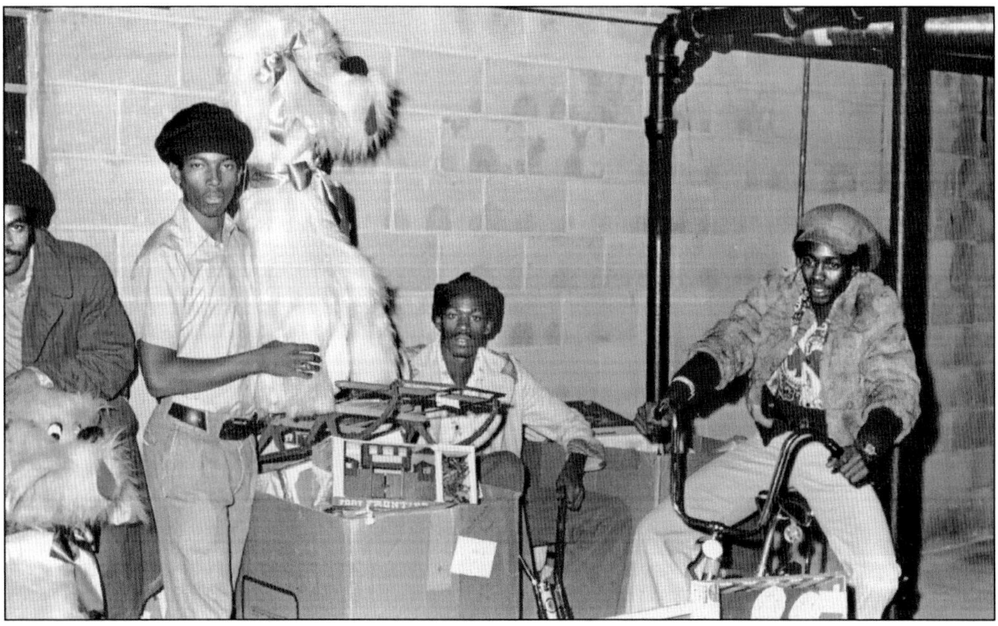

Members of the Gents Club prepare to distribute toys to underprivileged children in this picture taken before Christmas in 1973. Identified from left to right are Donnice Dabney (holding the stuffed animal), Danny Glenn (seated), and William Rucker (seated on the bicycle). (Courtesy of the Hall County Black History Society.)

Four

WHAT HAPPENED
Events

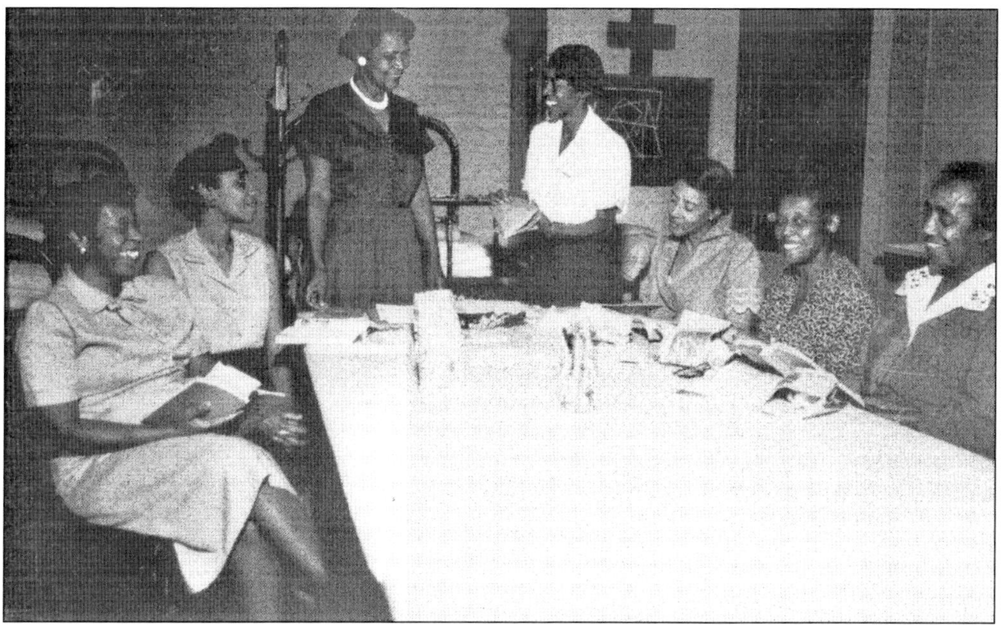

Public Health nurse Catherine Brown conducted Red Cross home nursing classes in the 1950s. Participants completing this home nursing class, from left to right, are Mrs. Doyce (Annie) Hughey, Mrs. Margaret Moorehead, Mrs. Martha Wilburn, Mrs. Catherine Brown (instructor), Mrs. Bessie Laws, Mrs. Sally Glover, and Mrs. Annie Davis. (Courtesy of Clinton and Inge Brown.)

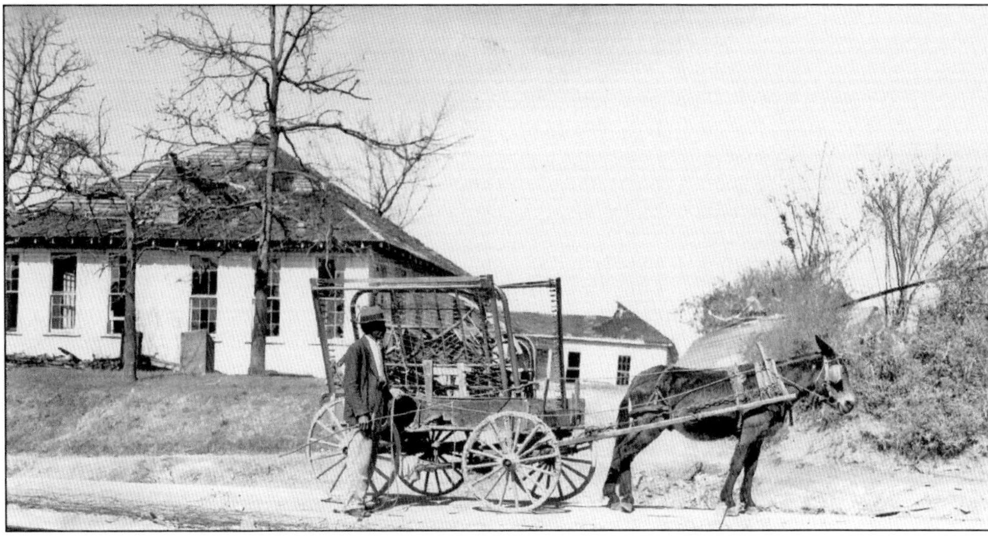

This borrowed mule and cart are carrying all that this man and family have left after the tornado of April 6, 1936. In the tornado, 25 African Americans, including 1 unidentified, died. The names of the dead are Emma Austin, Dee Byrd, Clifford Banks, Flora Bradley, George Cheek, Nicie Collier, Otis Couch, Mary Nell Davis, Carrie Lou Davis, Mary Dorsey, Lizzie Jones, Louise "Kitty" Moss, Montine Reynolds, Louellen Sadler, Charles Singleton, Lloyd Singleton, Leroy Strickland, Hattie Sadler, Joe Thompson, Ellen Waters, Edgar Lee Williams, Mollie Butts Williams, and Carrie Lou Williams. The Summer Hill School pictured in the background was also severely damaged by the tornado. (Courtesy of the Hall County Library.)

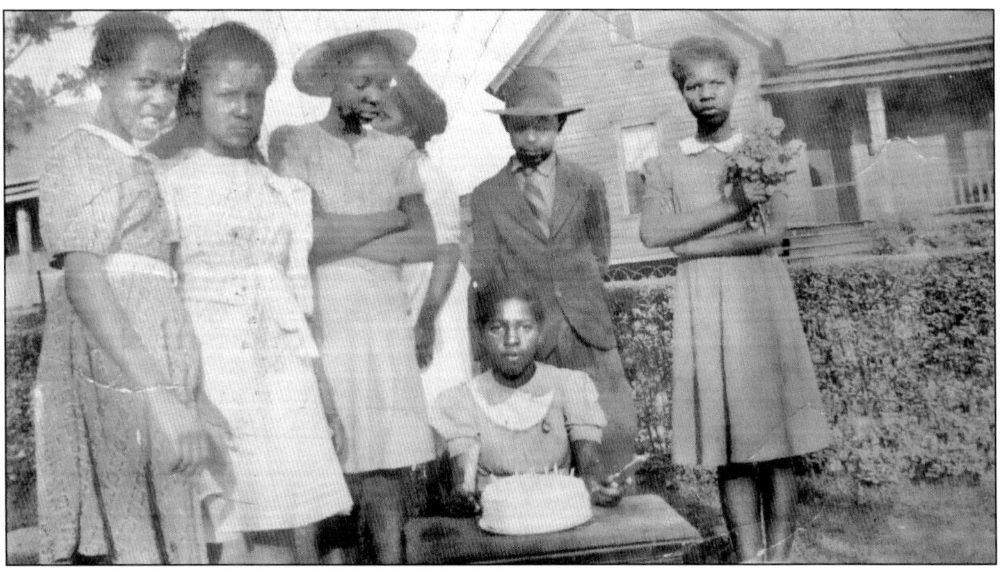

Seated at the table with her birthday cake is 12-year-old Luvercha Johnson. Attending Luvercha's birthday party, from left to right, are Queen Ester Dorsey, Jo Cox, Margaret Whelchel, Mary Byrd (partially seen), A.J. Bryant, and Fannie Pearl Dorsey. The party was held at the home of Mr. and Mrs. Virdell Lipscomb of Summitt Street in Gainesville. (Courtesy of Mrs. Margaret Osborne.)

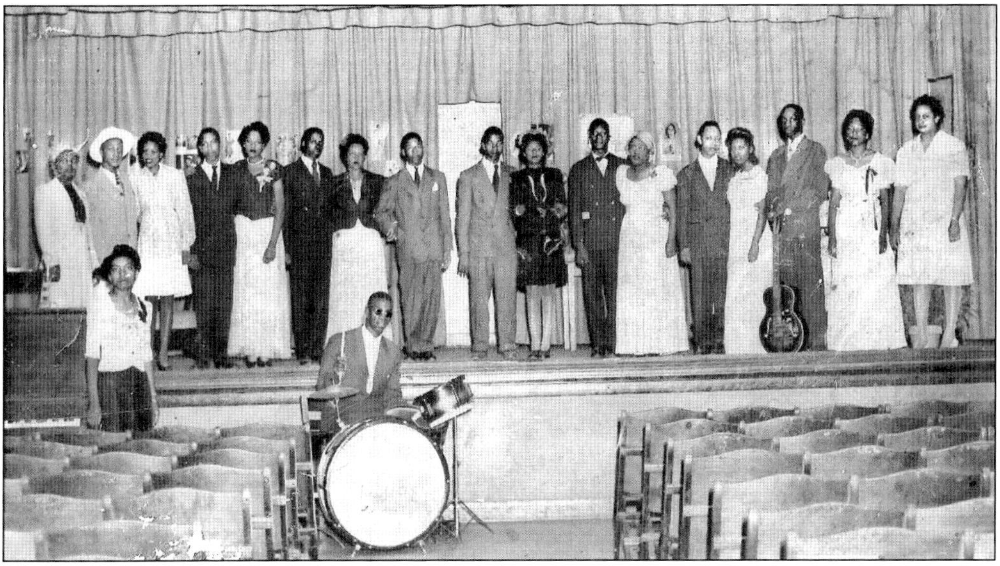

The cast of *Girl Shy*, the 1946 Fair Street High School Senior Class play, is pictured on stage in the Fair Street auditorium. Cast members on stage from left to right are Ruby Colbert, Billy Clyde, Viola Rucker, James "Jimmy" Morrow, Johnnie L. Deadwyler, Conchita Williamson, Cecil Ellis, Johnny Butts Jr., Douglas Randolph, Margie Butler, James Roper, Mary Byrd, Andrew J. Bryant, Eddie Bell Huitt, Fred R. Morton, Sammie Sue Law, and Mrs. J.B. Hylick. Maudine Thornton is shown standing on the floor and Samuel Thornton is pictured sitting at the drums. Not pictured are Bernice Morrow and Magnolia Smith. (Courtesy of Linda R. Hutchens.)

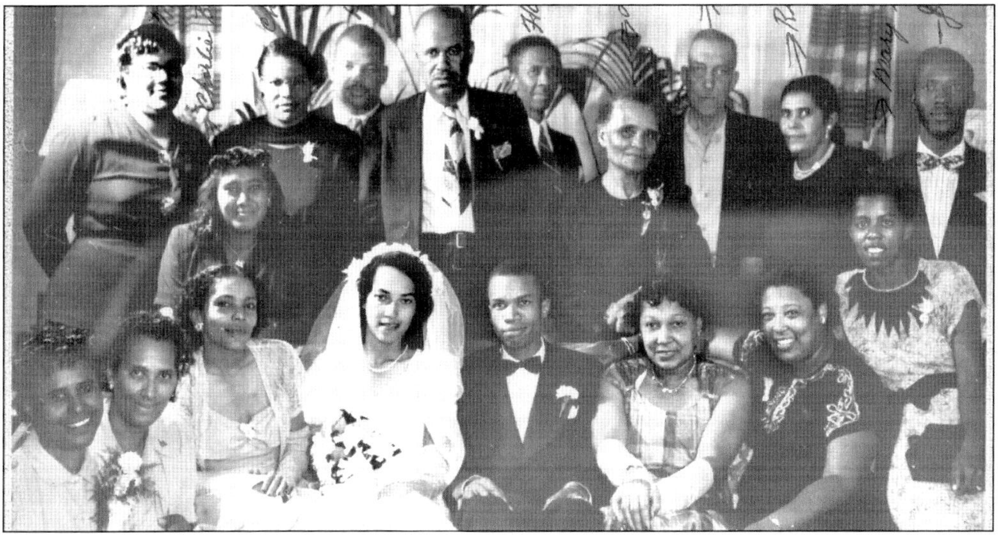

Mr. and Mrs. Benjamin(Annie Maude Lowe) Jenkins are pictured here with their wedding party. From left to right are (front row) Irene Lowe Hopson, Ila Butler Lowe, Mildred Lowe, Annie Maude Lowe Jenkins, Benjamin Jenkins, Johnnie M. Lowe, Clara Lowe, and Mary Glasper; (back row) Mattie Lowe, Charlie Bell Patterson Brown, Christine Lowe, D.S. Lowe Jr. , D.S. Lowe Sr. , Harvey Hopson, Lillie Lowe, Jim Lowe, Ruby Jackson, and Jackie Glasper. Mrs. Annie Maude Jenkins Hayward was a Gainesville educator. (Courtesy of Mattie Lowe)

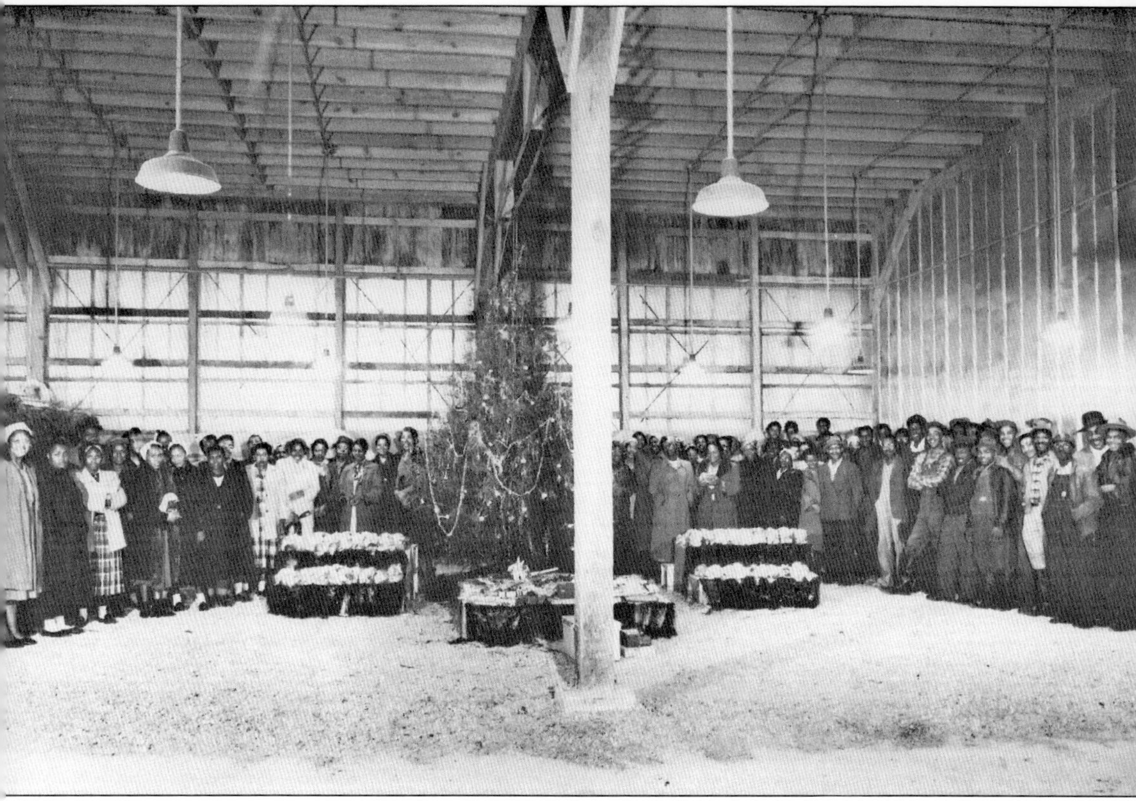

These employees of Swift and Company Poultry gathered in either December of 1953 or 1954 for a Christmas party. Located at 220 E. Myrtle Street, Swift was one of the many poultry processing plants that employed African Americans in Hall County and surrounding areas. Gainesville was known as the "poultry capital of the world." (Courtesy of Joyce Borders.)

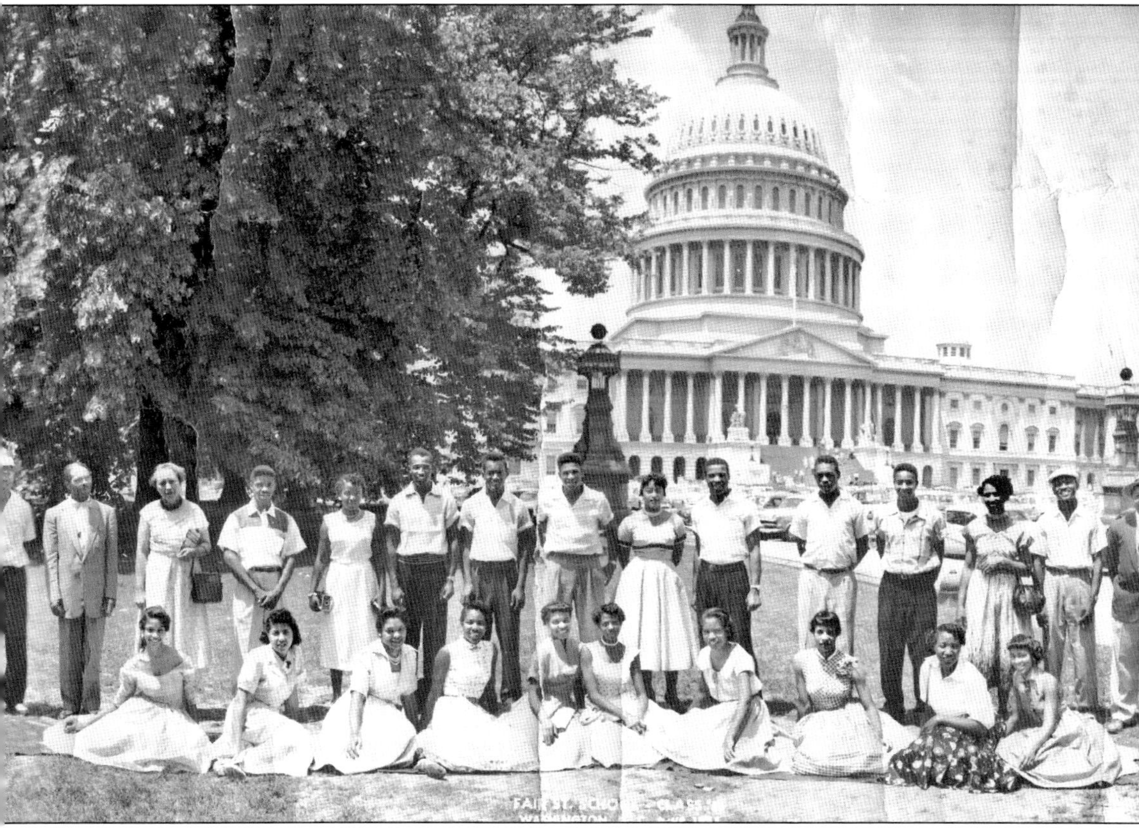

The Fair Street School Senior Class of 1955 traveled to Washington, D.C. From left to right are (seated) Eleanor Howell, Mary D. Jackson, Mary Christian, Mary Richardson, Joanne Ivory, Eloise Young, Anna Lois Martin, Thelma Jackson, Evelyn Jackson, and Annette Brown; (standing) Austin Brown (chaperone), Earnest Tolbert (teacher), Mattie Moon (teacher), Early Stephens, Patricia Brown, Maynard Brown Jr., Jimmy Thompson, Stanford Summerour, Barbara Peeks, Robert Cantrell, Noble Ross, Edward Hunter, Ruth Cantrell (chaperone), Verstee Howell (chaperone), and E.L. Cabbell (teacher). (Courtesy of the Fair Street Butler Alumni Association.)

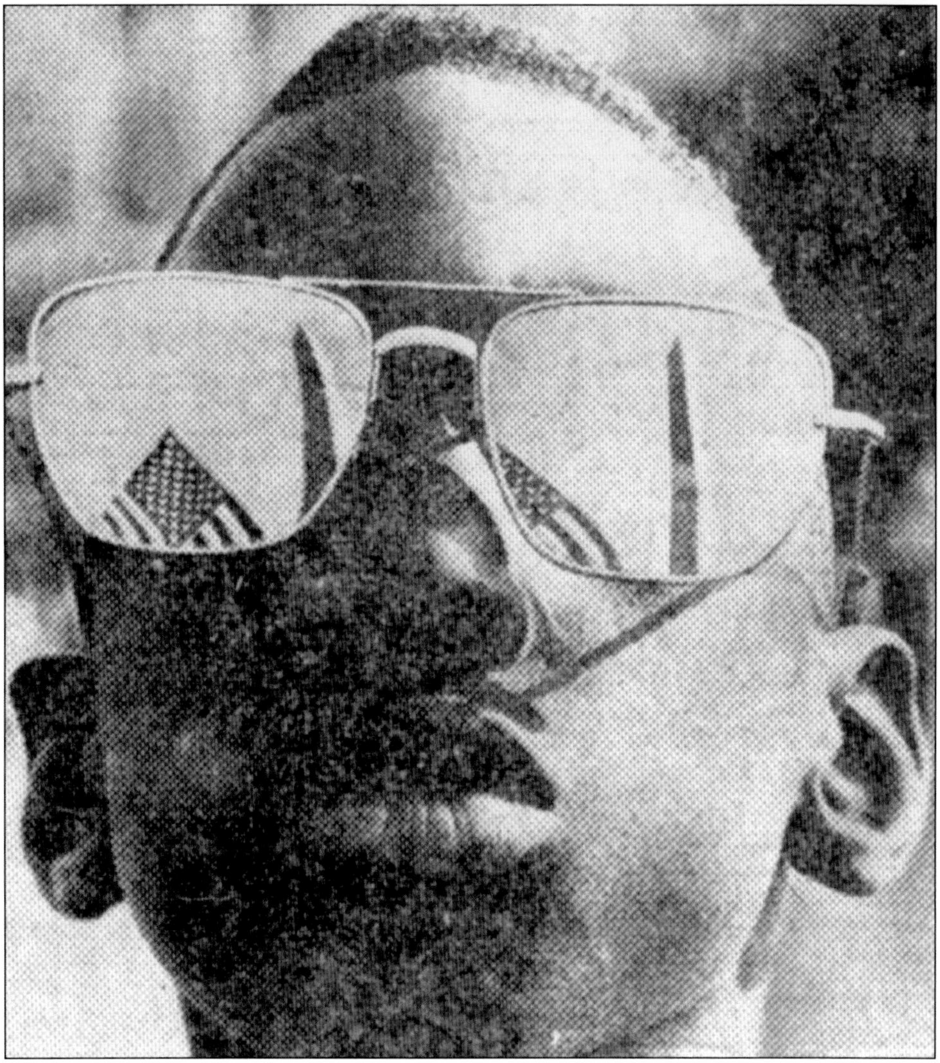

Published worldwide, this photograph of nine-year-old Clinton Brown of Gainesville, Georgia, became a symbol of the historic 1963 March on Washington. Reflected in Brown's sunglasses are the United States flag and the Washington Monument. (Courtesy of Clinton and Inge Brown.)

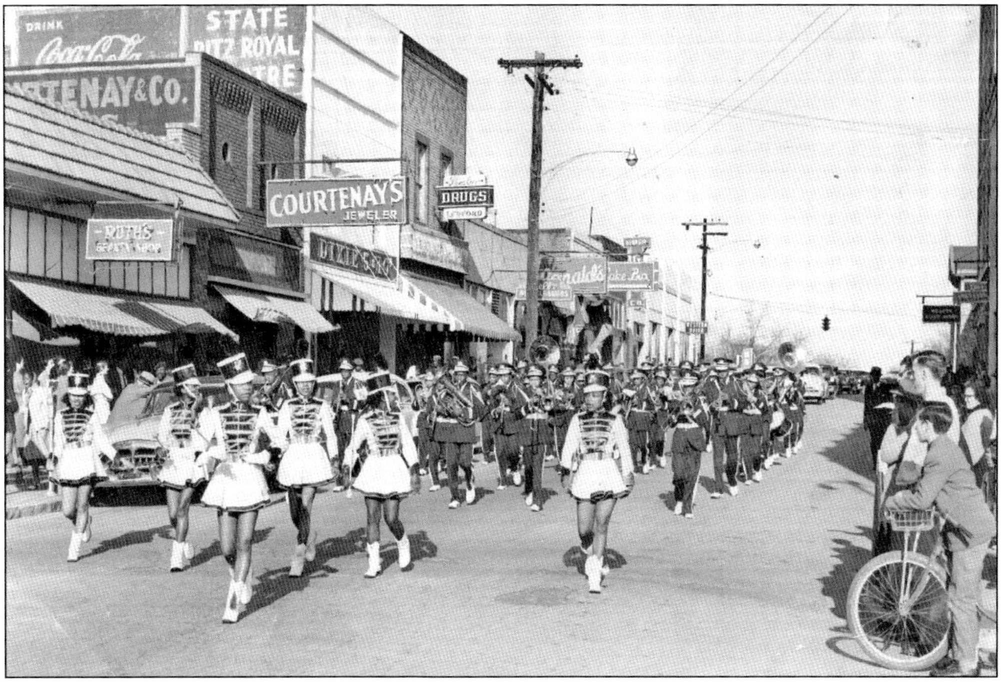

The Fair Street High School Band is seen marching down Washington Street towards the public square in downtown Gainesville in April 1954. This band was known for its excellence. (Courtesy of the Fair Street /Butler Alumni Association and Kenneth Robinson.)

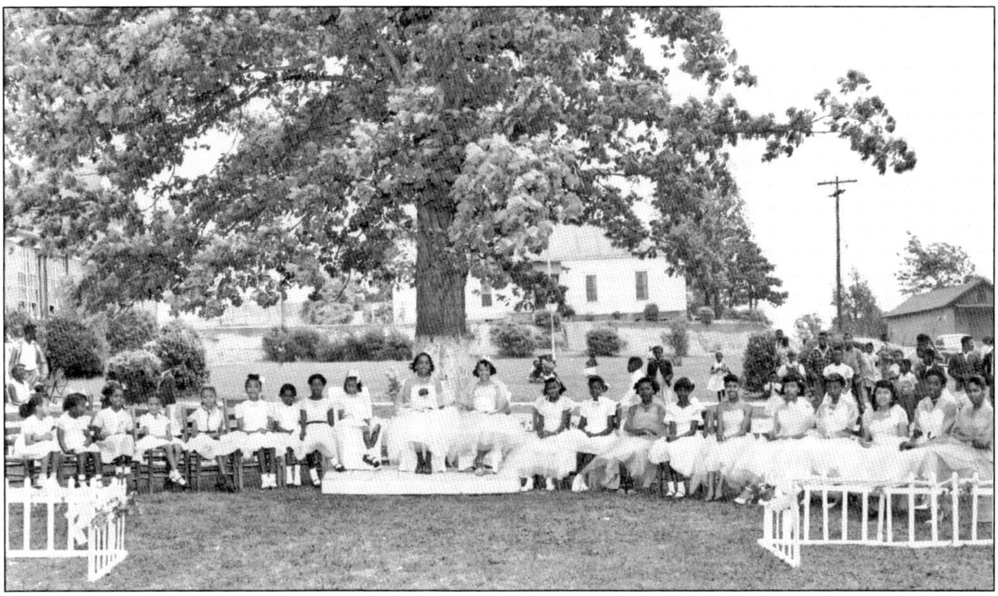

The 1954 May Day ceremony was held on the front lawn of Fair Street School. Pictured here are the May Day Queens. The building, which housed the school lunchroom and later the McCrary Branch of the Hall County Library, can be seen in the background. To the extreme left, across the street from the library, is Miss Marie Crosby's sweet shop or candy store. (Courtesy of the Fair Street/Butler Alumni Association and Kenneth Robinson.)

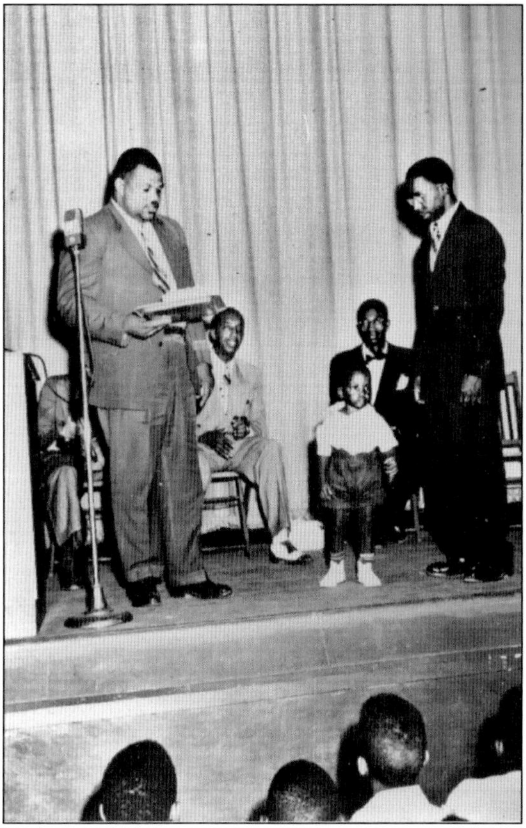

The Roxy Theater began serving its African-American patrons on August 31, 1946. Pictured on stage at its second anniversary celebration program, from left to right, are Dock S. Lowe Jr. (theater manager), Dr. E.E. Butler, two-year-old George Hutchens, Charles Westbrooks, and George Oscar Hutchens. Dock Lowe is presenting a birthday cake to young George, who was born on the opening day of the Roxy Theater. (Courtesy of George and Linda R. Hutchens.)

The Fair Street School Class of 1937 celebrated their 30th anniversary with a class reunion in July 1967. Attending this reunion from, left to right, are Robert Couch, Hazel Wright Meadows, Austin Brown, Lucy Carrington, and John Morrow Jr. The affair was held at the Dixie Hunt Hotel. (Courtesy of Clinton and Inge Brown.)

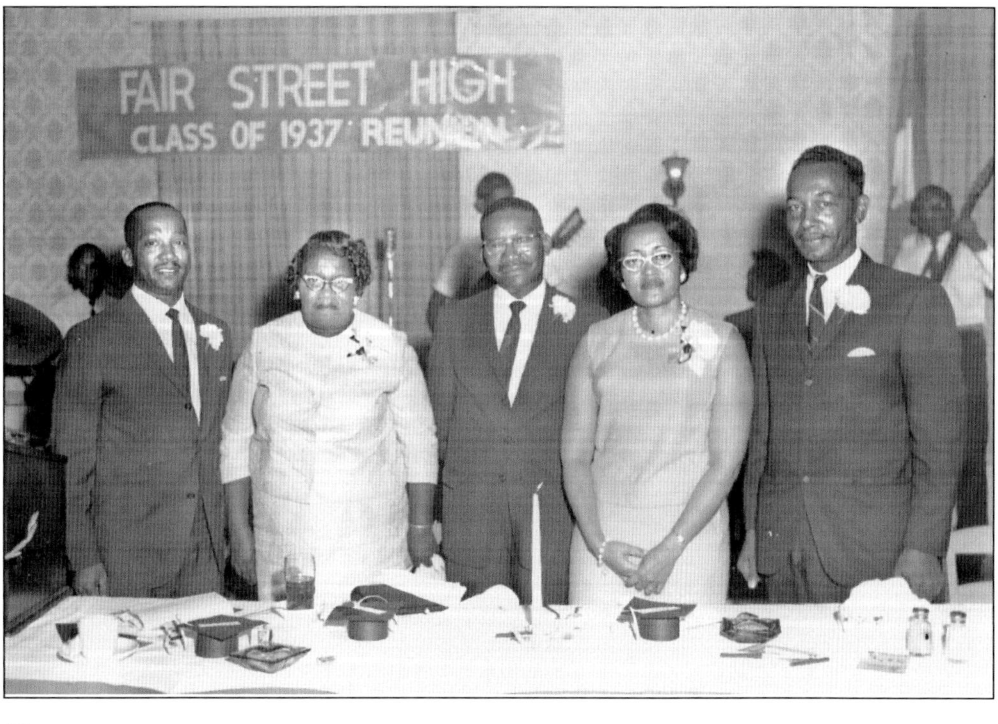

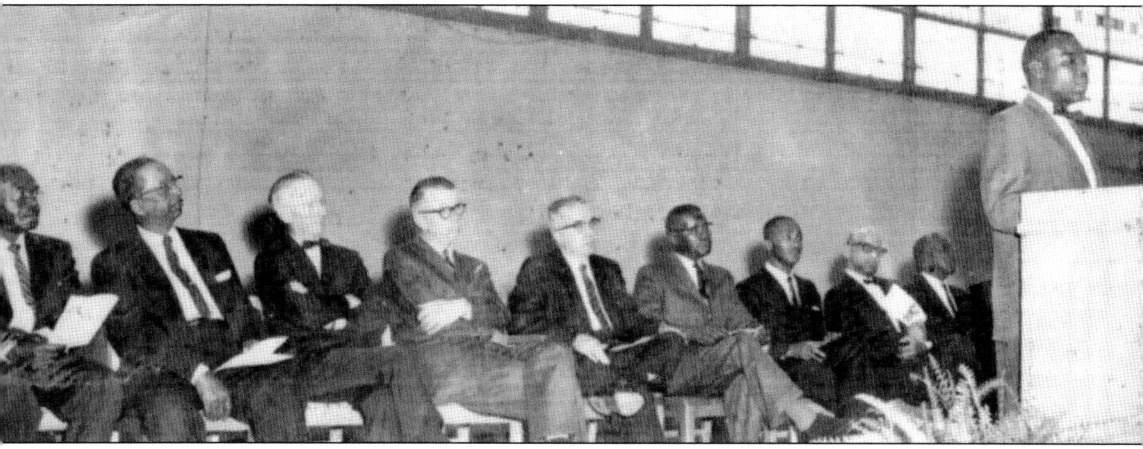

E.E. Butler High School was dedicated on Sunday afternoon, November 24, 1963 in Gainesville, Georgia. The platform guests participating in the dedication program, from left to right, included Rev. I.J. Watson, Rev. W.H. Brown, Mayor J. Milton Hardy, G.W. Moore (Gainesville Board of Education Chairman), T.H. Carmichael, Austin Brown, and Joseph Graham. E.E. Butler High School principal Ulysses Byas is shown standing at the podium. (Courtesy of the Fair Street/Butler Alumni Association.)

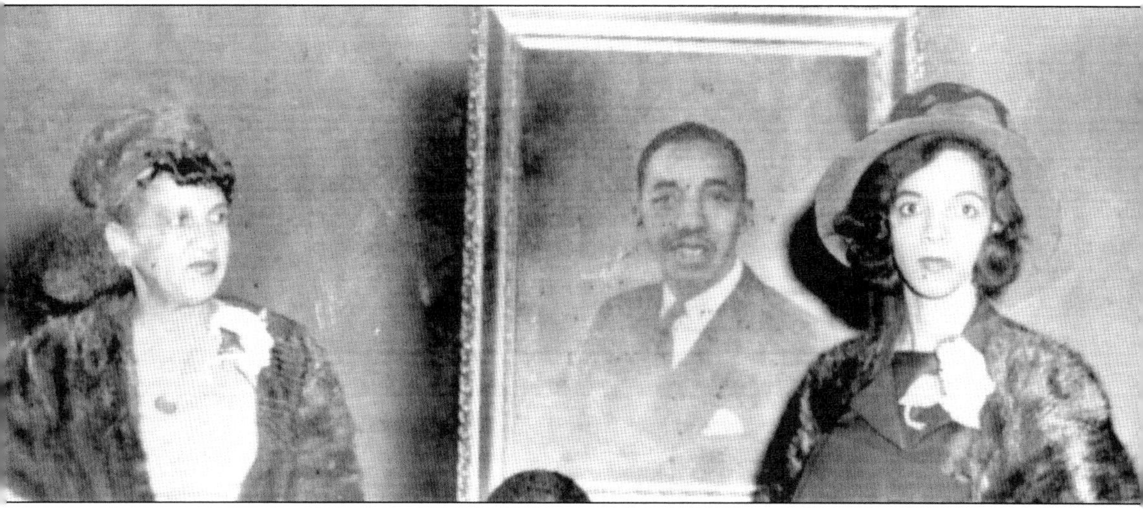

Dr. E.E. Butler's widow, Mrs. Lillian Butler, and their daughter are pictured standing before his portrait at the dedication ceremony of E.E. Butler High School. (Courtesy of the Fair Street/Butler Alumni Association.)

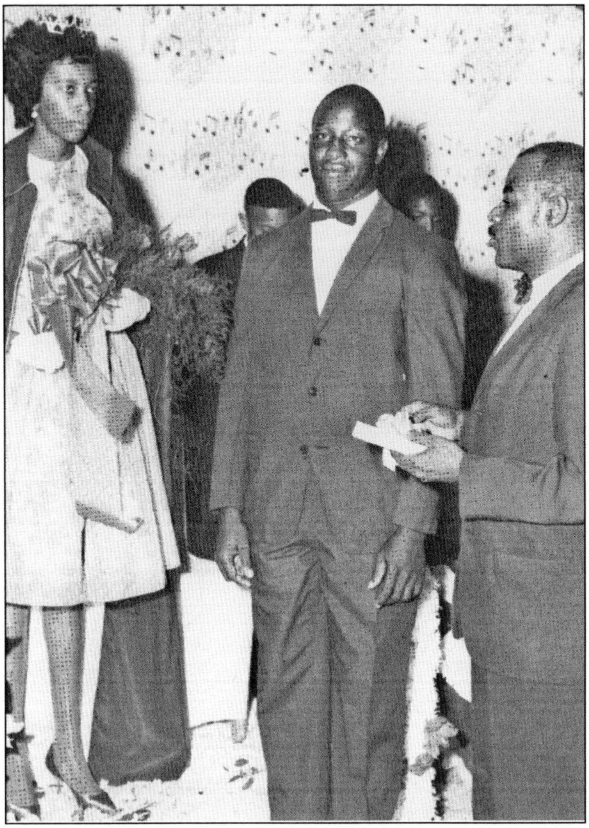

Deborah Keith Mack was the first E.E. Butler High School homecoming queen. She was crowned "Miss Butler High School" during the 1962–1963 school year. From left to right are Deborah Keith Mack, captain of the football team Roger Smith, and Ulysses Byas, principal of E.E. Butler High School. (Courtesy of the Fair Street/ Butler Alumni Association.)

Miss Butler High School and her attendants posed for this picture on the football field at Gainesville's City Park in 1965. The homecoming queen and her attendants, from left to right, are Vivian Goss, Pamela Law, Melinda Lipscomb, Shirley Brawner ("Miss Butler High School"), Linda Rucker, Ernestine Shields, and Beverly Moorehead. (Courtesy of the Fair Street/Butler Alumni Association.)

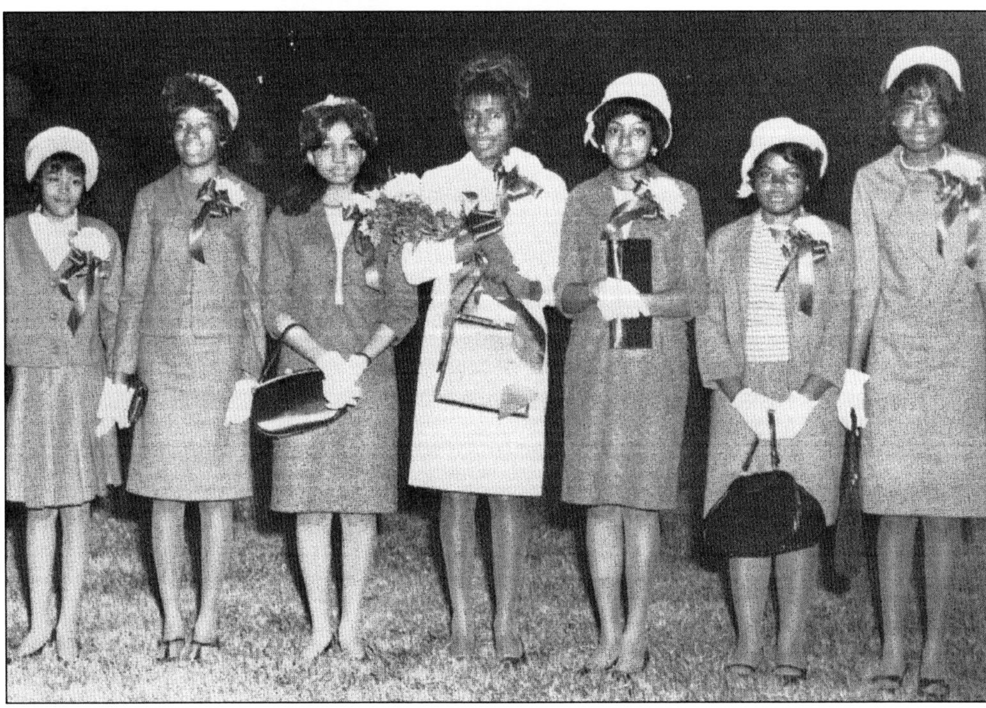

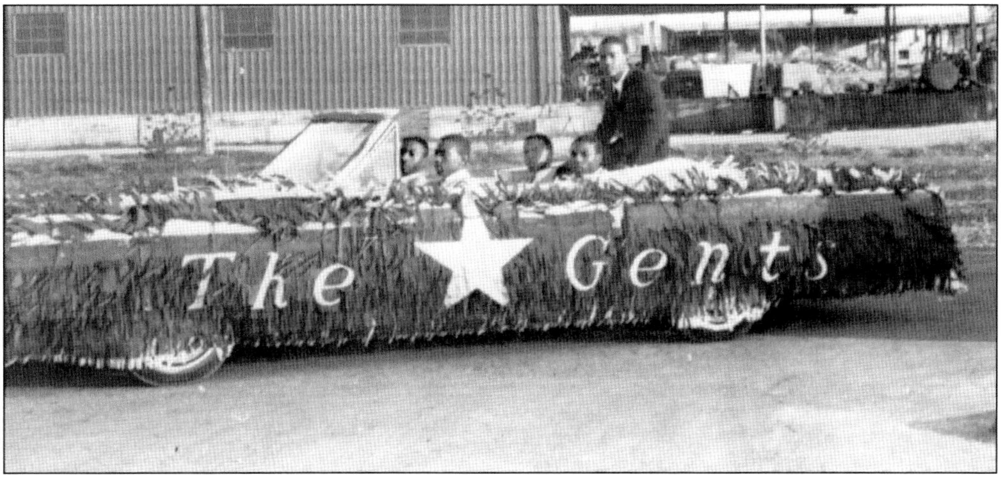

Members of the Gents Club are shown riding in a convertible in the E.E. Butler High School homecoming parade in 1968. (Courtesy of the Fair Street/Butler Alumni Association.)

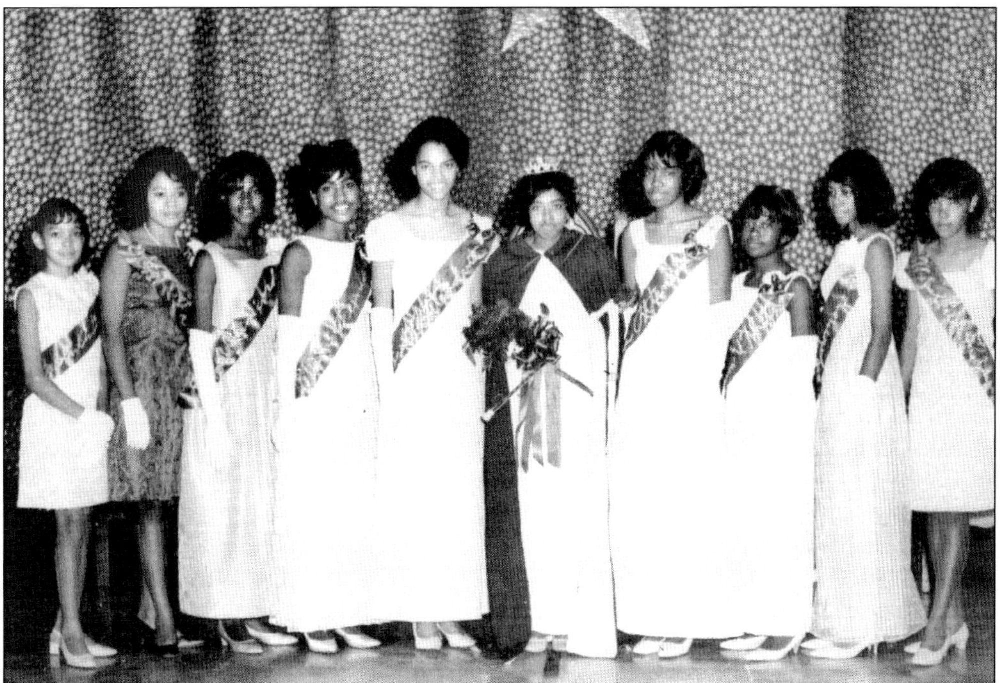

The coronation theme for the 1967–1968 Miss Butler High School Pageant was "A Shower of Stars." The homecoming queen and her court, from left to right, included Marcel Branch, Patricia Sims, Berlinda Turner, Carolyn Brawner, June Hayward, Linda Ann Cheeks (Miss Butler High School), Beverly Moorehead, Deborah Wells, Bobbie Jean Rucker, and Joyce Hayward. (Courtesy of the Fair Street/Butler Alumni Association.)

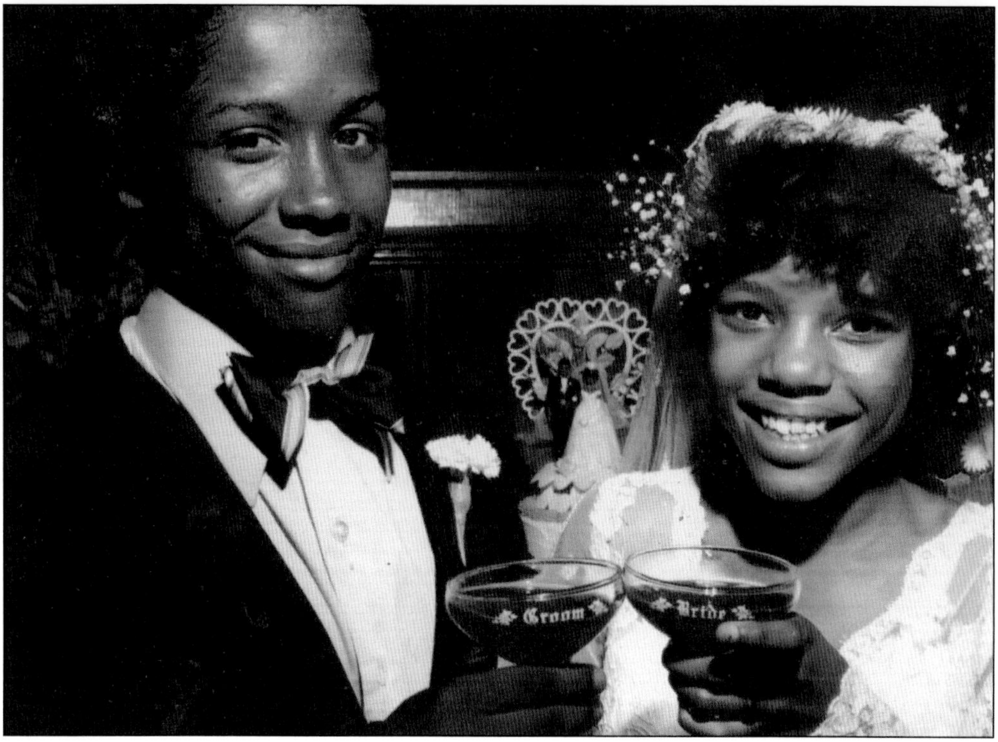

The Gainesville Chapter of the Housewives' League sponsored a Tom Thumb Wedding in 1978. The groom was Derrick "Squeak" Butts and the bride was nine-year-old Misty Burris. The wedding was held at Rucker Memorial Church in Gainesville. (Courtesy of Mary Alice Burris Fuller.)

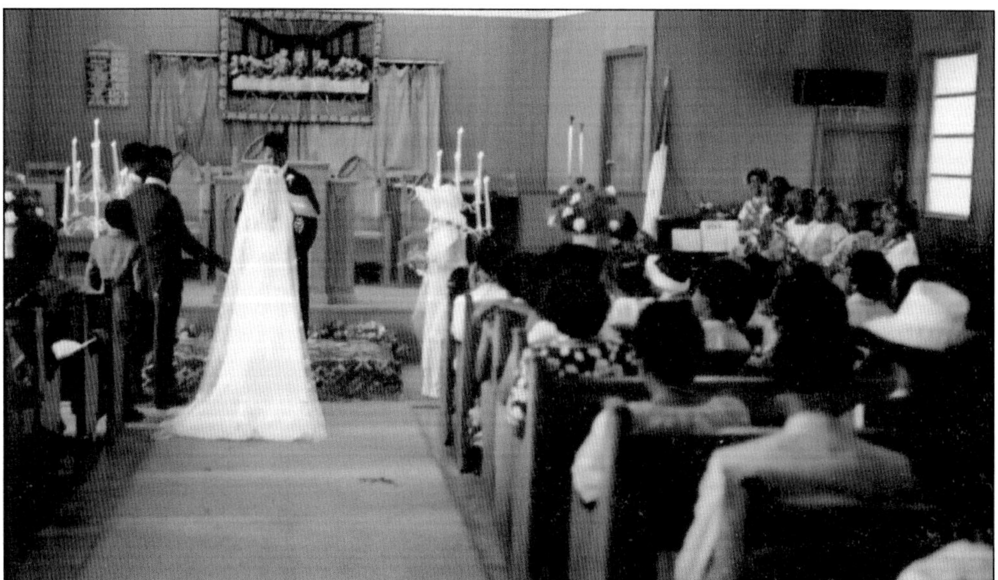

The Tom Thumb bride, Misty Burris, and the Tom Thumb groom, Derrick Butts, exchange vows before Curtis Wright, the Tom Thumb minister. (Courtesy of Mary Alice Burris Fuller.)

Five

DID WE HAVE FUN?
Sports and Recreation

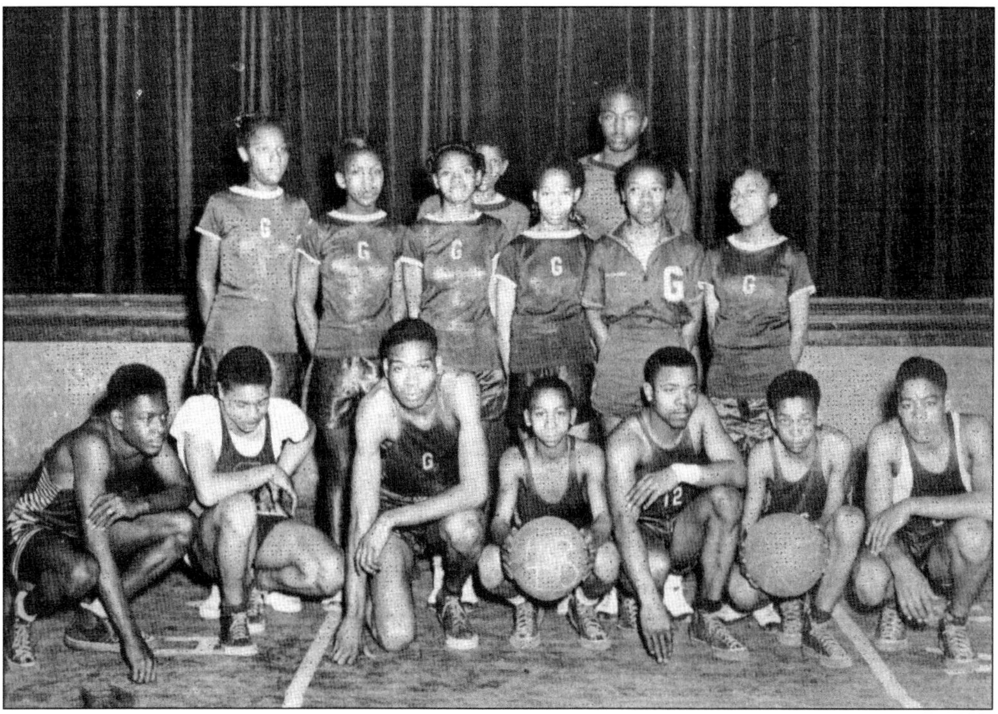

Members of the 1948 Fair Street School basketball team, from left to right, are (front row) William T. Harbin, James Ellison, Samuel Thornton, Haywood Clyde, Harold Anderson, Doyle Butts, and Kyle Moorehead Jr.; (back row) Virginia Blake, Mary Frances Moss, Minnie Hopps, Dorothy Thornton, Rebecca Thompson, and Carolyn Sadler; (extreme rear) Charles Harris and Julian Niles. (Courtesy of the Fair Street/Butler Alumni Association.)

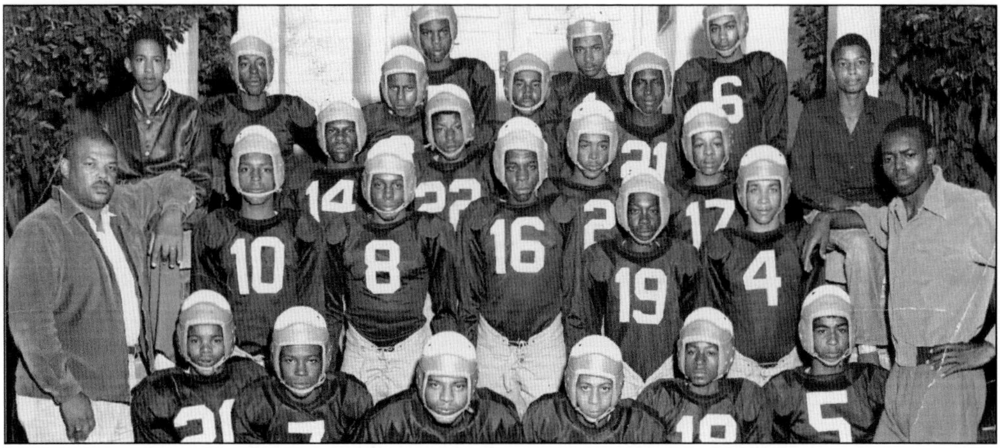

The Men's Progressive Club raised funds to establish Fair Street High School's first football team in 1950. Coaches and players pictured are, from left to right, (first row) Assistant Coach, Dock S. Lowe Jr., Tommy Holland, Leroy Wright, Cleo Sadler, Haywood Clyde, Asberry Turner, Douglas Morrow, and Coach Belton James; (second row) Raymond Hudson, George Goss, Winfred Cobb, Paul Wilkins, and Doyle Butts; (third row) Eugene Underwood, Amos Goudelock, Bobby Pittman, Robert Cantrell, Alvin Johnson, and Robert Morrow; (fourth row) Robin Hudson, Jack Pittman, Maynard Brown, and Walter Donahue; (fifth row, extreme rear) T. J. Holcomb, Scipio Jackson, and Charles Mitchell. (Courtesy of Maggie R. Lowe.)

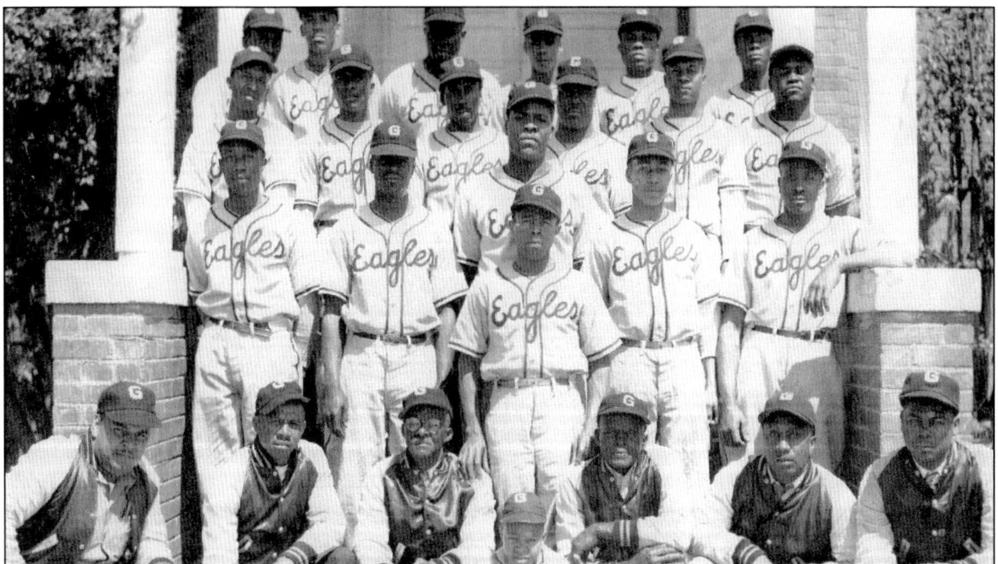

The Gainesville Eagles, a community baseball team, included from left to right (first row) Hubert Brooks, Tunic Davis, Jep Johnson, two unidentified, Lamb Shepard, and Bennie Rucker; (second row) Charles Johnson, Matt Randolph, Ollis Williams, Billy Clyde, and Cal Hart; (third row) James "Dude "Mack; (fourth row) Bennie Johnson, Herman Johnson Clyde Riley, George Banks, Edward Johnson, and Lovie Smith; (fifth row) Ralph Slaughter, Newt Randolph, Charles Mitchell, unidentified, Roger Wilmont, and Booth Roper. (Courtesy of James Brooks.)

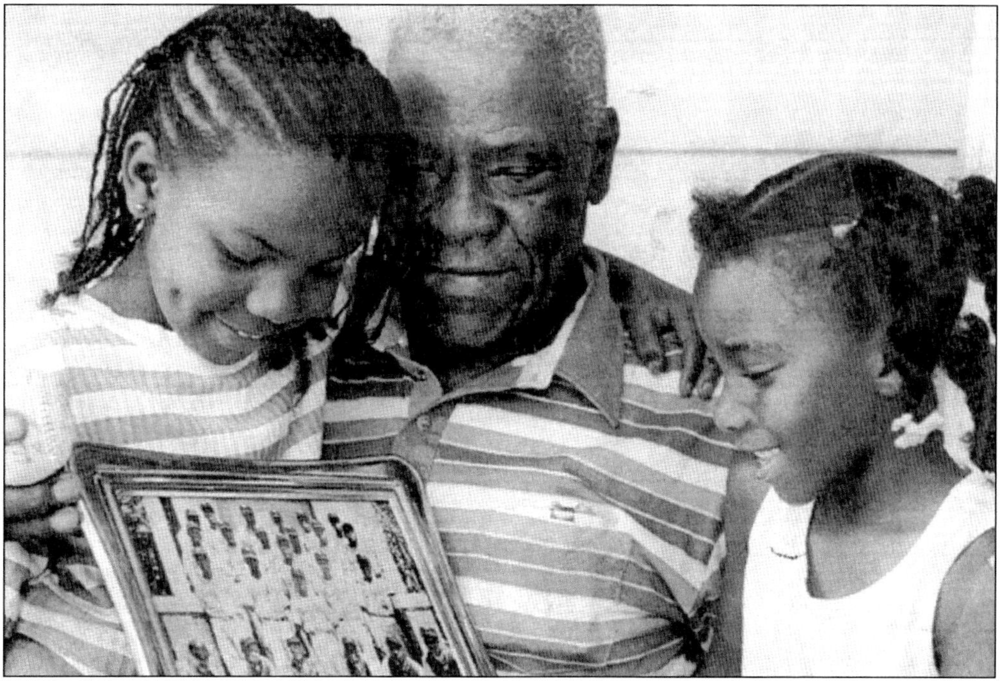

Gainesville's James Henry "Dude" Mack was the star pitcher of the Gainesville Eagles Baseball team in the 1940s and 1950s. He specialized in what he termed a "submarine pitch." Whenever Dude announced his intentions of pitching "the submarine," all of the outfielders would come into the mound. They would then sit and clap while Dude threw nine pitches to end the inning. (Courtesy of *The Times*.)

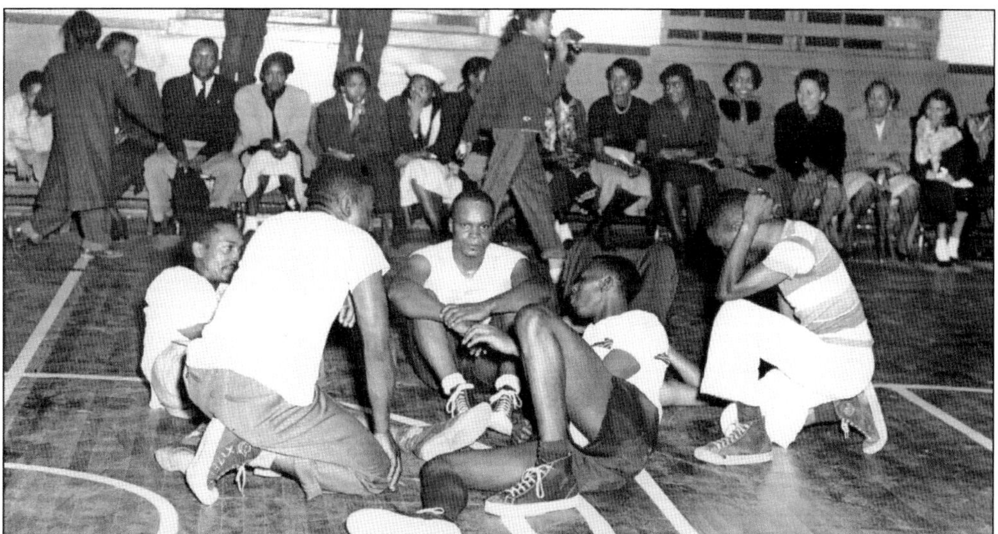

Spectators watch from the sidelines as members of the Men's Progressive Club play basketball in the Fair Street auditorium. The second person on the left, seated on the floor, is John Morrow. The fifth person from the left is Austin Brown Sr. (Courtesy of Clinton and Ingie Brown.)

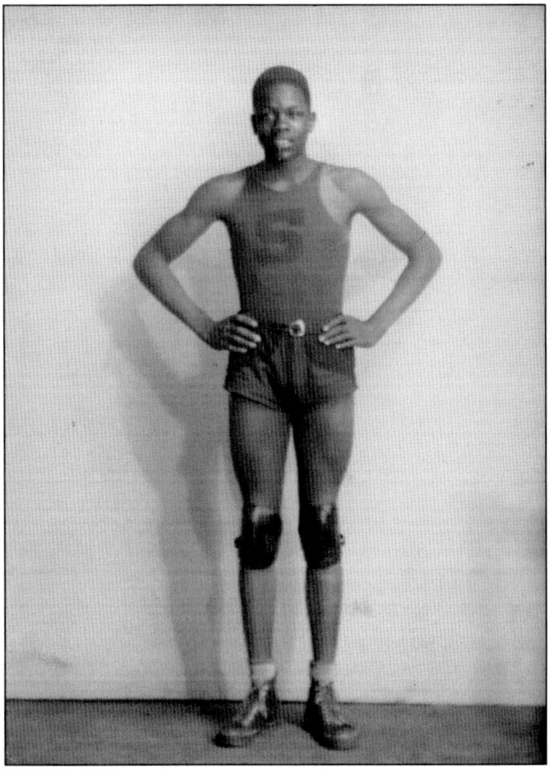

Lawrence Appleby posed for this picture wearing his basketball uniform. He was the first African-American lifeguard in Hall County. He practiced his skills at the Fair Street Pool in Gainesville. (Courtesy of Wilbur and Dixie Ramsey.)

The Fair Street Pool was constructed in 1948 to serve Hall County's African-American community. The pool is operated by the Gainesville Park and Recreation Department. (Courtesy of James and Alphia Wills.)

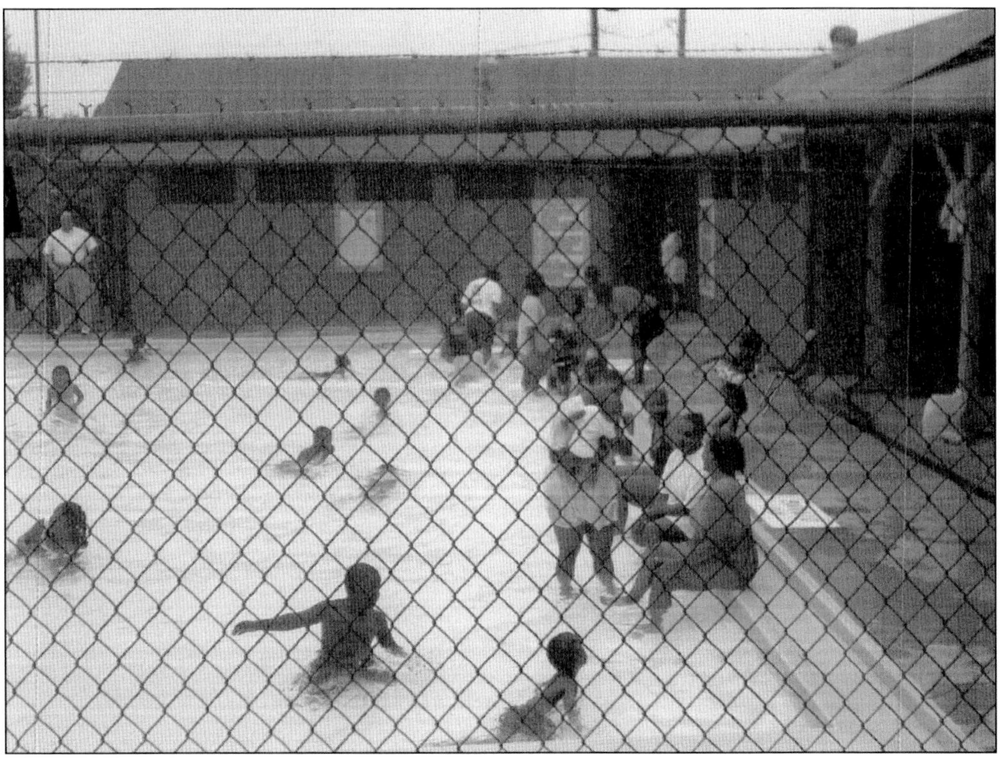

The American Legion was a popular nightspot in Gainesville during the 1950s. James Brown and the Famous Flames were frequent performers at The Legion. From left to right are Q.D. Brown, Flora Anderson, unidentified, Idell Martin, and Louise Littlejohn. (Courtesy of Linda Rucker Hutchens.)

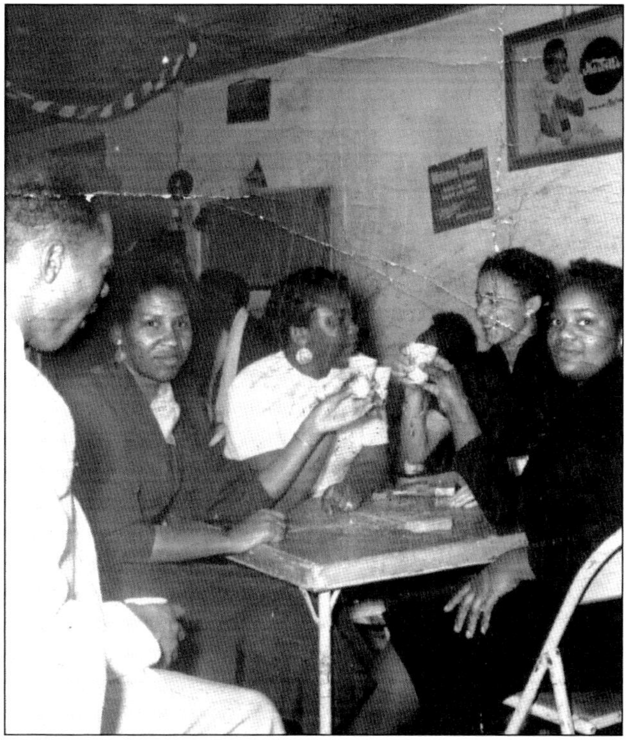

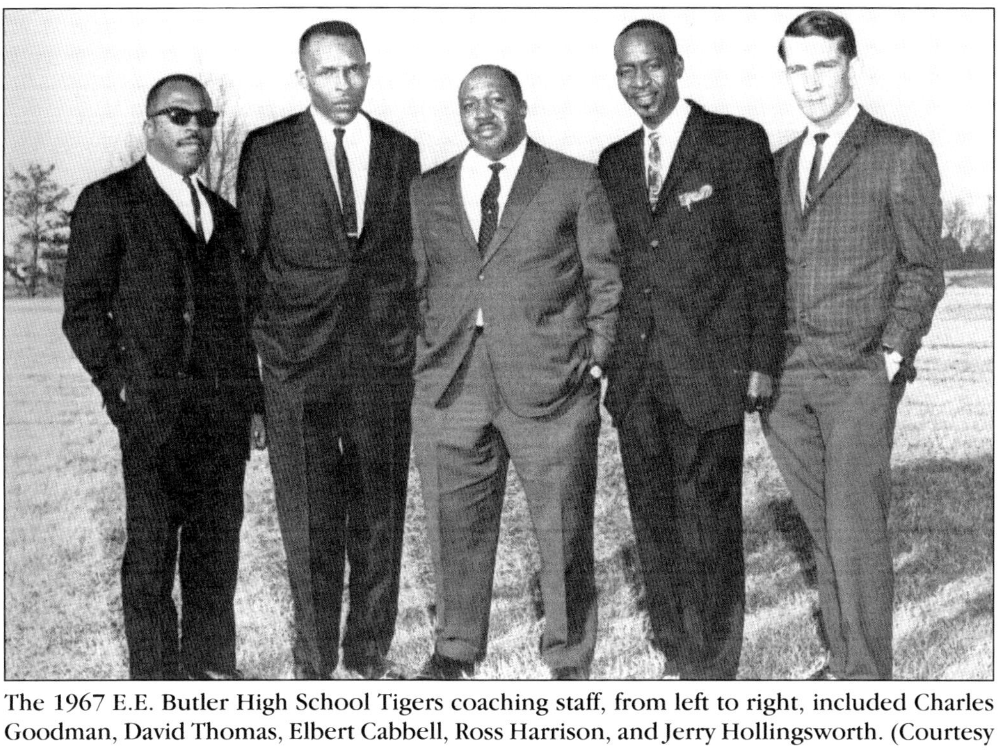

The 1967 E.E. Butler High School Tigers coaching staff, from left to right, included Charles Goodman, David Thomas, Elbert Cabbell, Ross Harrison, and Jerry Hollingsworth. (Courtesy of the Fair Street/Butler Alumni Association.)

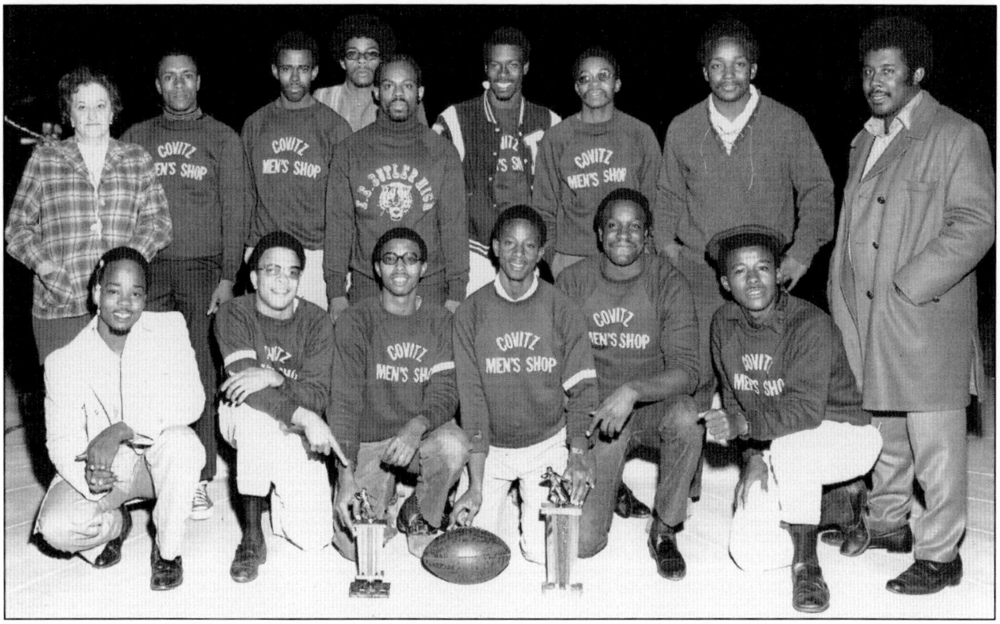

This Gainesville Park and Recreation football team was organized and sponsored by Lillian Covitz in the late 1960s. The team's players, from left to right, are (front row) Jimmy Clark, Paul Cheeks, Freddie Stephens, Douglas Turner, Billy Smith and Robert Hall; (back row) Lillian Covitz (sponsor) Tracy Collins, Eugene Brown, Nathaniel Montgomery, Jalasker Lyles, Billy King, Emory Turner, Jerry Castleberry, and Willie Ramsey (trainer). (Courtesy of the Hall County Black History Society)

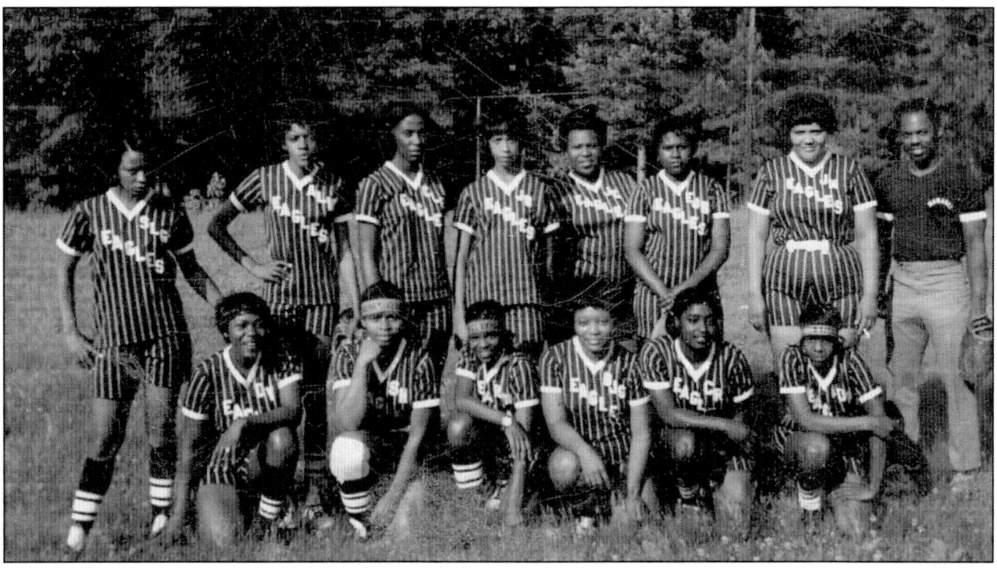

Members of the Eagles, Gainesville's first black ladies' softball team, from left to right, are (front row) Dorothy Young, Sandra Harris, Ruby Watson, Barbara Jean Glaze, Clara Bailey, and Ruth Watson; (back row) Sandra Turner, Annie Lee Smith, Constance Pulliam, Joyce Butts, Johnnie Carrington, Ella Jean Smith, Julia Randolph, and Coach Jalaska Lyles. (Courtesy of Ella Jean Smith.)

These youngsters are shown enjoying summer fun activities at the Butler Day Camp in the 1970s. This day camp was sponsored by the Gainesville Park and Recreation Department. (Courtesy of the Hall County Black History Society.)

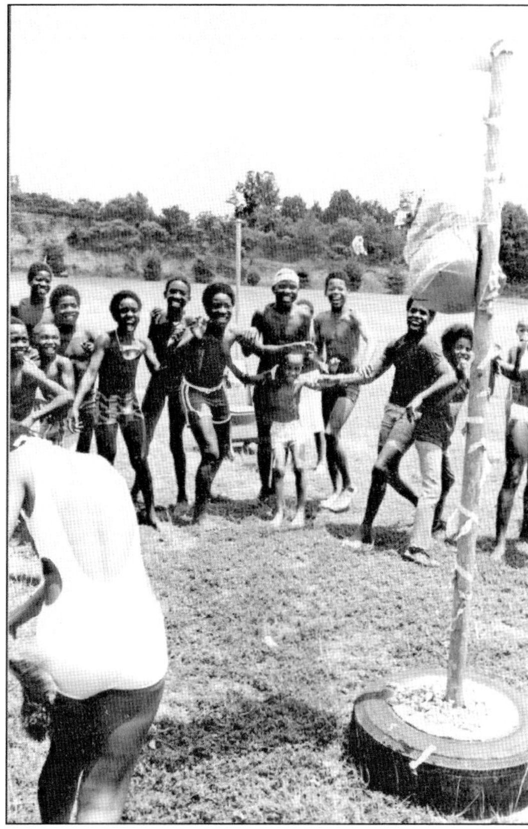

Emmett Walker on the left and Richard Haynes on the right are shown playing a game of table tennis at the Gents' Teen Center in Gainesville in this 1973 photo. (Courtesy of the Hall County Black History Society.)

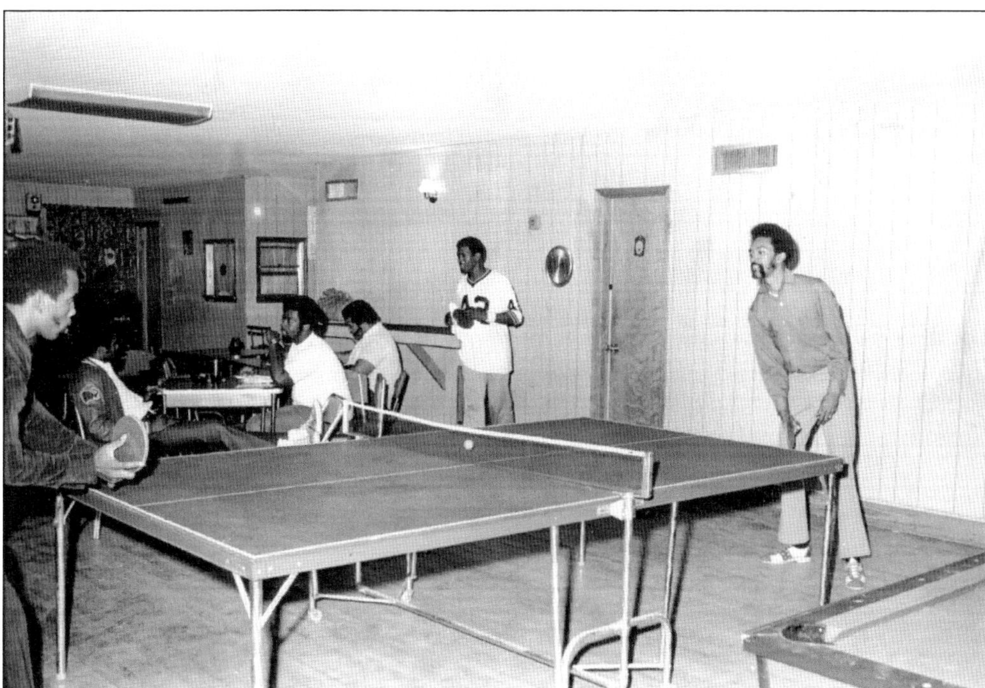

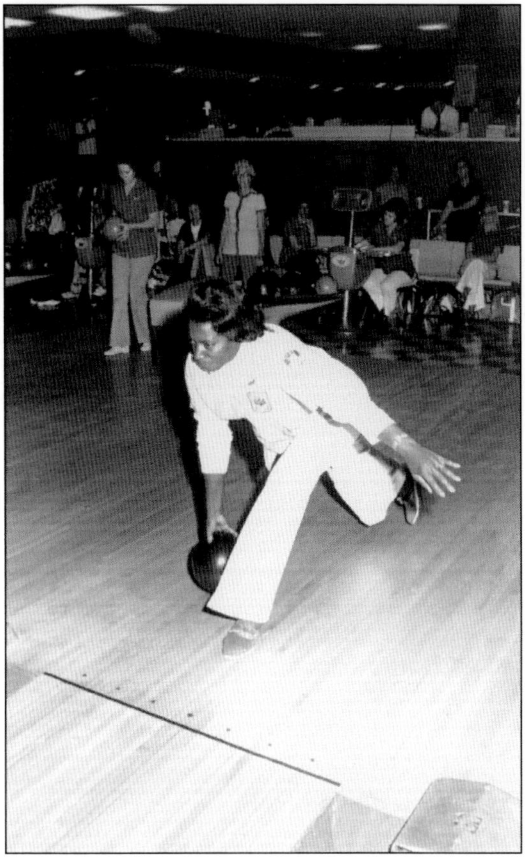

In April 1974, Ornie L. Whelchel of Gainesville became the reigning Women's Georgia State Bowling Champion. She rolled a total score of 1,706 to surpass all of the other female bowlers in Georgia. (Courtesy of the Hall County Black History Society.)

Members of the 1969 E.E. Butler High School basketball team, from left to right, are (front row) Jerry Hudson (trainer), Scott Randolph, Charles Sims, Charles Watson, James Willis, and Michael Gaither (trainer); (middle row) Kenneth Stephens (trainer), John Thompson, Terry Phillips, Robert Willis, Larry Robinson, and Wilburn Stringer; (back row) Osco Cantrell, Wallace Brawner, Edward Gaither, Tolman Merritt, and Emmett Walker. (Courtesy of the Fair Street/Butler Alumni Association.)

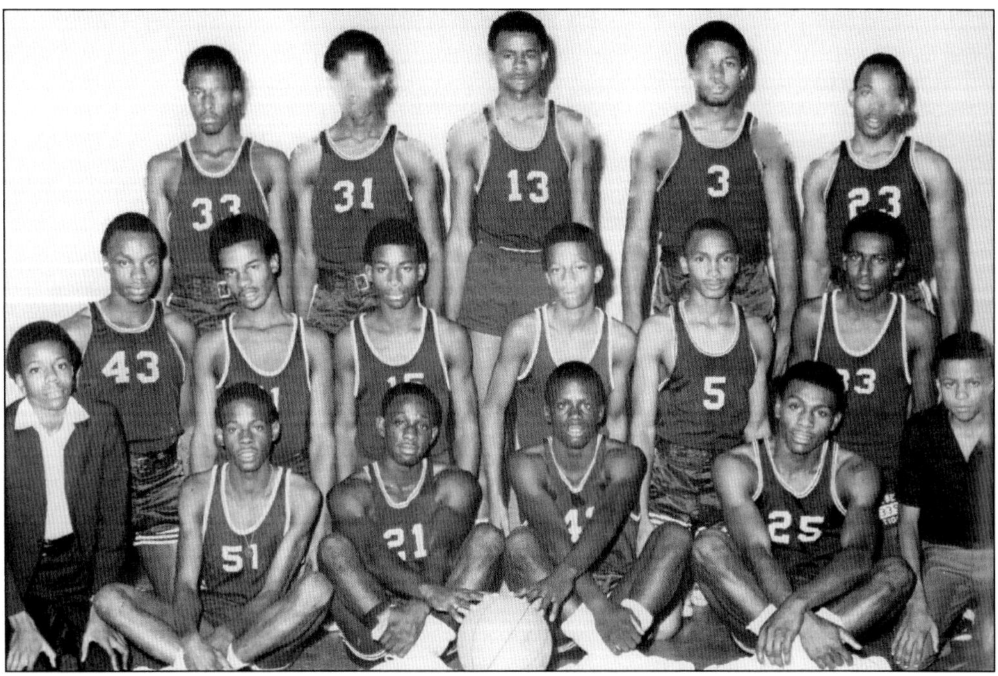

Six

The Three *R*s
Schools

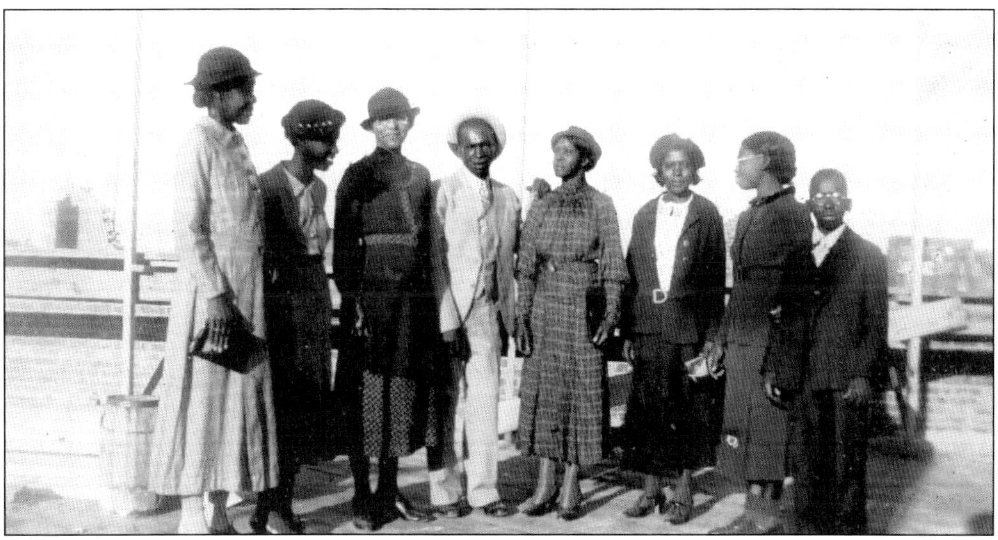

Construction began on Fair Street School in 1936. Standing on the foundation of the school at the construction site, from left to right, are Jennie Porter, Jennie Harris, Syna Maynor, Oscar Hutchens, Florence Hutchens, Alberta Anderson, Josie Nell Hutchens, and George Oscar Hutchens. Fair Street School was completed in 1937 after the tornado of 1936 severely damaged Summer Hill. (Courtesy of Josie Nell Billingsley.)

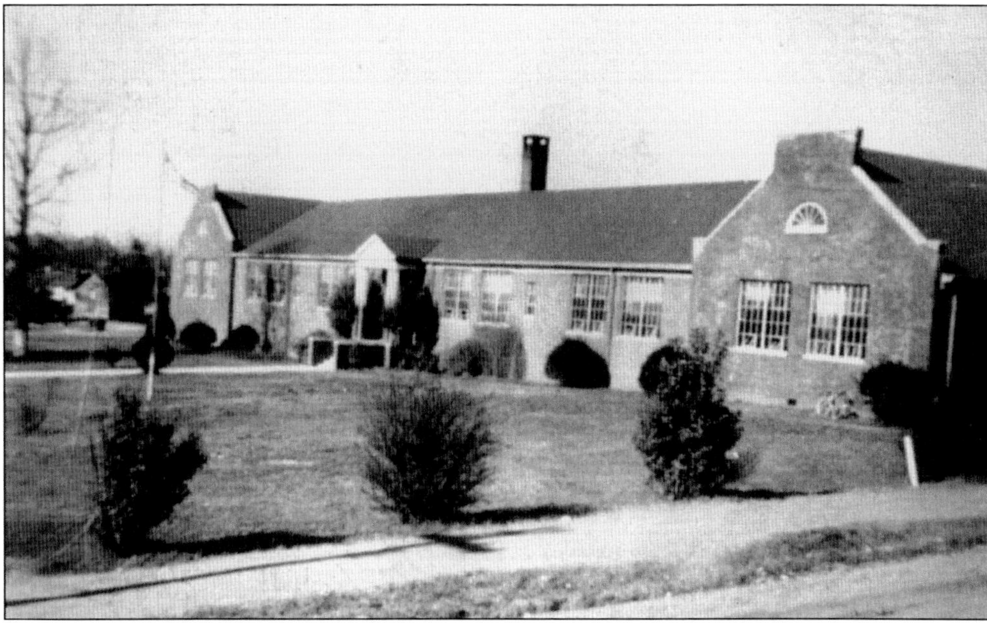

The original Fair Street School was constructed at a cost of $40,000 under WPA supervision after the 1936 tornado damaged Summer Hill School. The all-brick structure had a total of 14 classrooms with cloakrooms and an auditorium. (Courtesy of the Fair Street/Butler Alumni Association.)

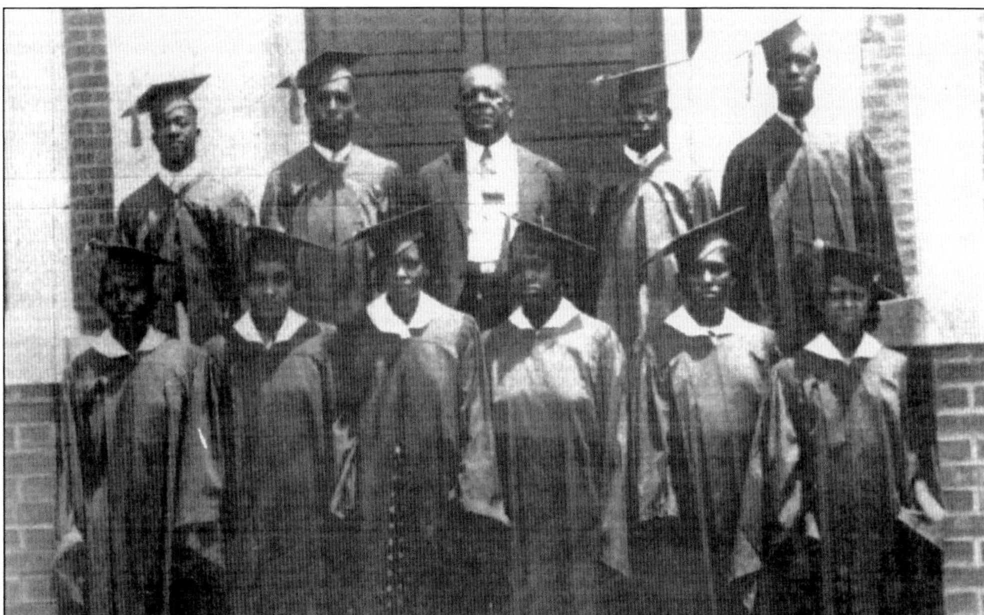

The Class of 1937 was the first class to graduate from Fair Street School. Identified in the front row, fourth from the left, is Hazel Wright. Pictured in the back row, from left to right, are Robert Couche, John Morrow Jr., W.H. Harper (principal), Austin Brown, and unidentified. (Courtesy of the Fair Street School Alumni Association.)

The 1948 faculty of Fair Street School included Principal C.W. Daniels and, from left to right, (front row) M.G. Bridges, S.G. Gannaway, D.L. Chamblee and G. Bryant; (middle row) B.E. Gambrell, J. Kimbers, and L. Gilbert; (back row) C.C. Miles, C. Poole, and L.G. Daniels. (Courtesy of the Fair Street/Butler Alumni Association.)

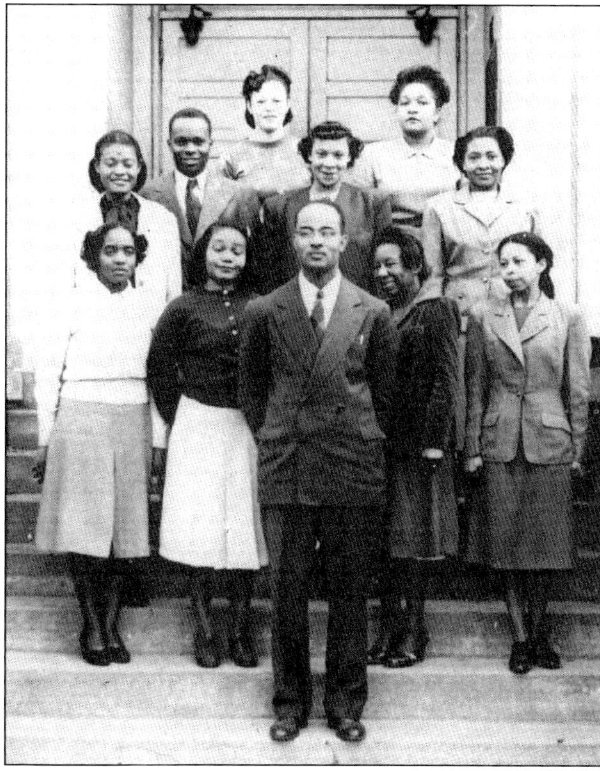

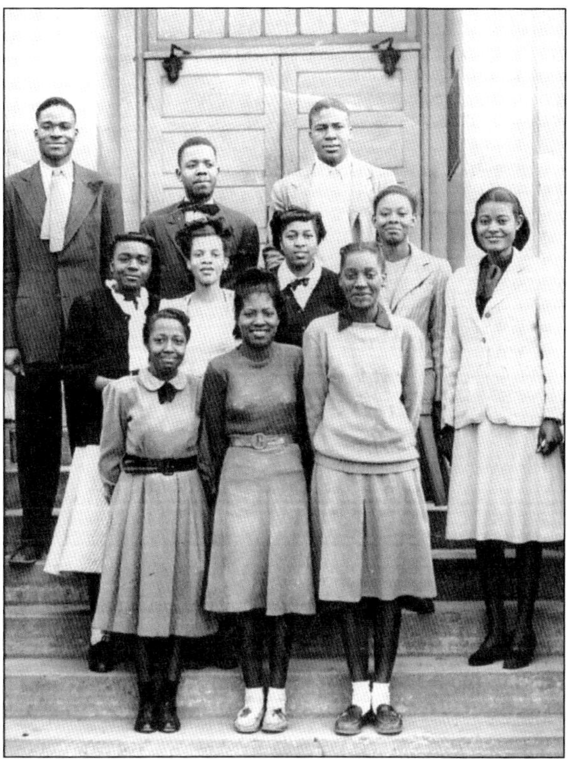

Pictured are members of the 1948 Senior Class. From left to right are (front row) Barbara Thompson, Elizabeth Waller, and Virginia Blake; (middle row) Martha Sullivan, Mattie Appleby, Luvercha Johnson, Margaret Wilburn, and Mrs. Gambrell (teacher); (back row) Samuel Thornton, Harold Anderson, and Charles Niles. (Courtesy of Fair Street/Butler Alumni Association.)

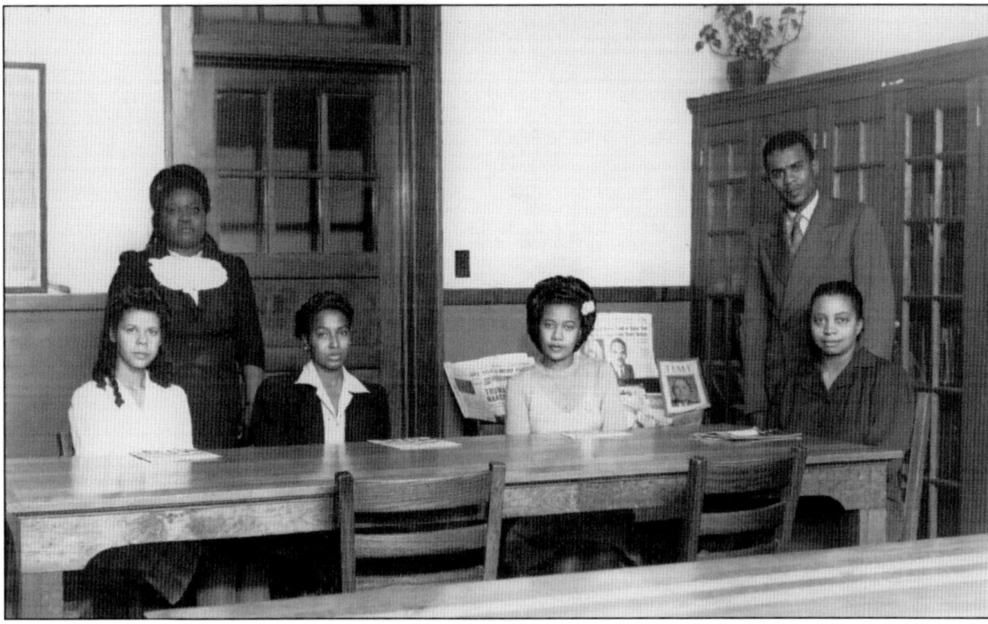

The setting for this picture was the Fair Street School Library in the late 1940s. Seated, from left to right, are Nannette Merritt, Luvercha Johnson, Sally Faye Jackson, and Mrs. J. B. Hylick (teacher); standing are Mrs. Benjamin (teacher) and J.B. Hylick (principal). (Courtesy of Wilbur and Dixie Ramsey.)

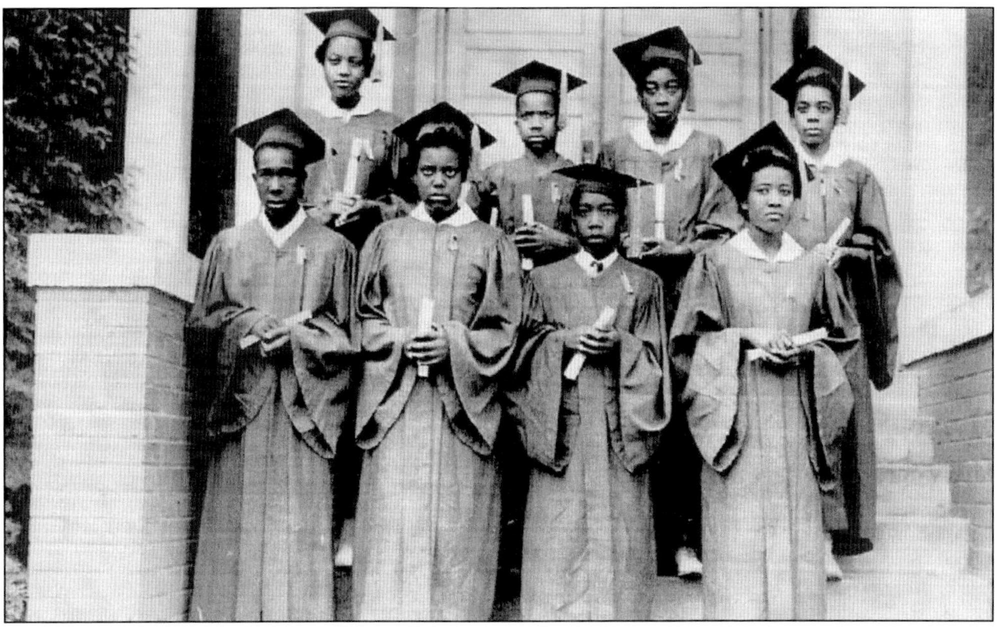

The 1943 eighth-grade graduates of Belton, Georgia's Public Colored School are, from left to right, (front row) G.B. Brown, Lezora Harvey, Jack Kid, and Christine Buffington Moon; (back row) Johnnie L. Deadwyler Rucker, Homer Bryson Jr., Ruby Moon Green, and Maudine Thornton Williams. Nancy Elrod (not pictured) was their teacher. (Courtesy of Linda Rucker Hutchens.)

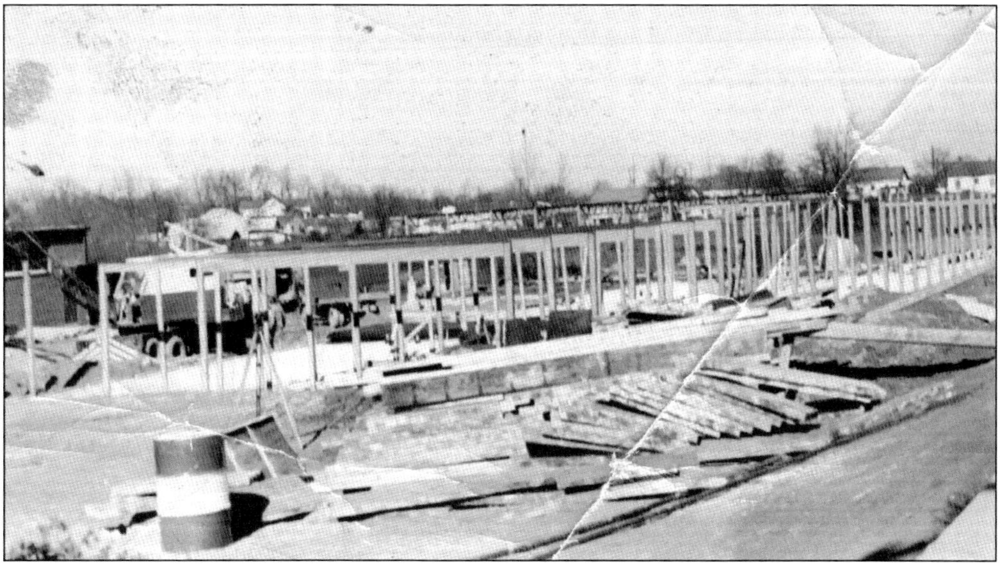

The construction of the upper-level addition to Fair Street School is shown in this picture. The new addition to the school was completed in 1958. (Courtesy of Evelyn Ware Glasper.)

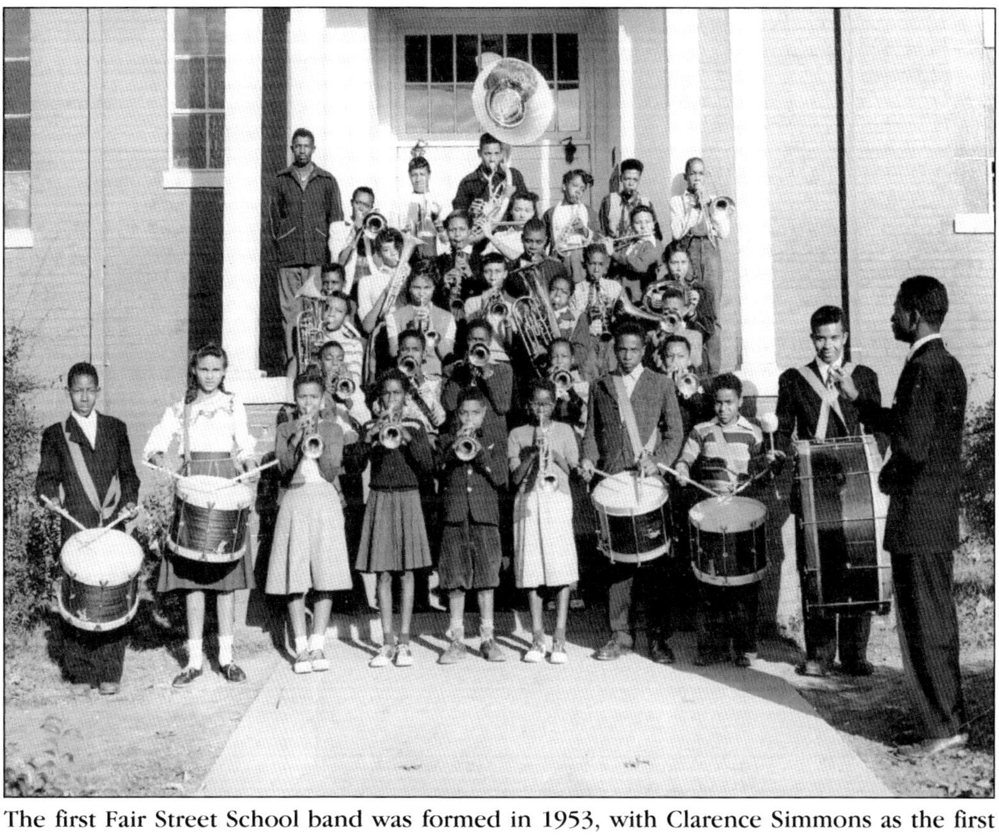

The first Fair Street School band was formed in 1953, with Clarence Simmons as the first band director. This picture was taken before the band received their uniforms. (Courtesy of the Fair Street/Butler Alumni Association.)

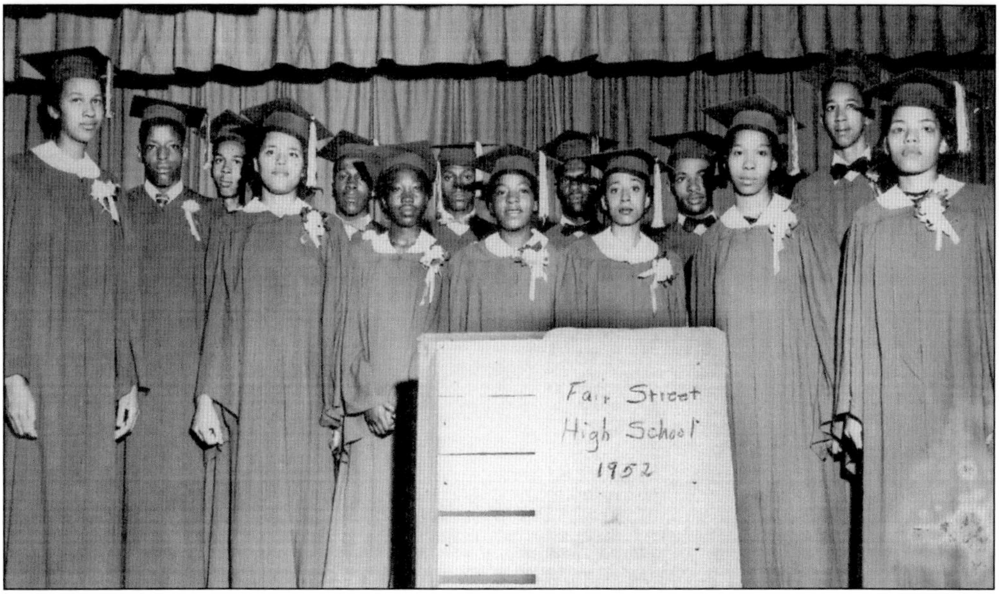

The graduates of the Fair Street High School Class of 1952 were, from left to right, (front row) Dorothy Williams, Lonnie Ann Wilkins, Martha Marshall, Bobbie J. Ellison, Dorothy Thornton and Doris Evans; (back row) unidentified, Bobby Pittman, George Moody, George Goss, Jack Pittman, Amos Guodelock, Scipio Jackson, and Eugene Underwood. (Courtesy of Doris Evans)

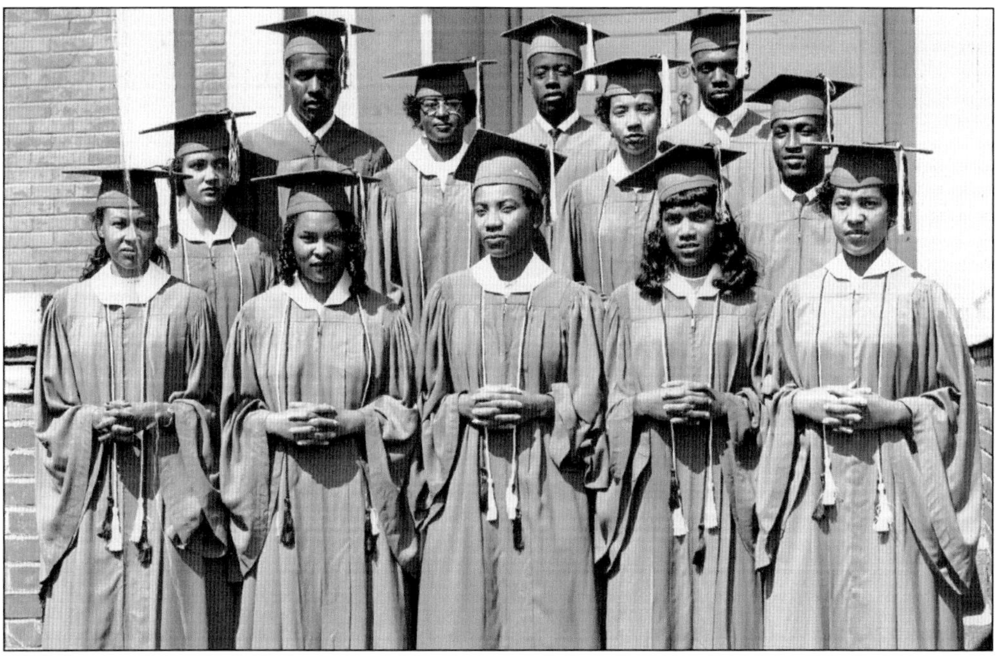

The 1956 graduates of Fair Street High School, from left to right, are (front row) Catherine Buffington, Mary Christian, Alice Faye Law, Hazel Martin, and Geraldine Williams; (back row) Eva Carter, Herman Moss, Lillie Young, John Turner, Mary Alice Cantrell, Royce Stephens, and Leroy Williams. (Courtesy of the Fair Street/Butler Alumni Association.)

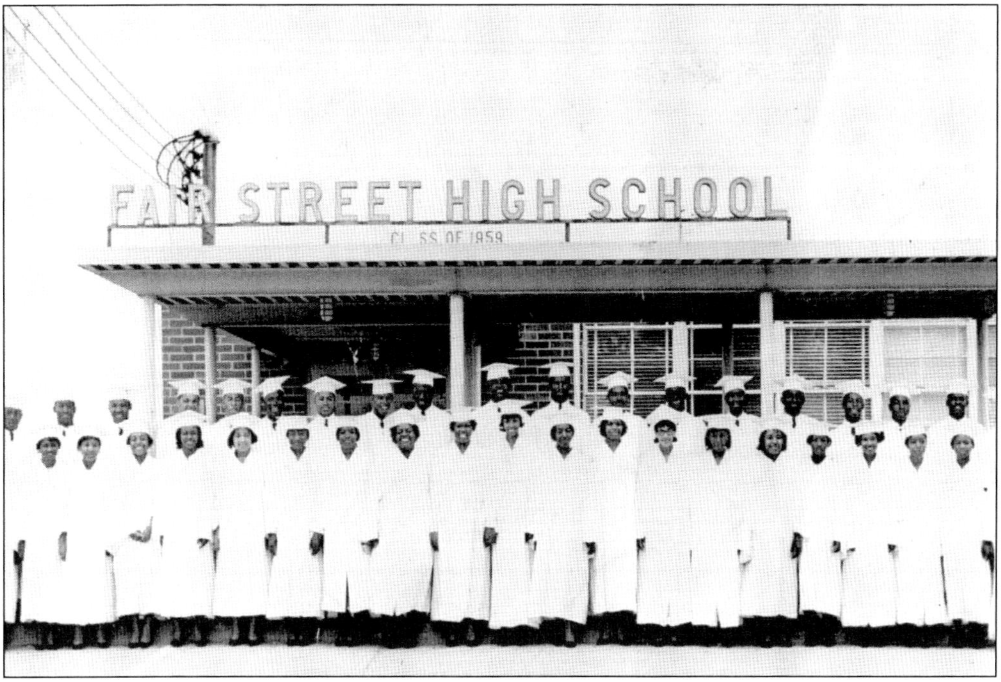

The Class of 1962 posed in front of the upper level of the Fair Street High School for this picture. This class was the last one to graduate from Fair Street School. (Courtesy of the Fair Street/Butler School Alumni Association.)

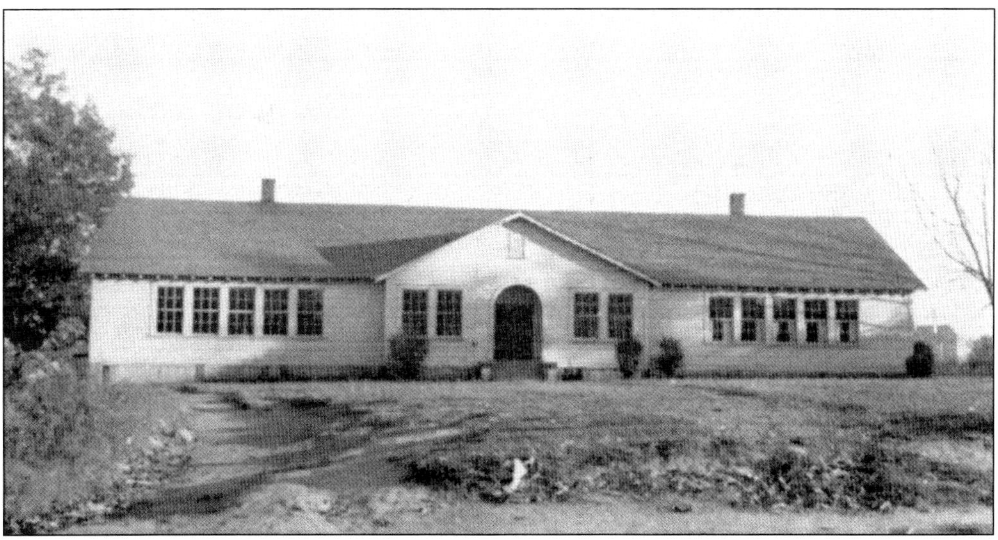

Northwestern Normal and Industrial School was established and maintained by the Northwestern Baptist Association. Plans for this school were presented to the association by its moderator, Rev. Green Hunter, in 1883. The school was erected on East Myrtle Street in Gainesville, at a cost of $1,200. Later, a girl's dormitory was added. This school was leased by the City of Gainesville in the mid-1950s to house its African-American students until construction of an addition to Fair Street School could be completed. (Courtesy of Fair Street/Butler Alumni Association.)

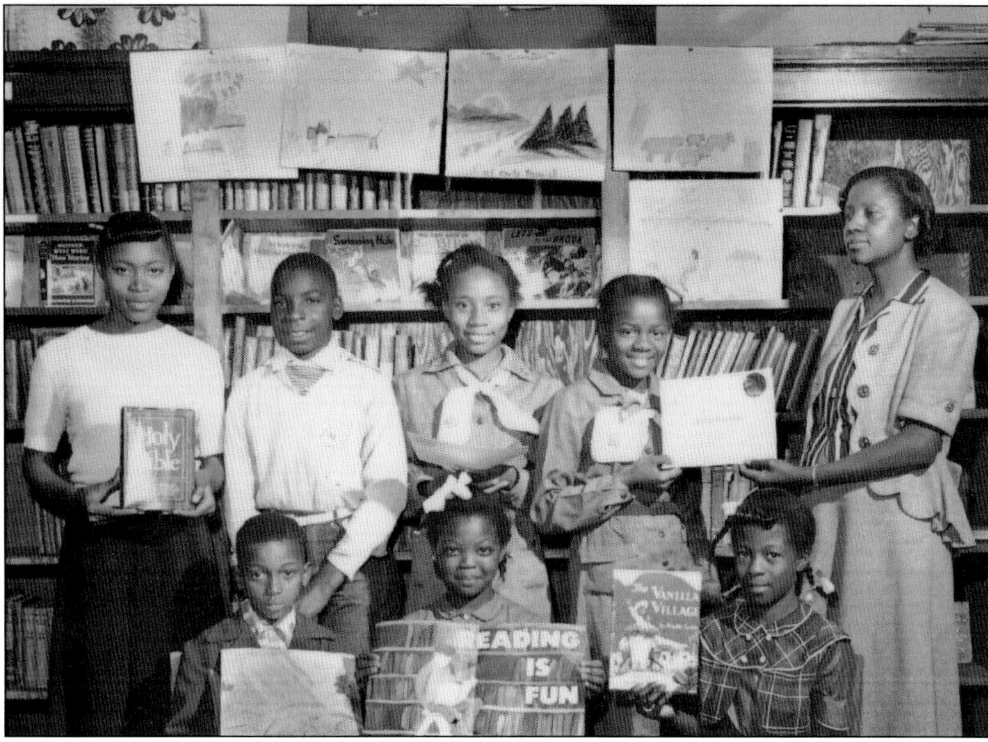

Students receiving reading certificates and awards in the library at Northwestern School, from left to right, are (front row) Bobby Joe Anderson, Sarah Carruth, and Alma Jane Hunter; (back row) Marion Thomas, Thomas Lawrence, Mattie R. Millsap, and Catherine Bryant. Clara B. McCrary, the school librarian (extreme right, back row), presented the awards. (Courtesy of Cathy McCrary Kimbro.)

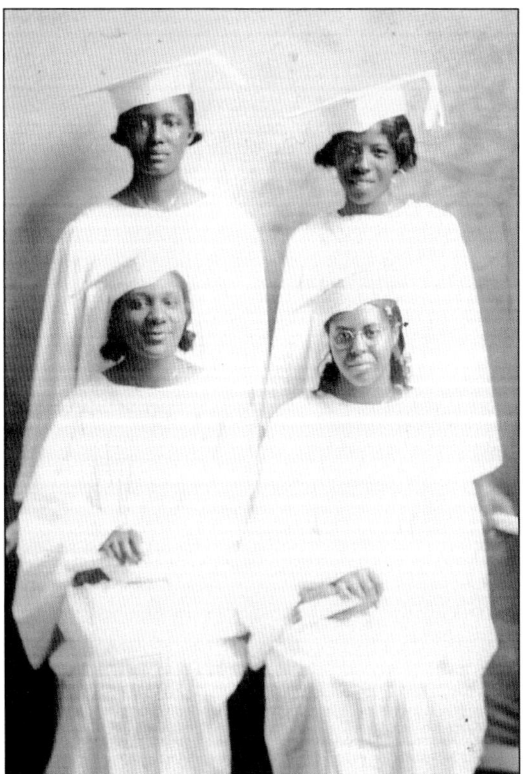

There were four graduates of the Beulah Rucker Industrial School in 1940. Seated, from left to right, are Eleanor Goss, Bertie M. Jackson, Jenell Thomas, and Carree Oliver Bailey. (Courtesy of Wilbur and Dixie Ramsey.)

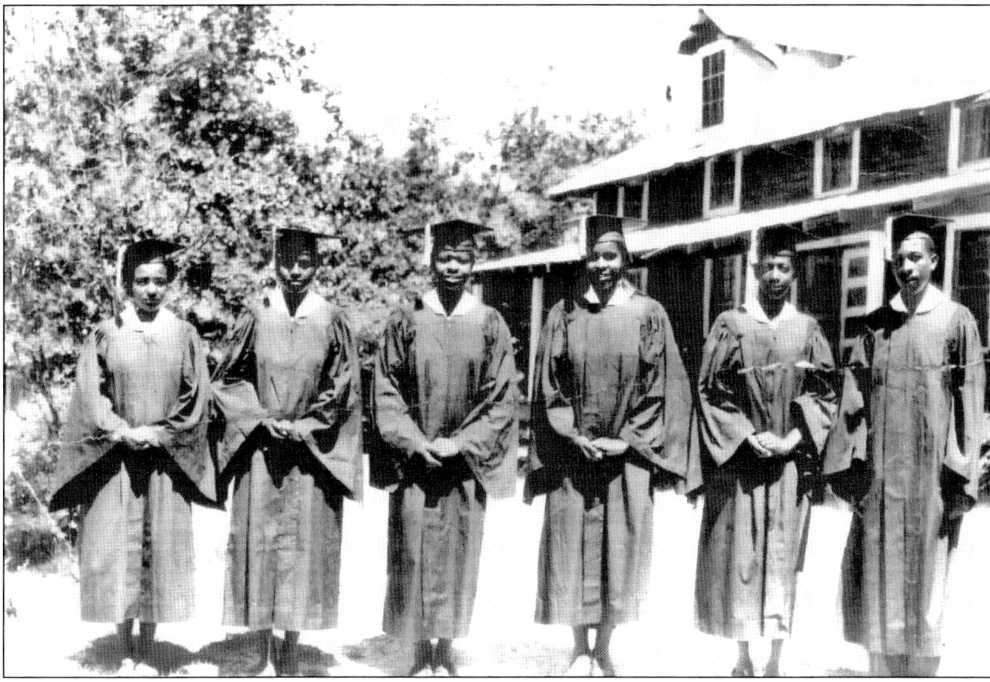

Members of the 1948 Graduating Class of the Beulah Rucker Industrial School posed for this picture. The graduates, from left to right, are Darline Allen, Ruby Nell Hudson, Lois Camp, Hazel Camp, Odessa Kelley, and Artrice Kelley. (Courtesy of Doris Thomas.)

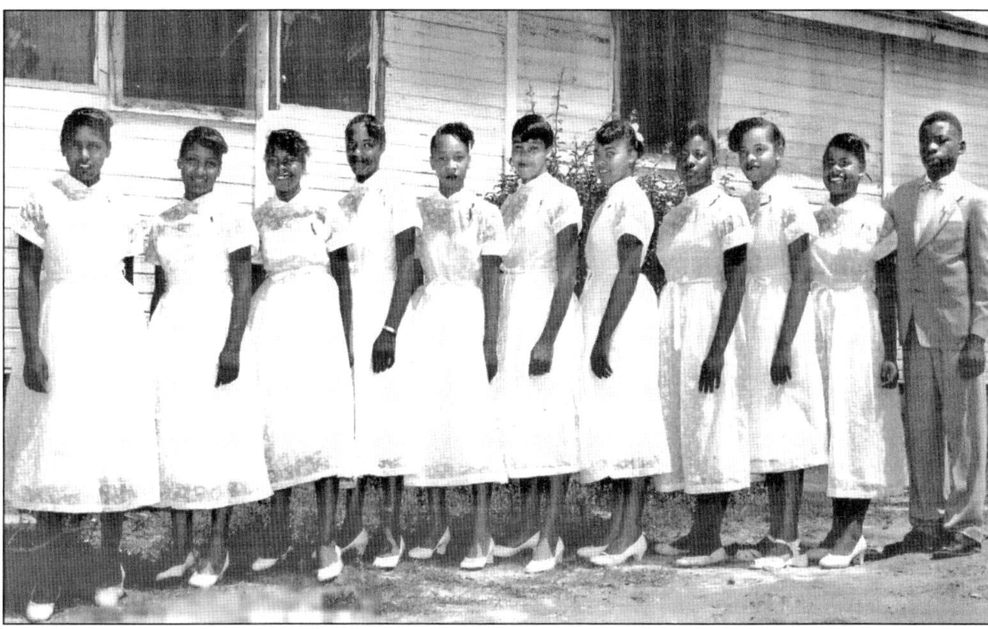

The eleven 1955 graduates of the Beulah Rucker Industrial School, from left to right, are Mamie Lee Lipscomb, Annette Lipscomb, Geneva Randolph, Irene Young, Thelma Harris, Georgia Randolph, Louise Hendrix, Mattie Mae Williams, Ernestine Williams, Annie Lois Bell, and Leroy Evans. (Courtesy of Doris Evans.)

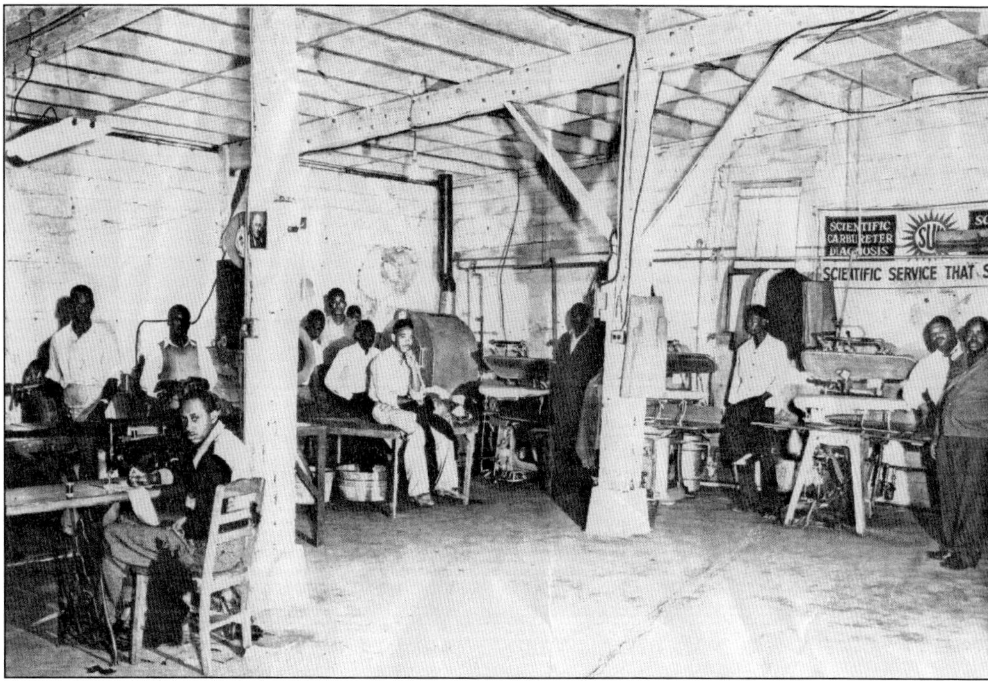

The Hall County Vocational School offered instruction in shoe repair, body and fender work, tailoring, and upholstery. C.C. Miles was the supervisor. (Courtesy of Jennie Harris.)

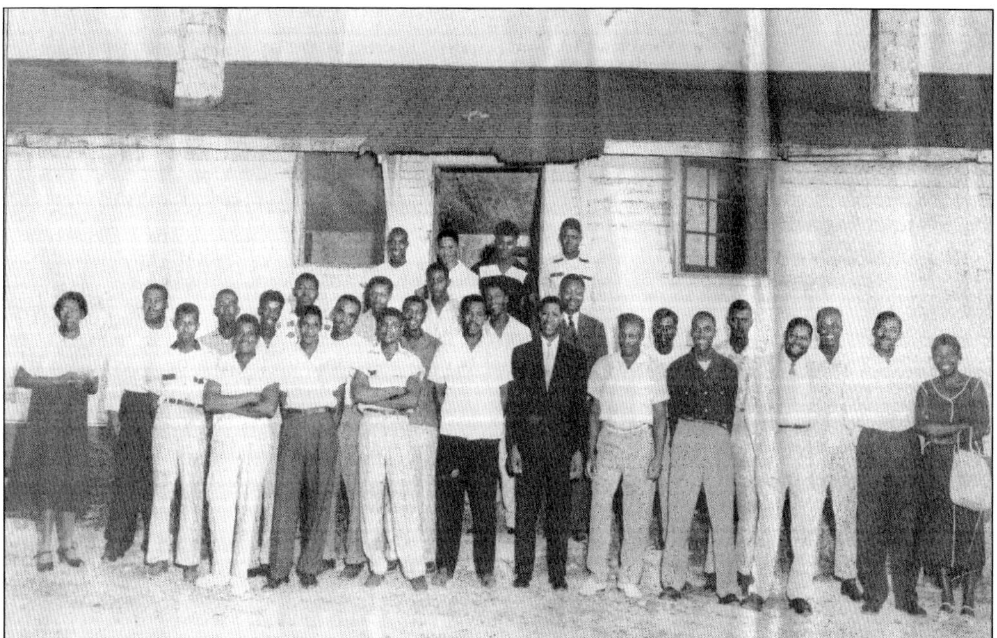

Mrs. Beulah Rucker Oliver, pictured on the left, conducted night classes for World War II veterans at her industrial school on Athens Highway in Gainesville. The students pictured in this class are being taught masonry skills. Dorothy Rucker, daughter of Mrs. Oliver, is pictured on the extreme right. (Courtesy of Eddie Dabney.)

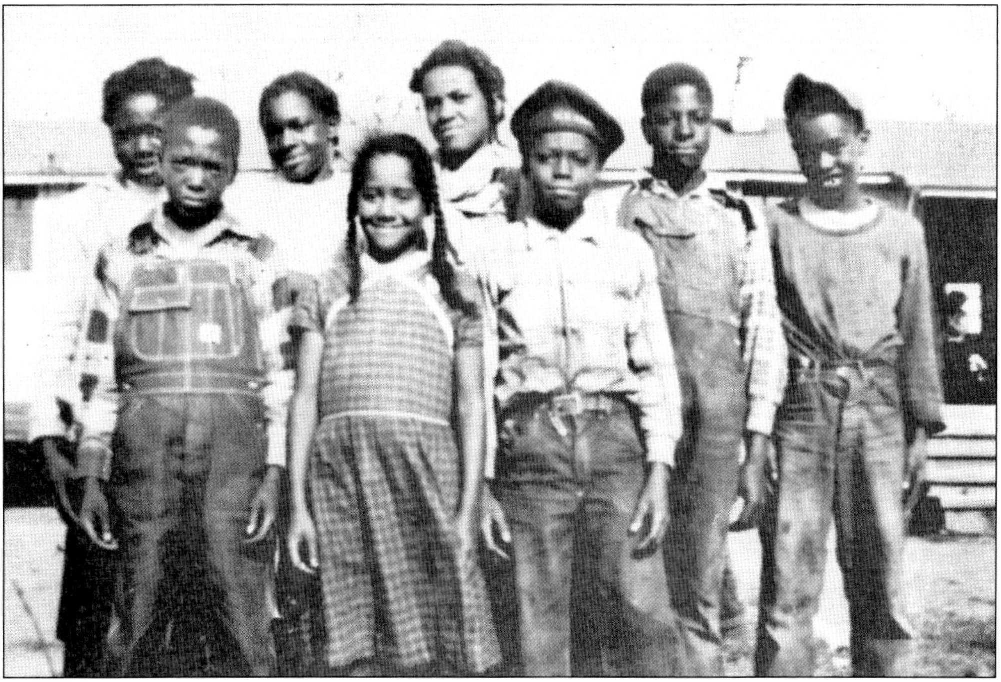

These students attended Mt. Zion School in Oakwood, Georgia, prior to the consolidation of Hall County's public schools in 1957. After consolidation, Hall County's African-American students were bused to Fair Street School in Gainesville. (Courtesy of Doris Evans.)

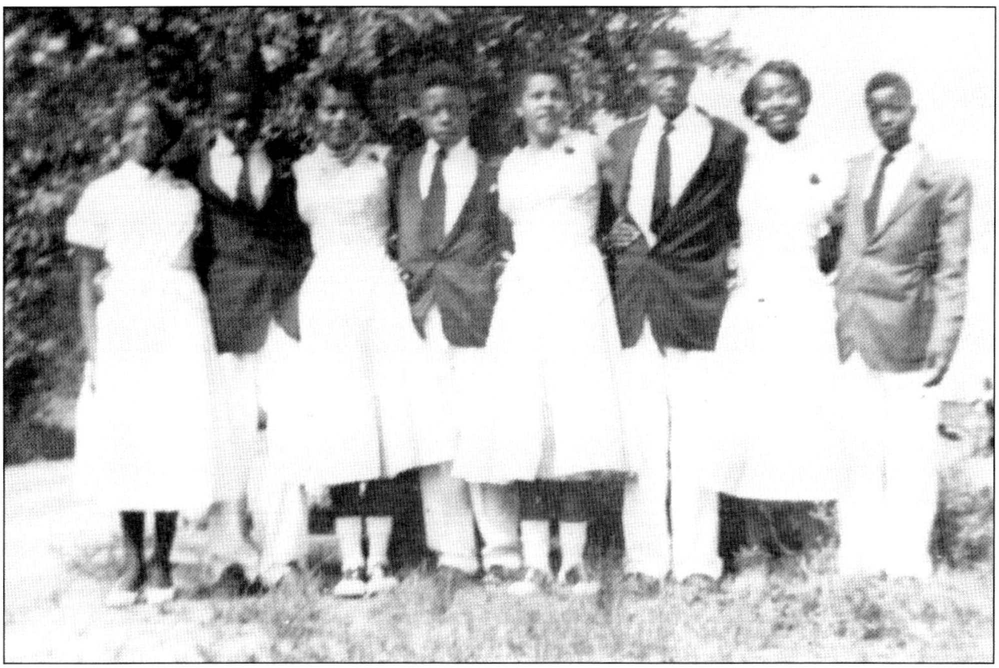

The 1955 Mount Zion eighth grade class included, from left to right, Ruby Millsap, Harold Cunningham, Betty S. Cheeks, Ollie B. Stephens, Annie L. Cheeks, James Poole, Doris Tanner, and Bob Dorsey. (Courtesy of Doris Evans.)

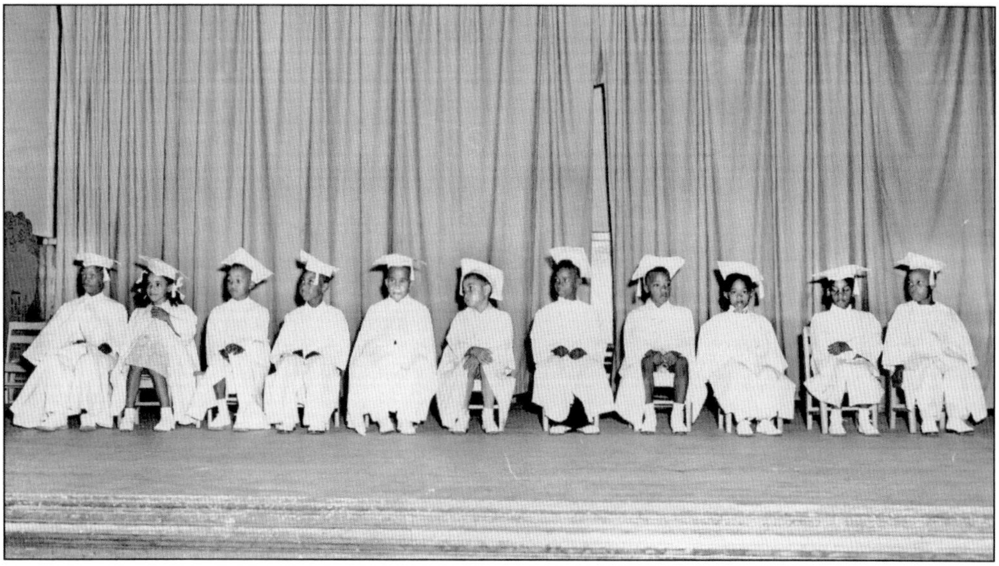

The 1955 graduates of Green Hunter Nursery, from left to right, were Donald Charles Wright, Theodora Merritt, Benjamin Rucker Jr., Gary Maxey, Eddie Dean Christian, Michael Graham, Bill Joe Randolph, Eugene Harris, Charles Glasper, Larry Morrow, and Michael Hancock. Mrs. Dan Syfan, president of the Gainesville Junior Service League and the nursery's sponsor, presented the diplomas to the graduates. (Courtesy of Linda Rucker Hutchens.)

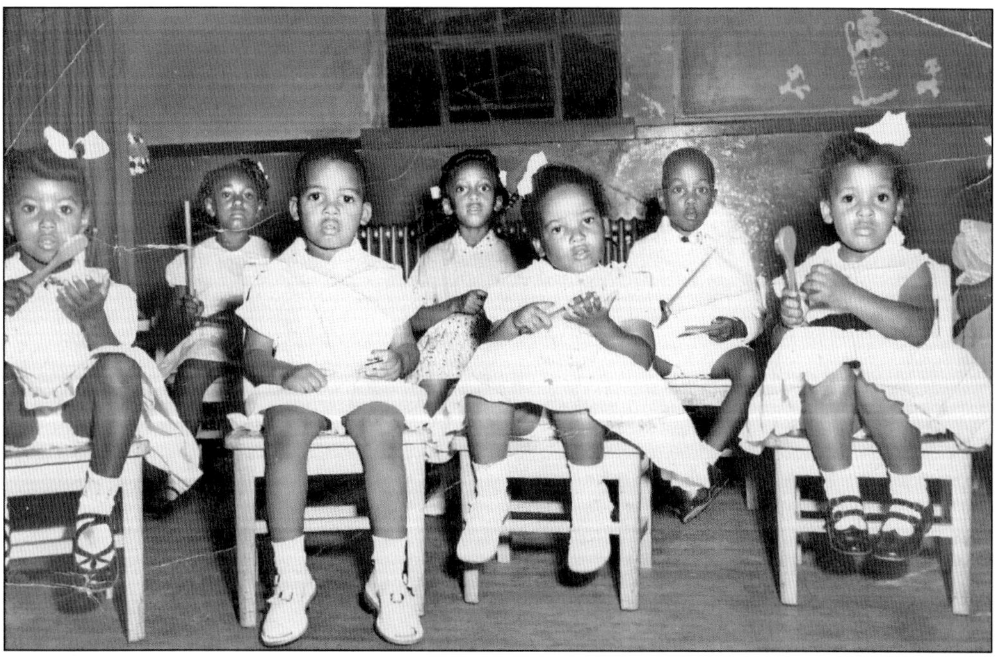

Children enrolled in Green Hunter Nursery in 1953 are shown as they present a musical program to parents and friends assembled at the nursery. Seen from left to right are (front row) Peggy Price, Tolman Merritt, Pamela Law, and Linda McMullen; (back row) Ophelia Ramsey, Dorothy Gilmore, and Benjamin Rucker Jr. (Courtesy of Linda Rucker Hutchens.)

Doris Evans was the director of the Fair Street Child Development Center. She is shown here with a group of children who are preparing to have snacks. (Courtesy of Doris Evans.)

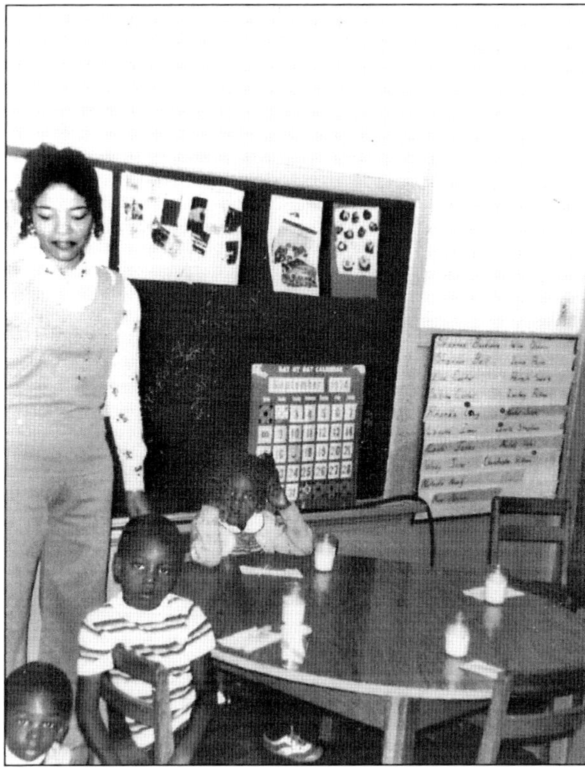

Todd Evans, Arnie Evans, and Ricky Davenport are pictured at play in a classroom at the Fair Street Child Development Center. (Courtesy of Doris Evans.)

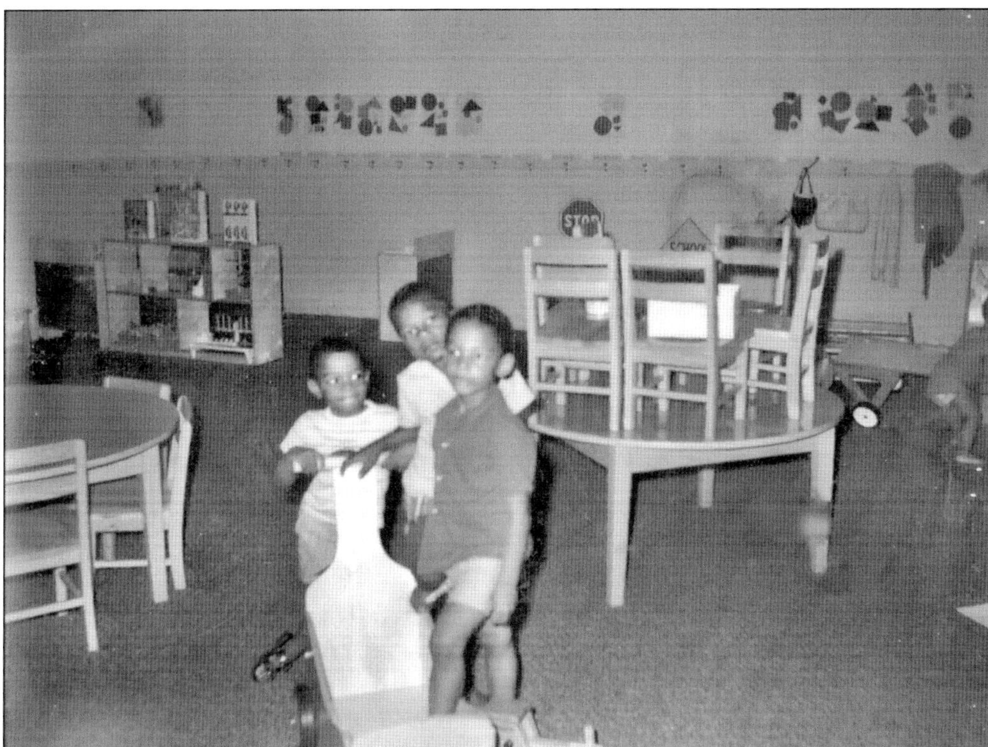

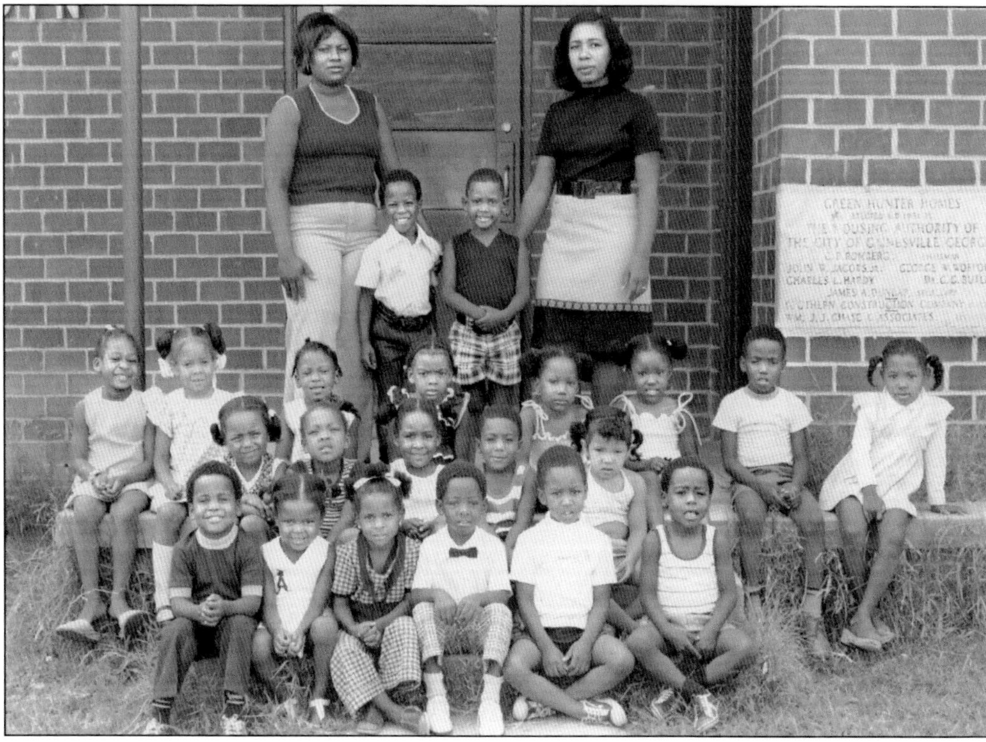

The Green Hunter Nursery Class of 1974 included, from left to right, (first row) Maurice Cantrell, Candace Cantrell, Tamela Webb, George Blackwell, Chadwick Hughey, and Quincy Brown; (second row) Swangala Hudson, Sarita Ivory, Marsha Brawner, Leman Riley, and Sharon Hardnett; (third row) Rhonda Davenport, Andrea Cheeks, Natasha Smith, Cheryl Carruth, Sonya Stephens, Tonya Stephens, John King, and Queenie Tanner; (fourth row) Ella Jean Smith (teacher), Walter Shea Smith, Barry Carruth, and Ruby Curry (teacher). (Courtesy of Barbara Brown.)

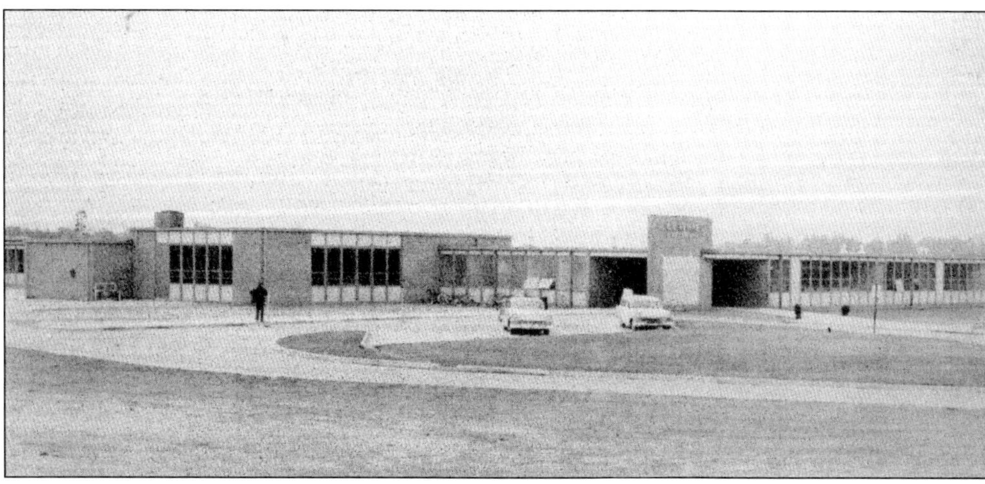

E.E. Butler High School, which was named in honor of Dr. E.E. Butler, opened in the fall of 1962. It served as a high school for African-American students until the local schools were integrated in the fall of 1969. (Courtesy of the Fair Street/Butler Alumni Association.)

Seven

Minding Our Own *Businesses*

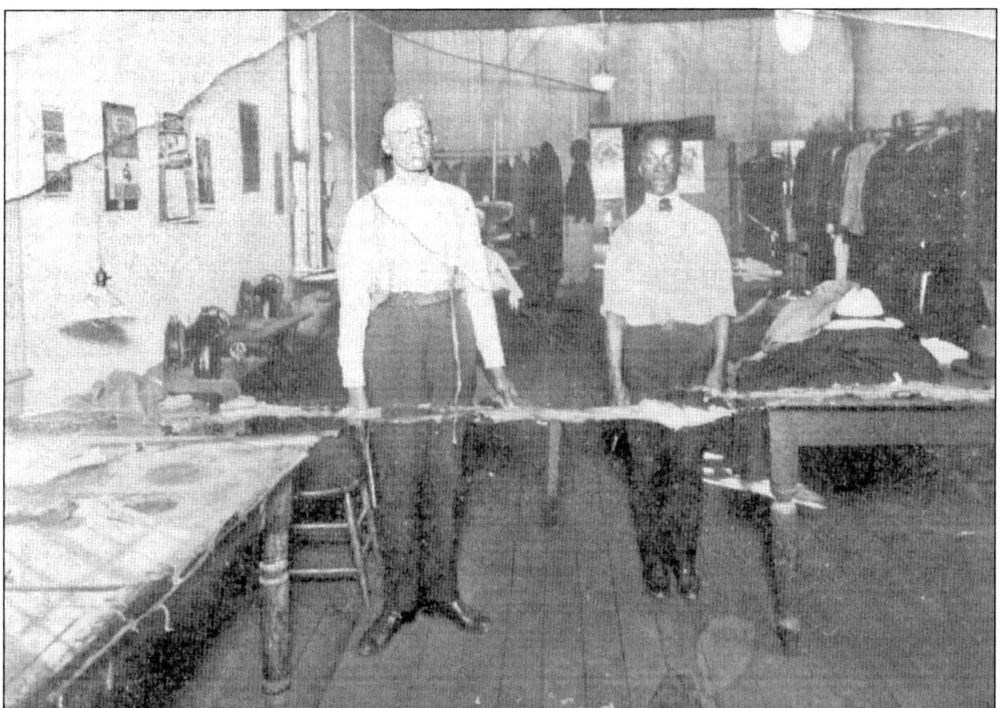

George Stephens (left) is pictured with his apprentice Howard Patterson in his tailor's and pressing shop. George Stephens opened his first shop in 1906 in the Hudson House, which later became the Princeton Hotel in Gainesville. In 1907, he moved to the Gaston House. A big fire in 1925 caused him to relocate his business to Maple Street, where he remained until 1943. That year, he sold his cleaners, but kept a tailoring shop in the backyard of his home on College Avenue. (Courtesy of James Brooks.)

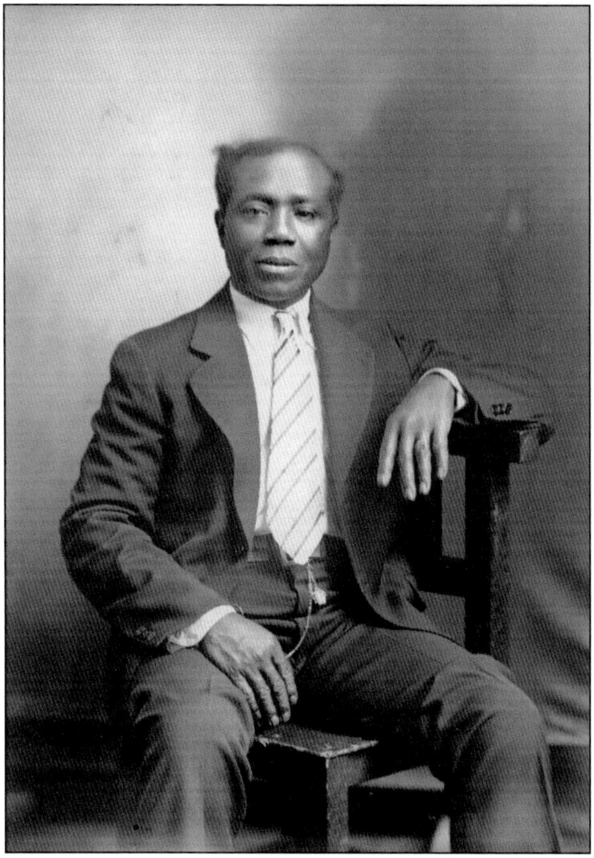

Leonard B. Barksdale Sr. was the owner of a neighborhood grocery store on Norwood Street in Gainesville. In the 1920s, he owned and operated a restaurant in the black community. (Courtesy of Wilbur and Dixie Ramsey.)

Leonard B. Barksdale's restaurant is pictured here in the 1920s. (Courtesy of Hall County Library.)

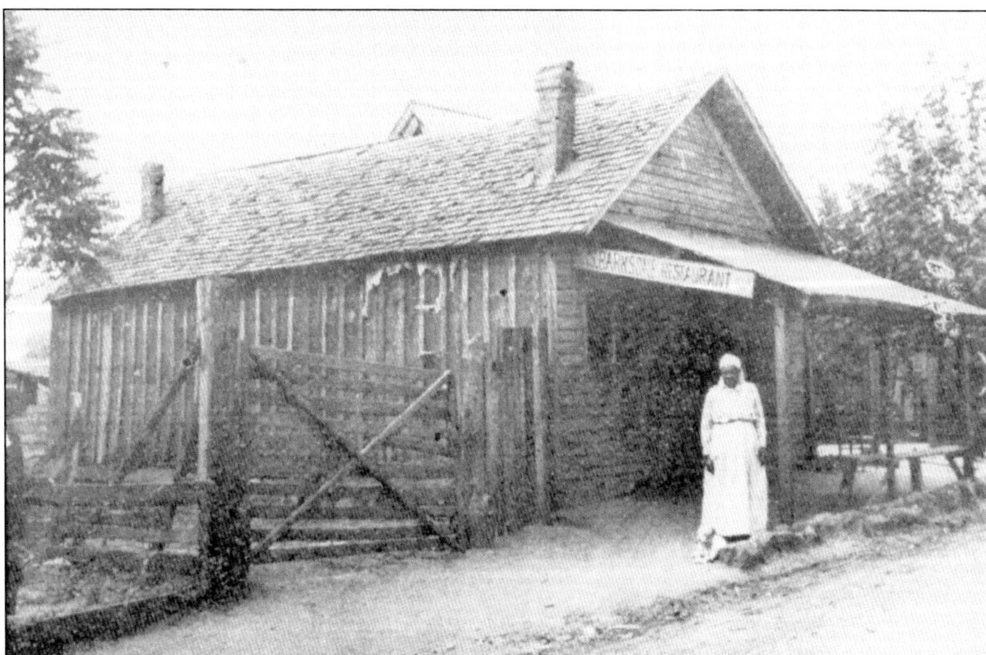

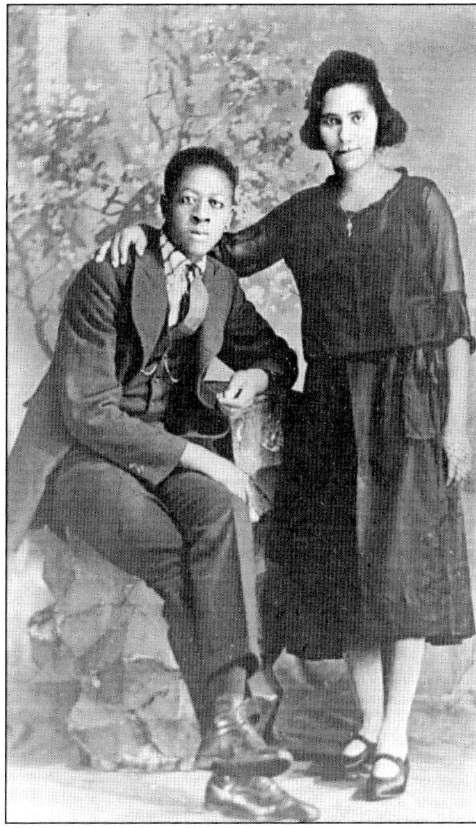

Rev. and Mrs. Alvertus J.(Velma L.) Butler are pictured here. President Lyndon B. Johnson honored Reverend and Mrs. Butler with a presidential visit to their home store located on the corner of College Avenue and Race Streets in Gainesville on May 8, 1964. The President came to Gainesville to tour and inspect prospective urban renewal areas as part of his War against Poverty Program. Reverend Butler invited the President into his home after Mr. Johnson inquired about his store. The President accepted Reverend Butler's invitation and stepped briefly into his home store. (Courtesy of Mattie Lowe)

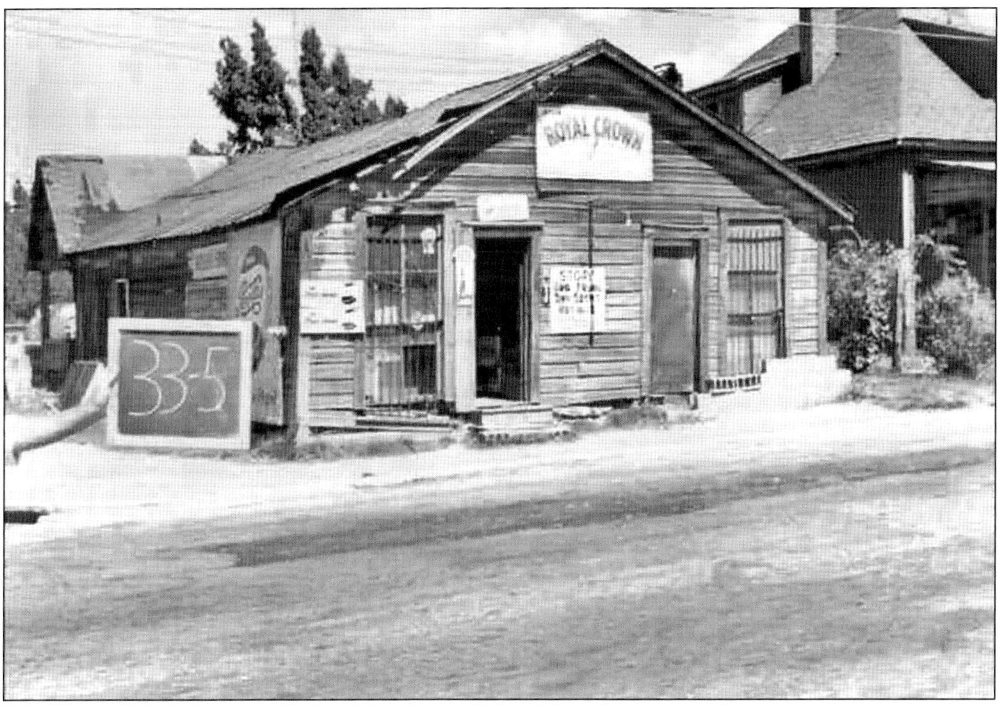

This home store was owned by Rev. and Mrs. Alvertus J. (Velma) Butler. President Lyndon B. Johnson briefly interviewed Reverend Butler about his home store during his visit in May 1964. Reverend Butler told the President that he had lived at this location since 1938. He also shared his dream of building a new home and store through the Urban Renewal Program with Mr. Johnson. (Courtesy of the City of Gainesville)

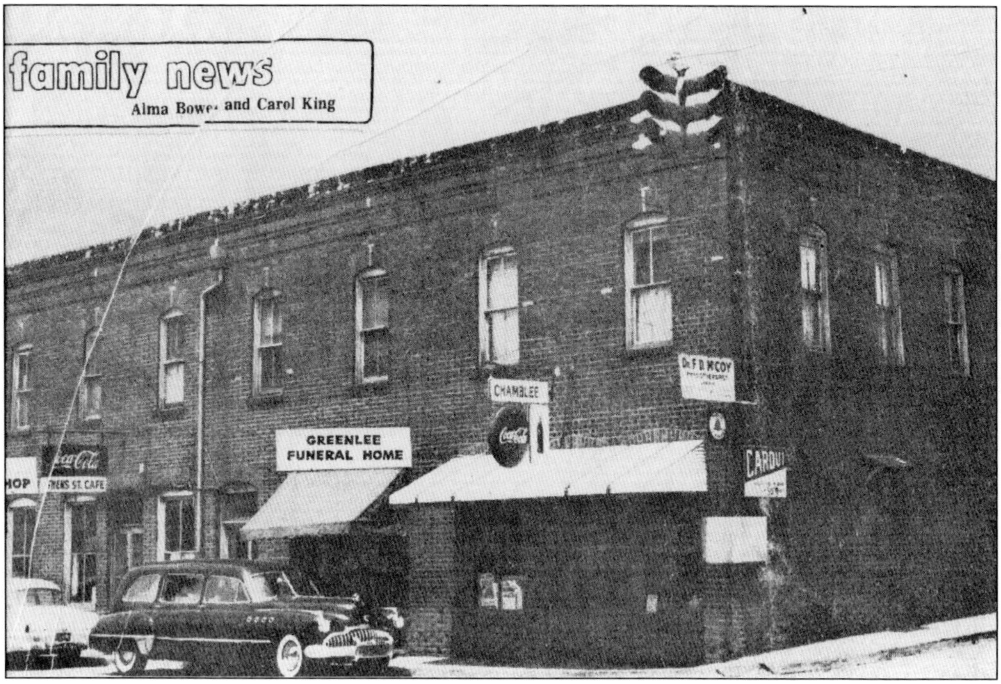

Athens Street was the main thoroughfare for African-American businesses in Gainesville before the onset of urban renewal in the 1970s. Pictured in this 1950s photo is the Oddfellow Building, which housed Burn's Barber Shop, the Athens Street Cafe, Greenlee's Funeral Home, Chamblee's Drugstore, and Dr. F.D. McCoy's upstairs office. Chamblee's Drugstore was originally owned by Dr. N.A. Doyle, the first black physician in Hall County. (Courtesy of the Newtown Florist Club and *The Times.*)

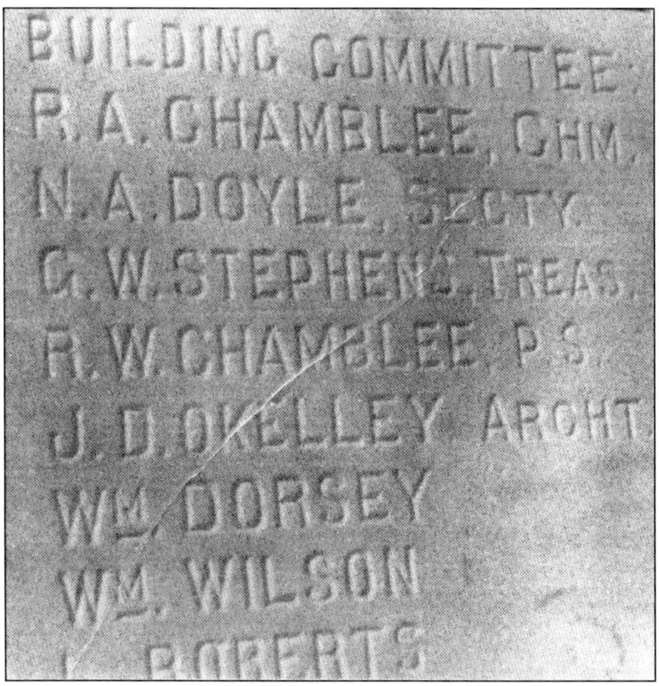

The names of the Oddfellow Building Committee are recorded on this cornerstone. The building committee included R.A. Chamblee (chairman), N.A. Doyle (secretary), G.W. Stephens (treasurer), R.W. Chamblee (P.S.), J.D. O'Kelly (architect), William Dorsey, William Wilson, and J. Roberts. (Courtesy of the Newtown Florist Club and *The Times*.)

Raymond Maxey was the chef at Riverside Military Academy. In 1944, he and his wife, Mattie Maxey, moved their family-style restaurant to Athens Street, where they both worked until his death in 1964. (Courtesy of W.H. Maxey.)

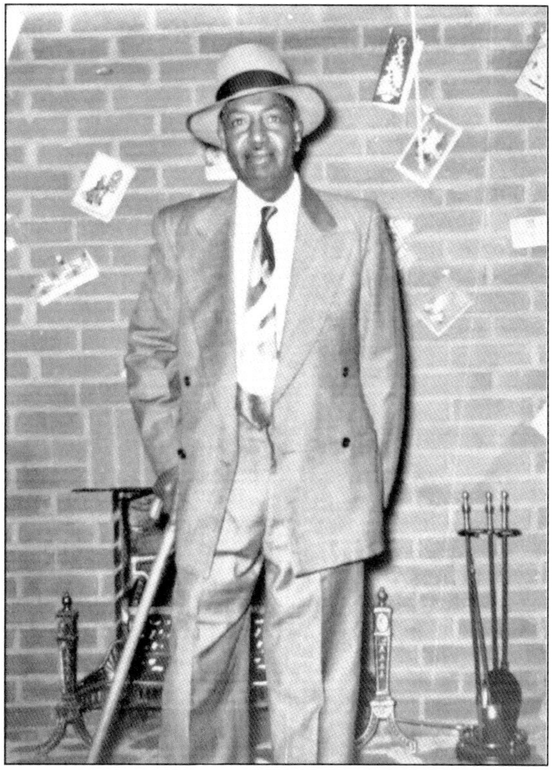

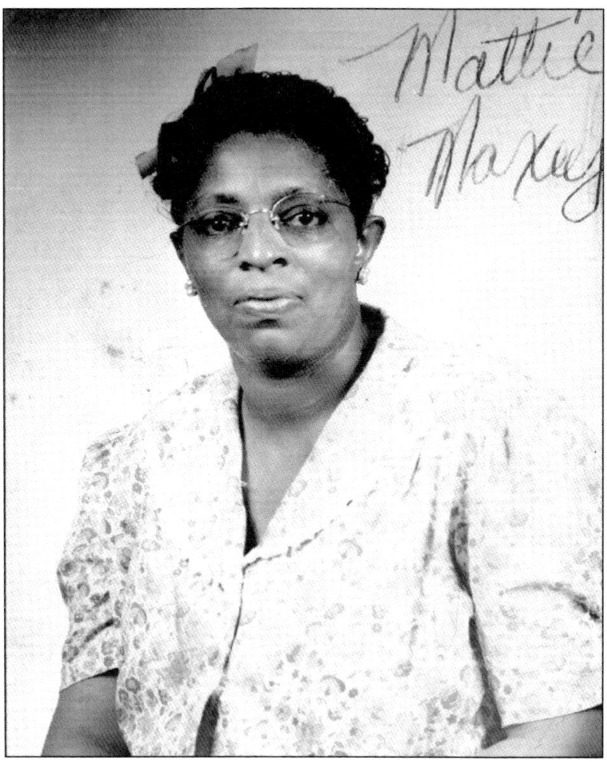

Mattie Mae Maxey, wife of Raymond Maxey, opened a family-style restaurant on Summitt Street in 1942. It was the only black restaurant to serve three meals a day. Other black restaurants operating at this time served sandwiches at night. (Courtesy of W.H. Maxey.)

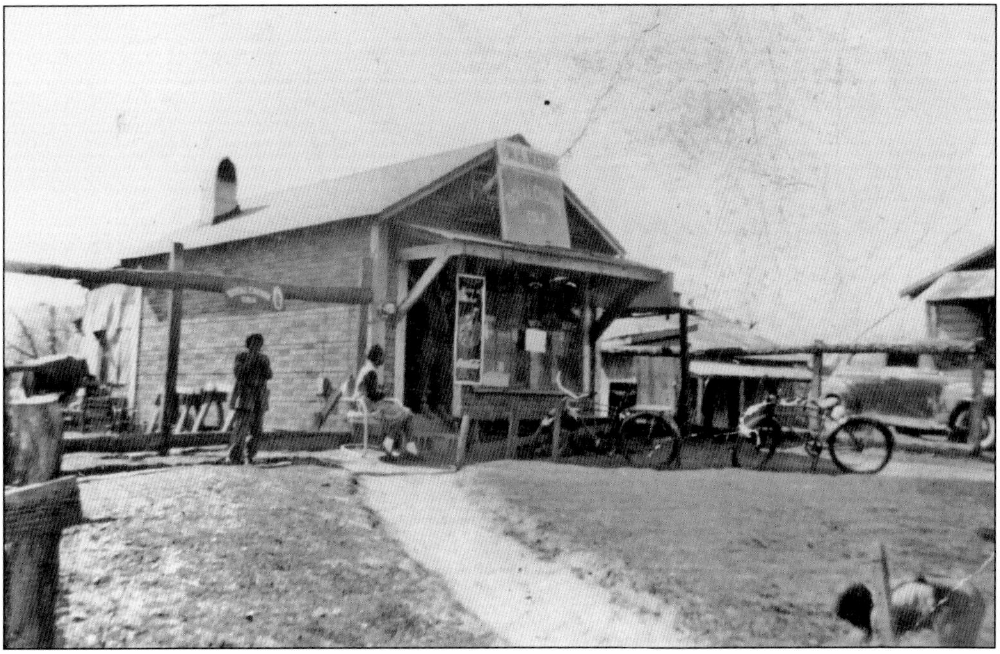

Maxey's grocery store was located in Jewell's Alley in 1946. It was owned and operated by Raymond and Mattie Maxey. (Courtesy of Royce Stephens and James Brooks.)

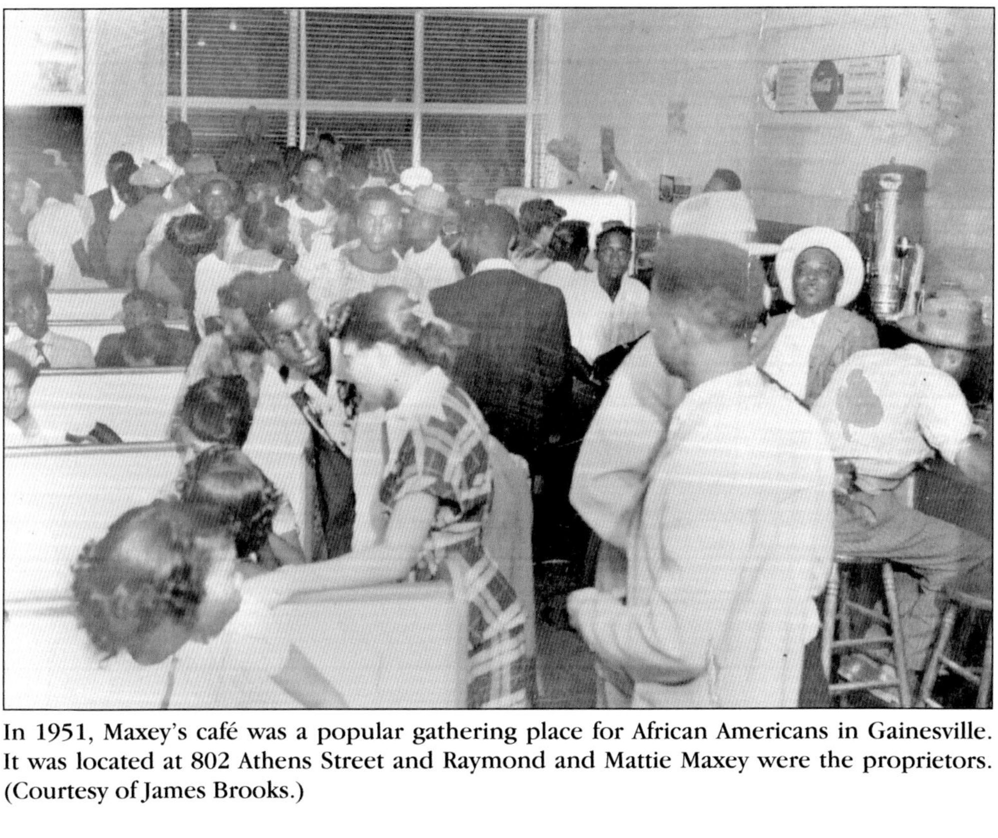

In 1951, Maxey's café was a popular gathering place for African Americans in Gainesville. It was located at 802 Athens Street and Raymond and Mattie Maxey were the proprietors. (Courtesy of James Brooks.)

James (Jimmy) Morton was a tailor. He owned and operated a pressing shop or dry cleaning establishment at 739 Athens Street in Gainesville for many years. In this picture, James Morton is shown standing in the doorway of his shop in the 1930s. (Courtesy of Frances Law Williams.)

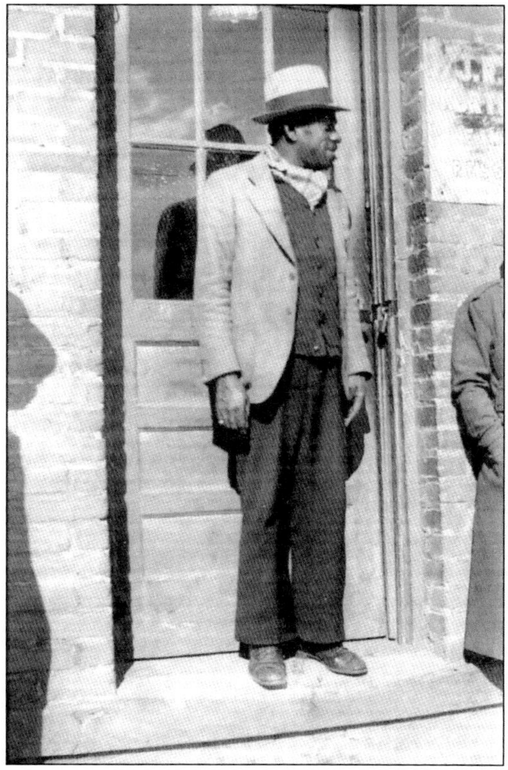

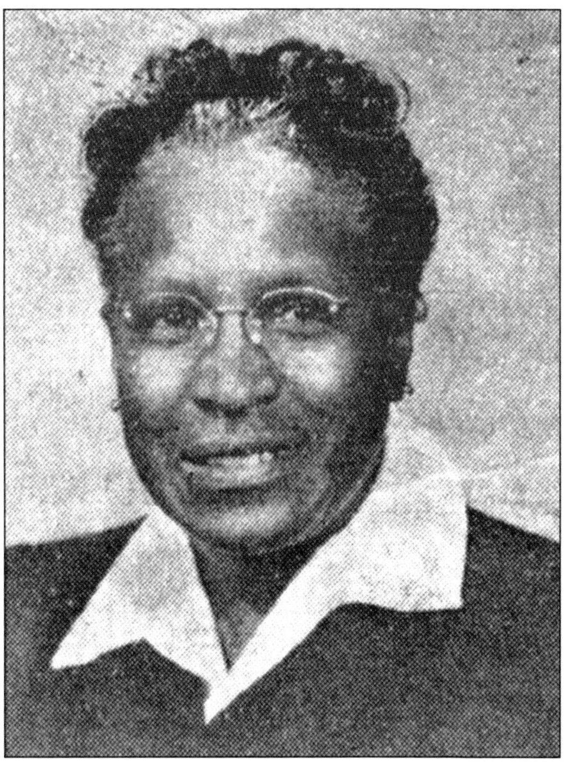

Rena Bush Harrison was one of the first black female entrepreneurs in Hall County. She owned and managed simultaneously a boarding house for teachers, a small café on Athens Street, several rental housing units, and the cooks at Gainesville's Brenau College. (Courtesy of the Fair Street/Butler Alumni Association.)

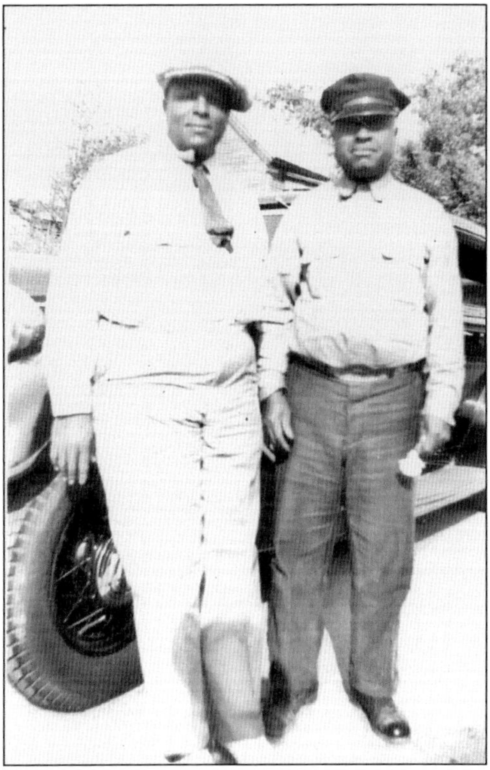

Redric Pete Harrison (left) and his brother Dock F. Harrison (right) were the operators and owners of Pete's Taxi in Gainesville. This business, established *c.* 1932, was probably one of the earliest of its type in Gainesville-Hall County. (Courtesy of Katie Earle.)

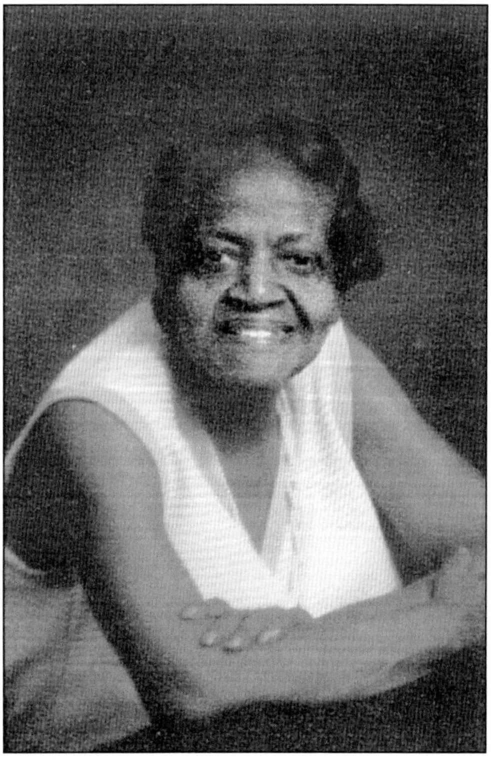

Daisy Harrison was a vital member of the successful Harrison Taxi team. She was the business's receptionist, secretary, and dispatcher. (Courtesy of Katie Earle.)

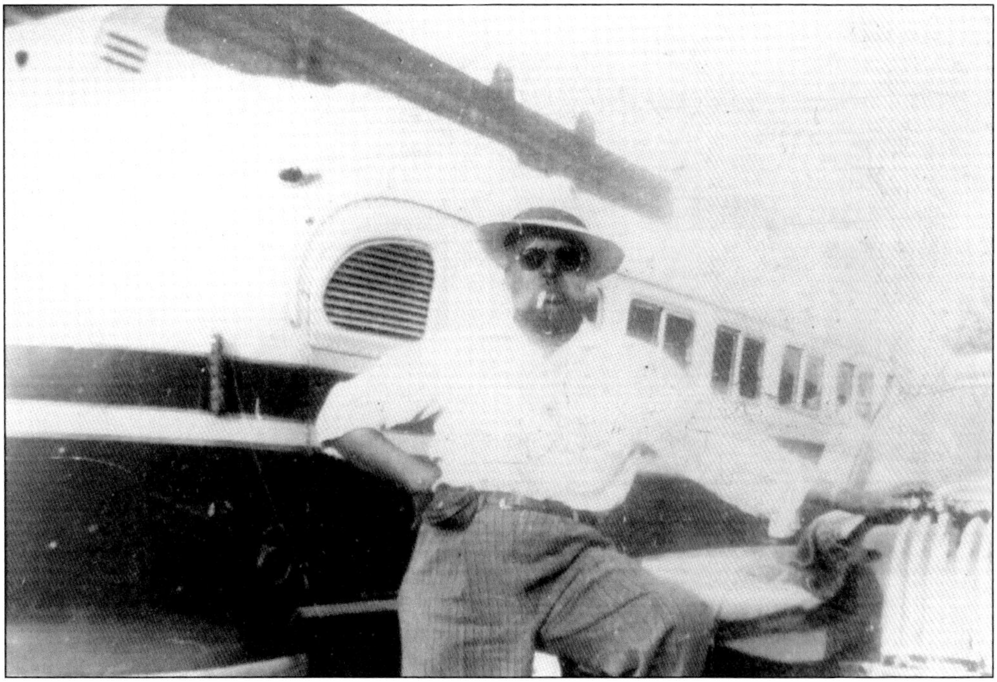

George Neal operated a taxi service for many years. He is seen here at the train station in Gainesville, Georgia, where cab drivers often picked up their passengers. (Courtesy of Annette Cantrell.)

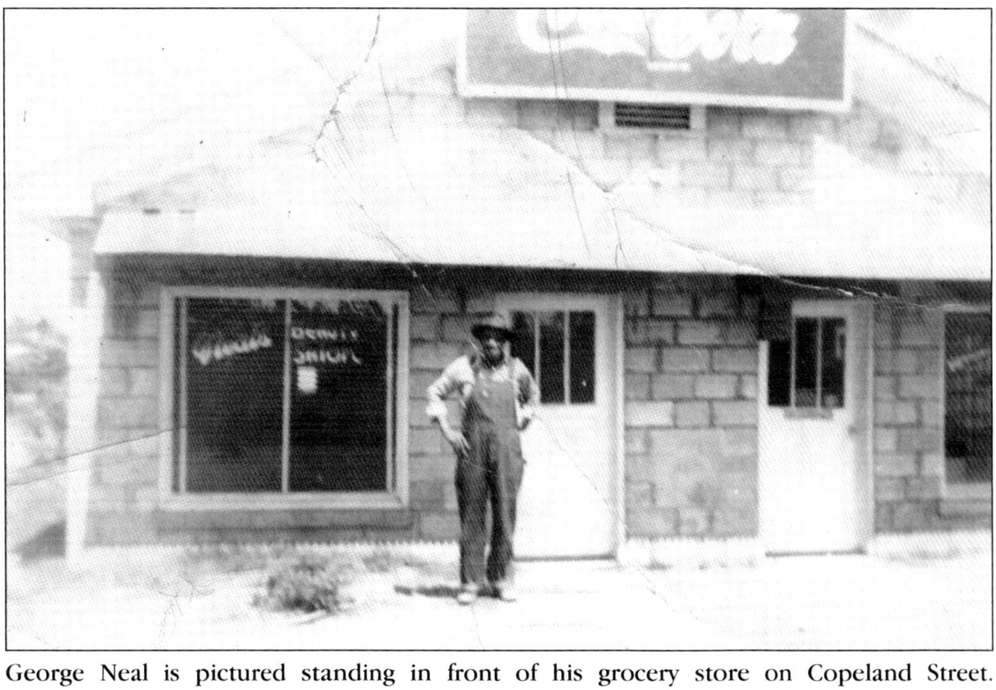

George Neal is pictured standing in front of his grocery store on Copeland Street. His wife, Pearl Neal, operated a beauty salon on the left side of the building. (Courtesy of Annette Cantrell.)

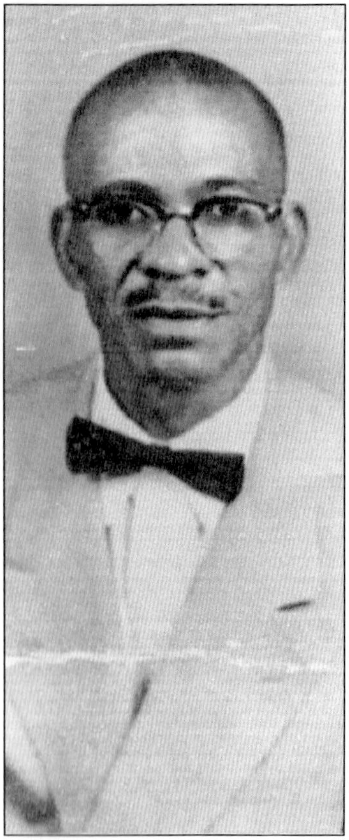

Fletcher and Pecolia Randolph built and operated the second black-owned neighborhood grocery store on the corner of Desota Drive and Harvey Street in 1943. In 1946, they built two houses on Athens Highway, a store, and a café. People came from miles away to get their delicious barbecue and Brunswick stew every weekend. (Courtesy of Inez Randolph Yarbrough.)

Peccolia Moon Randolph, wife of Fletcher Randolph is pictured here. She was a member of Bethel Church of the Nazarene, the Eastern Star Evergreen Court #7, the Service Home League, and a bell ringer for the Salvation Army. A part-time employee of the Gainesville division of the Georgia department of Family and Children Services, she is especially remembered for her kind and compassionate nature. She often visited area hospitals and nursing homes where she prayed and distributed "get-well" cards. (Courtesy of Inez Randolph Yarbough)

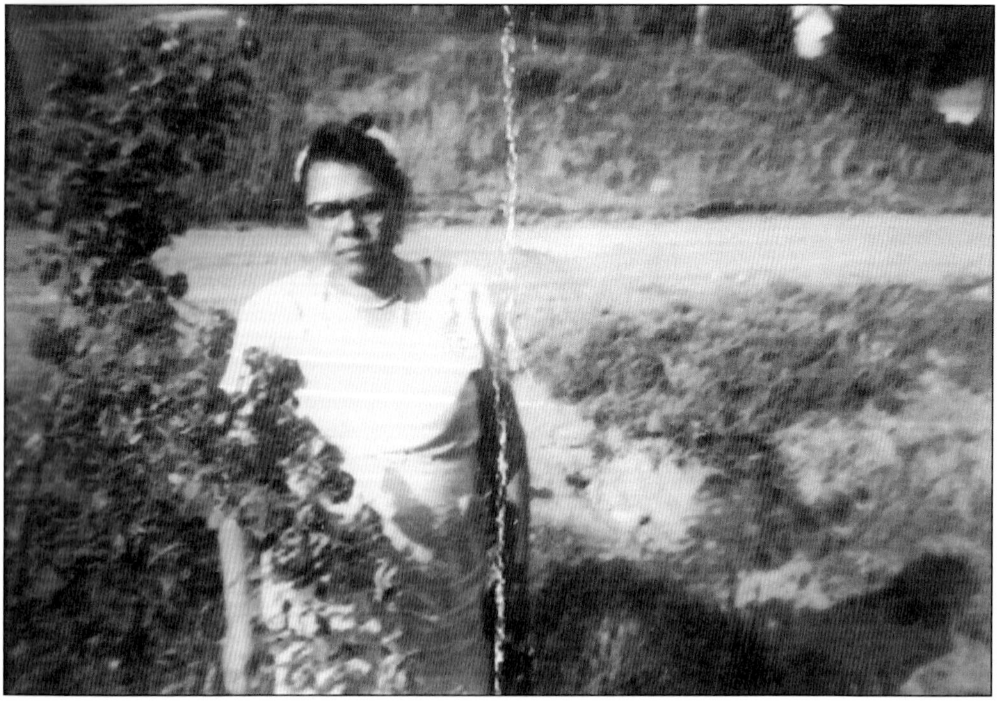

Mrs. Polly Robinson and her husband, J.D. Robinson, operated a combination grocery and variety store on the first floor of the old Good Samaritan Lodge Building, located on the corner of Race and College Avenue. When the 1936 tornado destroyed this building, they reopened their store in a small house next door to their home on College Avenue. (Courtesy of Wilbur and Dixie Ramsey.)

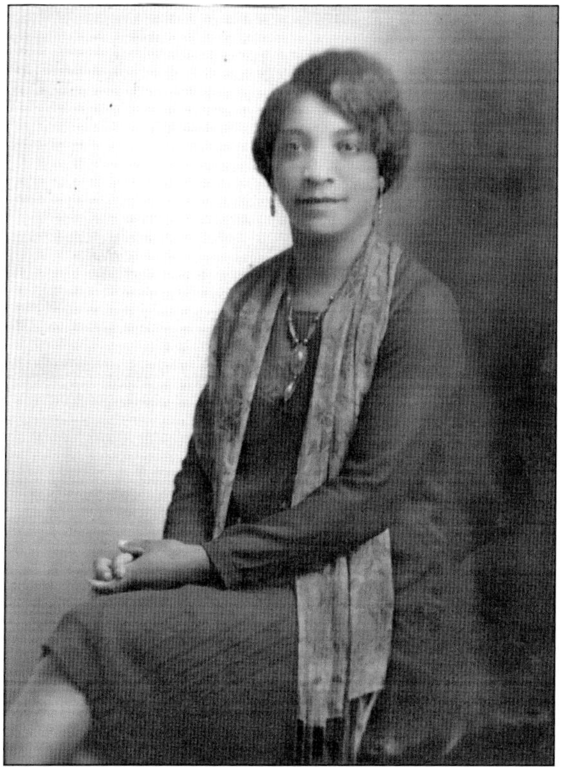

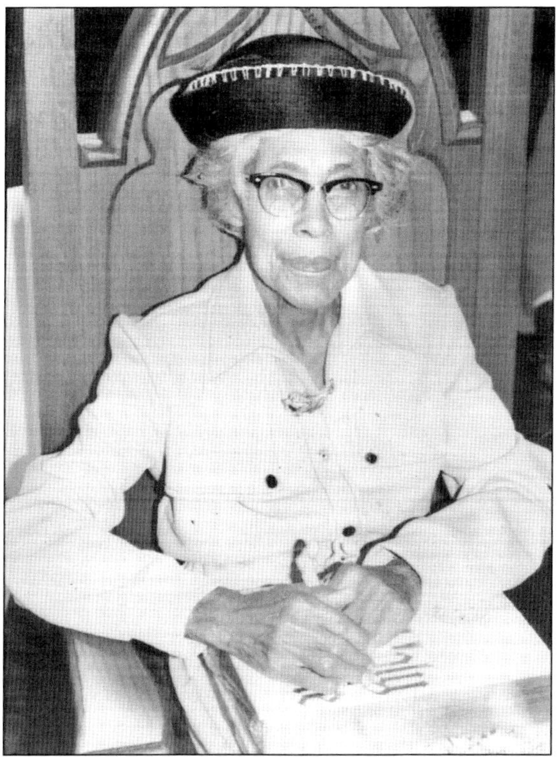

Annie Hawkins was a teacher and principal at Timberidge School in Hall County in the 1930s. She also operated a neighborhood store from her home on College Avenue in Gainesville in the late 1920s. (Courtesy of Janet Maxey Stephens.)

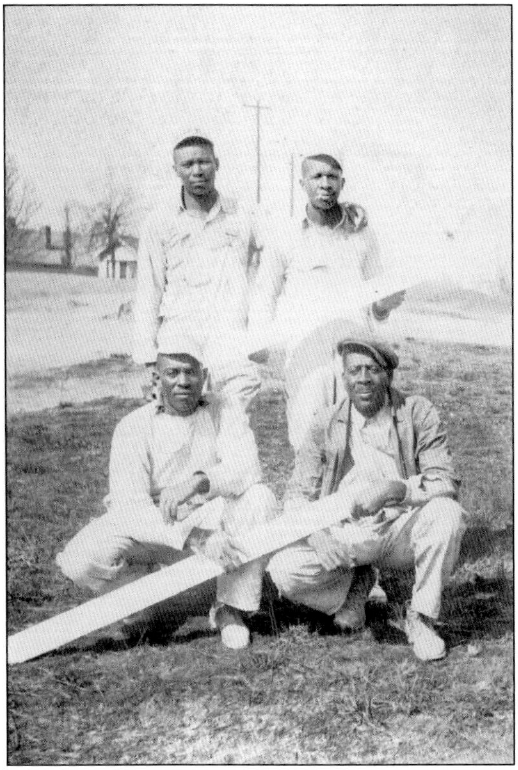

The Johnson brothers were plasterers. This trade was passed on to them by their father, Jep Johnson. Shown from left to right are (front row) Charles Johnson and William Johnson; (back row) Harold Johnson and Bennie Johnson. (Courtesy of Tashiana Cheeks.)

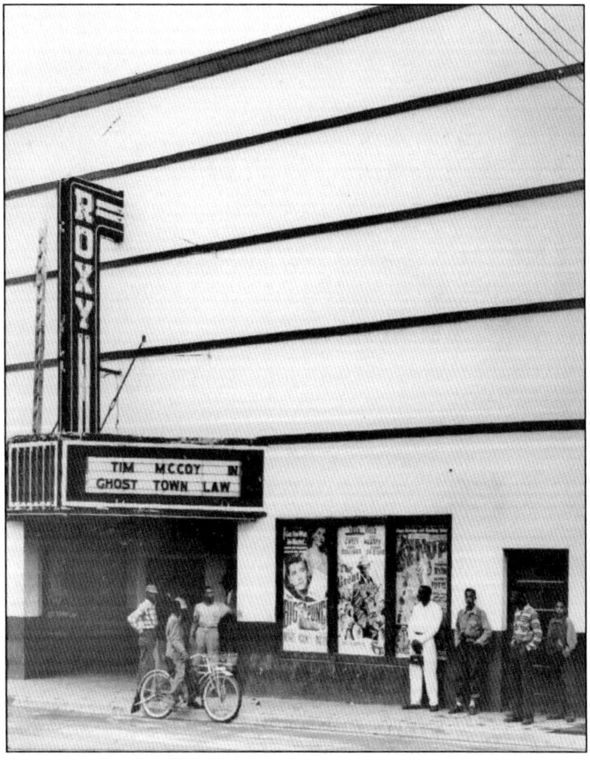

The Roxy Theater was located in the Kidd Building on Athens Street in Gainesville. It offered its African-American patrons family-style entertainment. (Courtesy of the Hall County Library.)

Arthur Henry Jones, a community photographer, was employed by Hardy's Studio of Gainesville. Mr. Jones is credited with producing many of the photographs taken in Hall County's African-American community. (Courtesy of Johnny Jones.)

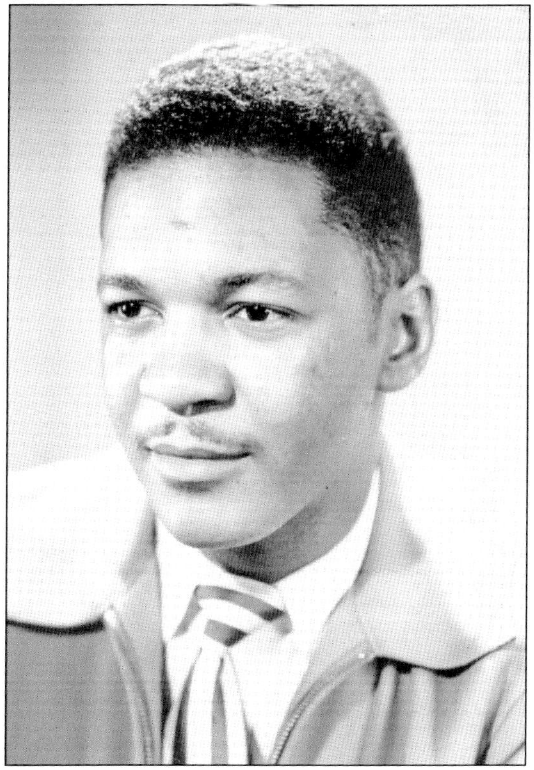

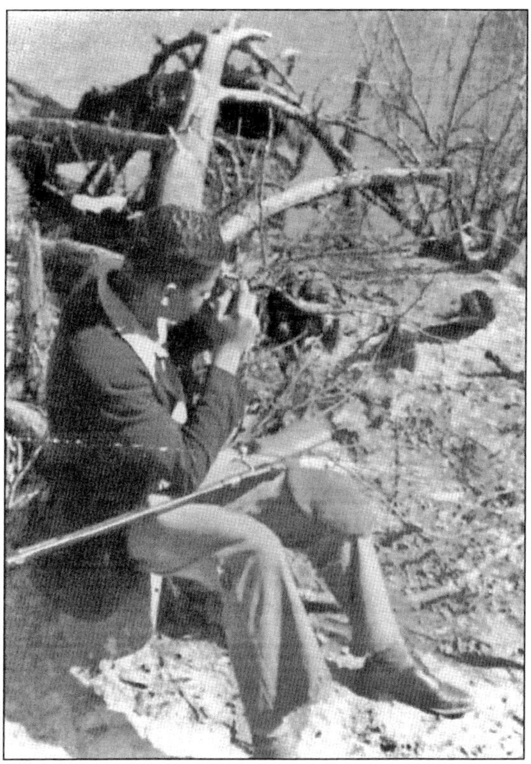

Arthur Henry Jones is seen here photographing Harrison Lake. (Courtesy of Johnny Jones.)

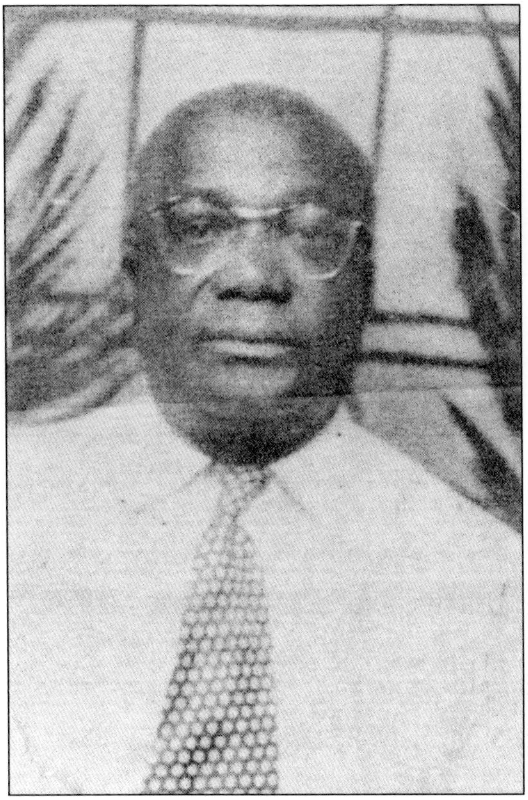

Willie B. Young established W.B. Young's Funeral Home in 1932; it was located at 715 Athens Street in Gainesville. Young was a church and community leader. He was a faithful member of Cross Plain Baptist Church, where he served as President of the Ushers' Board, and was also a member of the Trustee Board of the Northwestern Baptist Association, the Southside Chamber of Commerce, and the Georgia Practitioners of Funeral Services. (Courtesy of Annette Cantrell.)

The back of this fan advertised East Side Funeral Home, which was managed and owned by Willie B. Young in Gainesville. (Courtesy of Frederick A. Young.)

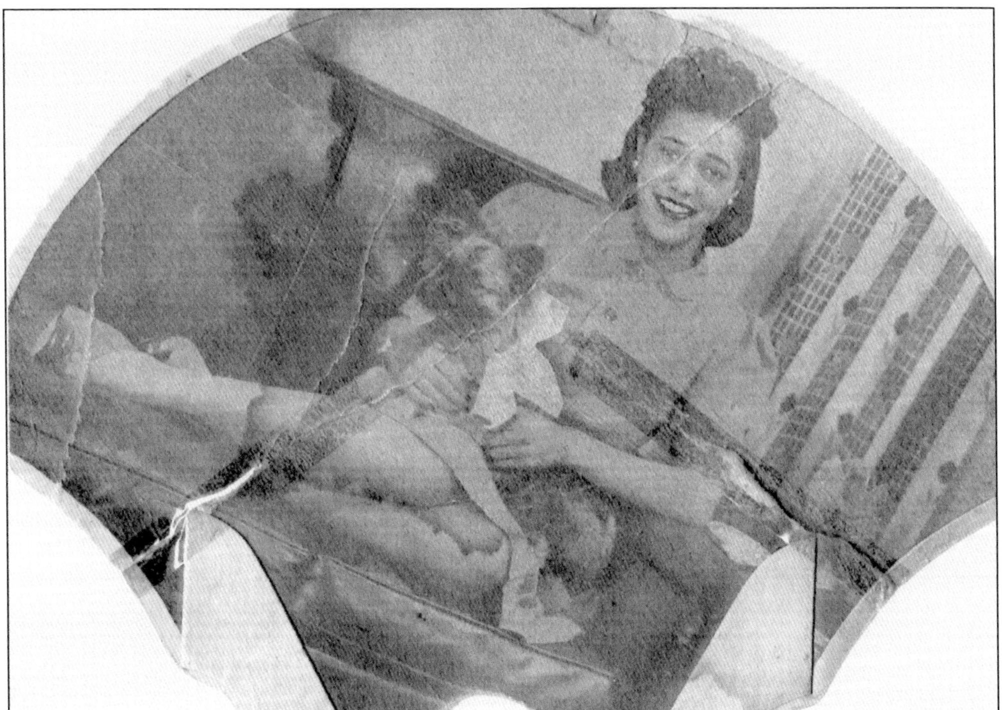

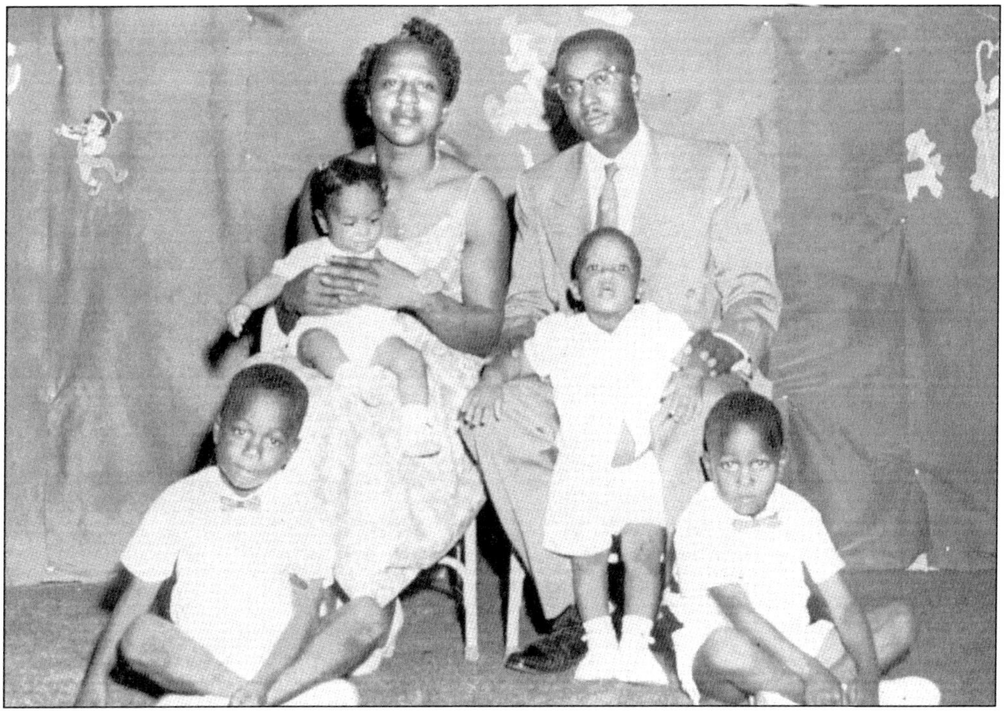

Grover Young is pictured here with his wife, Estelle (a local school teacher), and their children. He owned and operated a funeral home on Old Athens Highway in Gainesville. His business offered complete funeral and ambulance services. (Courtesy of Jennie Harris and Eddie Dabney.)

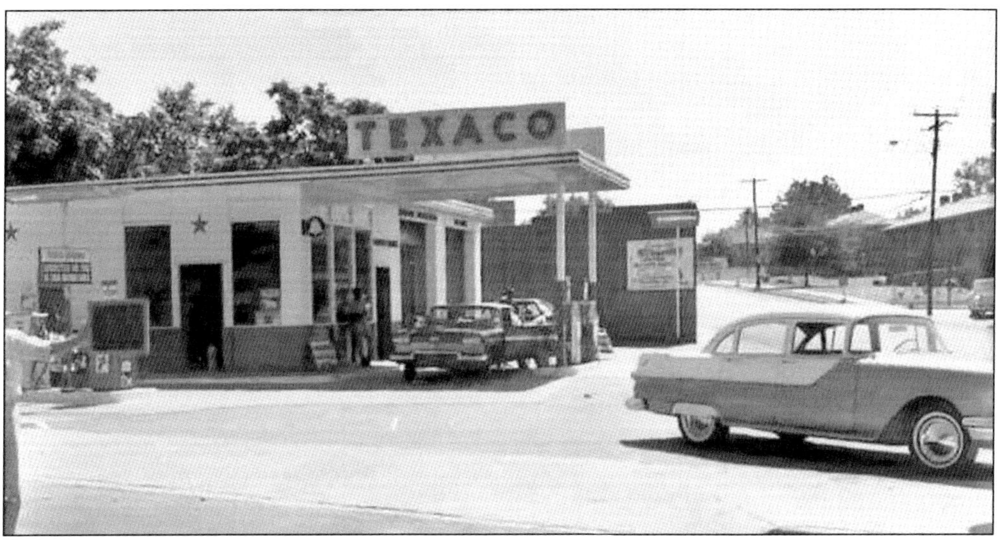

Grady Cheeks owned and operated this Texaco service station, located at 607 Athens Street in 1964. Two buildings of the Green Hunter Homes, or Atlanta Street projects, and the Mount Calvary Church of God are seen on the right. Other service stations operated by African Americans in Gainesville were Arthur Lipscomb's Gulf Station on Athens Highway and Eldon Goss's Shell Station on Spring Street. (Courtesy of the City of Gainesville.)

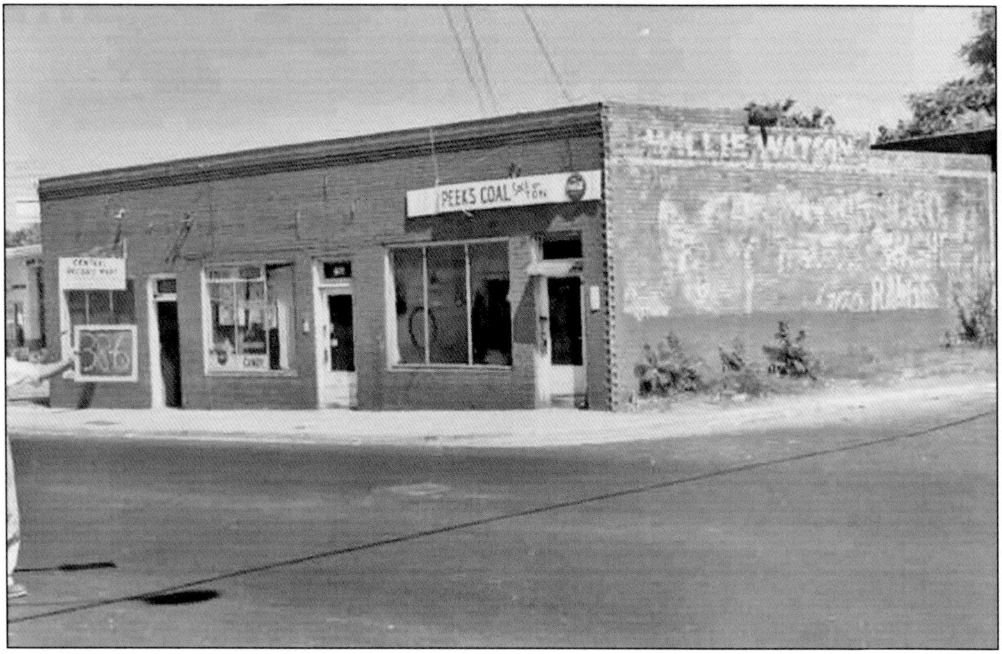

Central Record Mart, a record store, was located in the left side of this building. In 1964, it was located at 615 Athens Street. John Butts Jr. was the proprietor. (Courtesy of the City of Gainesville.)

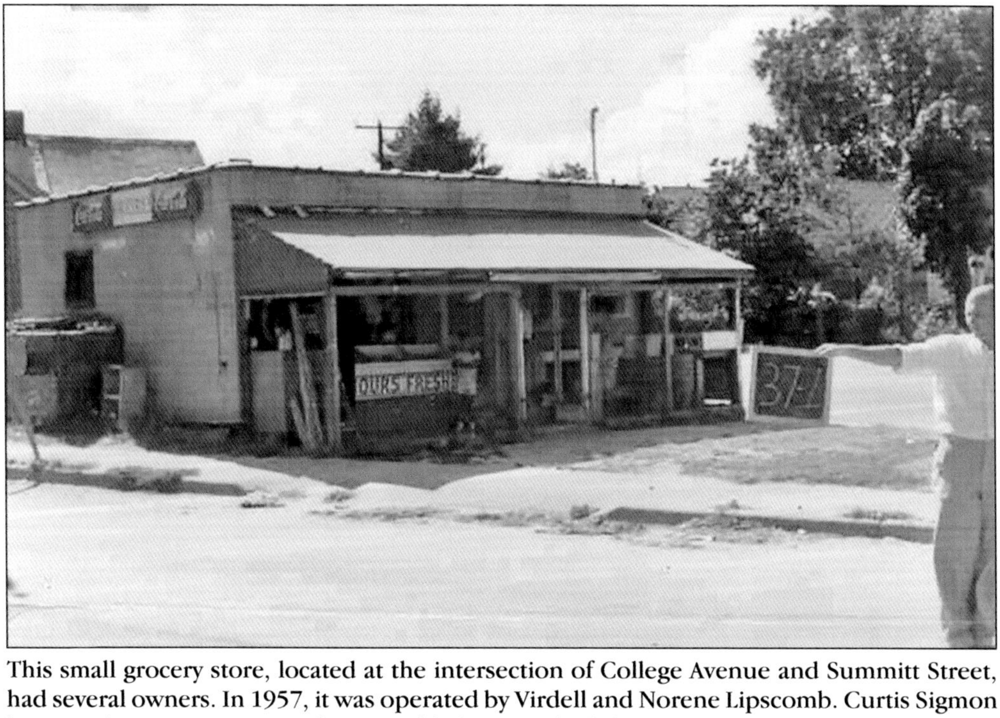

This small grocery store, located at the intersection of College Avenue and Summitt Street, had several owners. In 1957, it was operated by Virdell and Norene Lipscomb. Curtis Sigmon became the proprietor in 1960. By 1964, the store had changed hands again and was under the management of T.O. Jenkins. (Courtesy of the City of Gainesville.)

This building, located at the intersection of Myrtle (Martin Luther King Drive) and Carlton Streets, served as a grocery store and barber shop. The building was owned by the Blake Family. (Courtesy of Mr. James Brooks.)

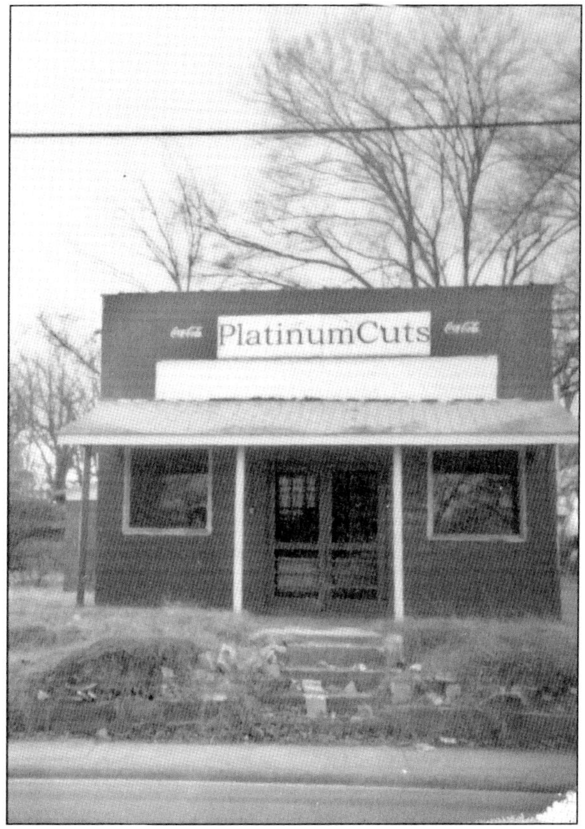

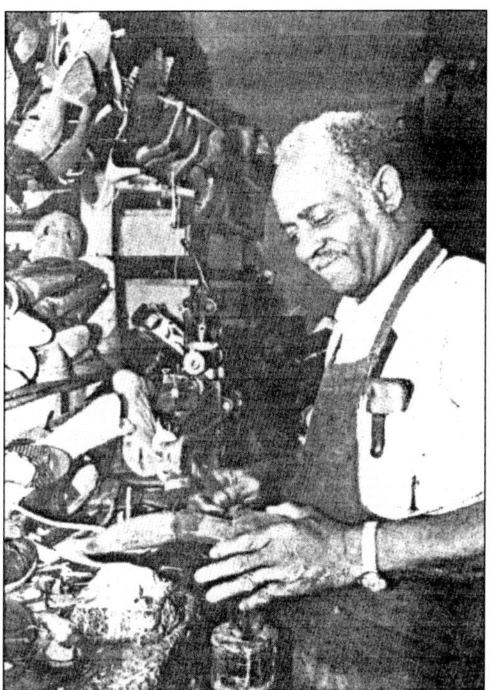

Thomas Hawthorne Carter established Carter's Shoe Shop on Athens Street after the tornado of 1936. His left leg was ripped off by a falling telephone pole during the tornado and as a result, he attended school to study shoe repair. Mr. Carter was commissioned to dye all of the shoes used in the well-known movie *Gone with the Wind*. He earned his first $100 bill upon the completion of this job. His business slogan was, "We mend the rips, patch the holes, dye for you and save your sole." In addition to operating a business, Mr. Carter served faithfully as an elder of Mt. Calvary Church of God Holiness and taught shoe repair at the Hall County Vocational and Rehabilitation School for Veterans in Gainesville. (Courtesy of Fralil Carter Walker)

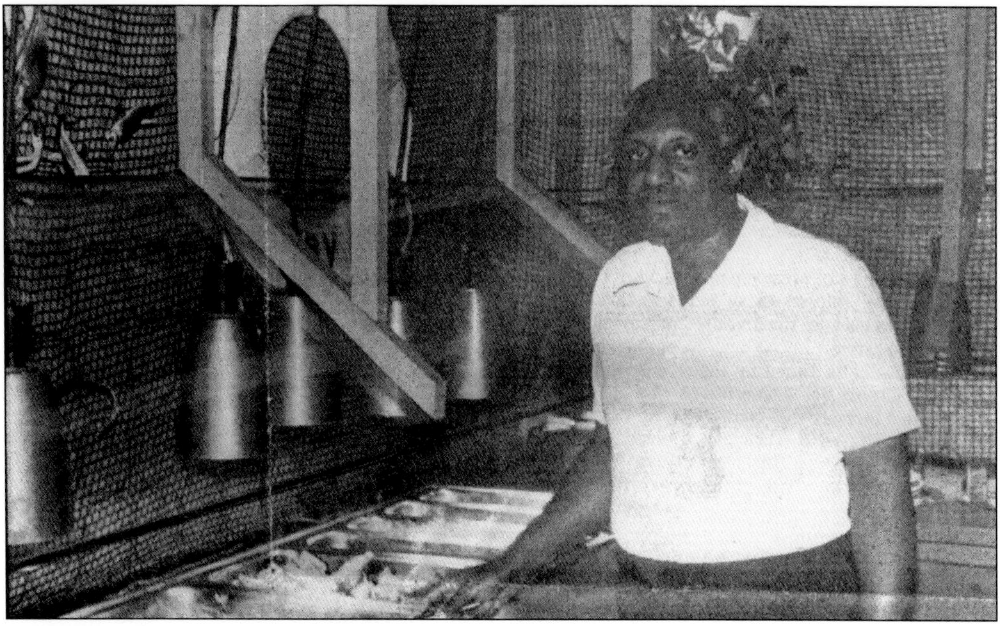

William Henry Maxey has spent a lifetime in the restaurant business. He began his career in 1948 as a cook at Dixie Hunt Hotel. Later, he worked in the restaurant on Athens Street, which was owned by his father, Raymond Maxey. In 1965, he operated "Food-To-Go," the first fast-food restaurant on the Southside of Gainesville. He then worked at the Holiday Inn and the Elks Club. After leaving the Elks Club, he completed an eight-year stint at Holly's Landing as vice-president of operations. (Courtesy of *The Times)*

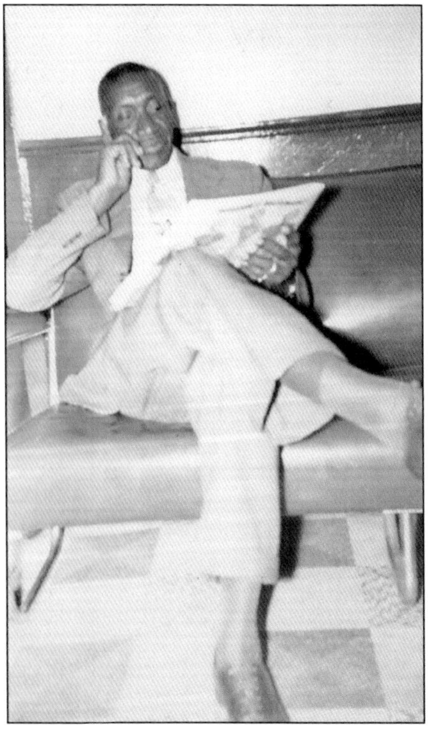

Levi G. Greenlee operated a grocery store in Gainesville. In 1938, he became the founder of Greenlee Funeral Home. He also established Eureka Cemetery. He and his son, T.J. Greenlee, continued to operate the funeral home until his death in 1968. (Courtesy of Margaret Greenlee.)

Eight

Certain People
VIPs

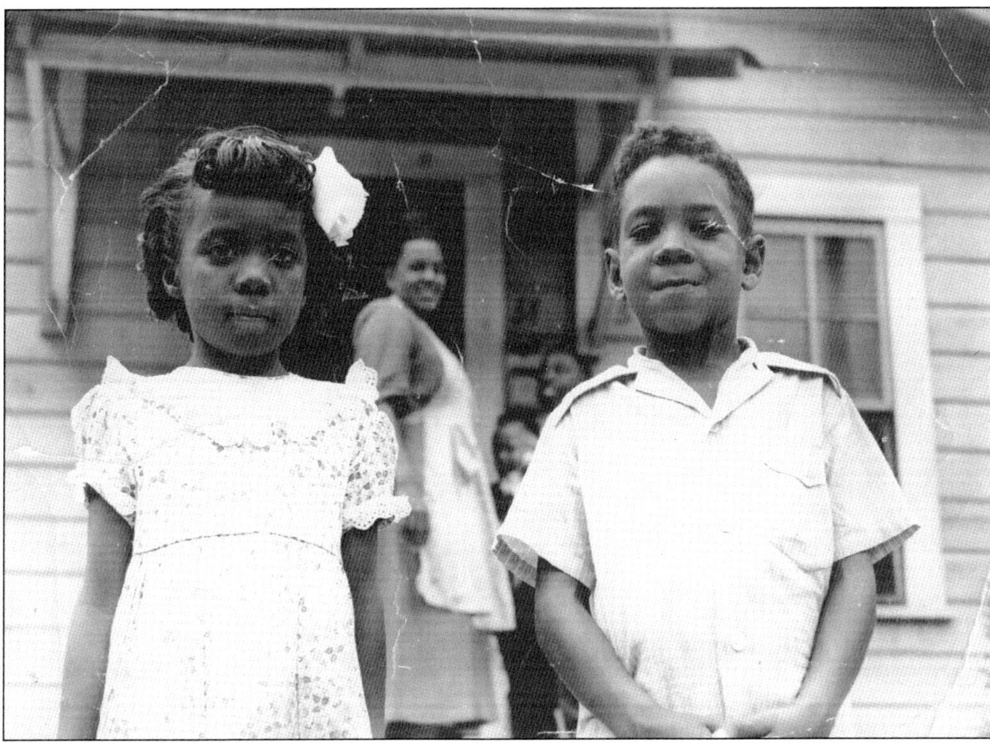

Siblings Dorothy and Kenneth Robinson are pictured in a scene from *Palmour Street*, a locally produced film set in the early 1950s about black family life. This film, which was made under the direction of the Hall County Health Department, was distributed to district health departments in the state and nationwide. This docudrama featured the J. Wesley Merrit Sr. family and included some of their Palmour Street neighbors. In the background from left to right are Mrs. Mildred Merrit, baby Vernon G. Merrit, and James Wesley Merritt Jr. (Courtesy of Kenneth Robinson)

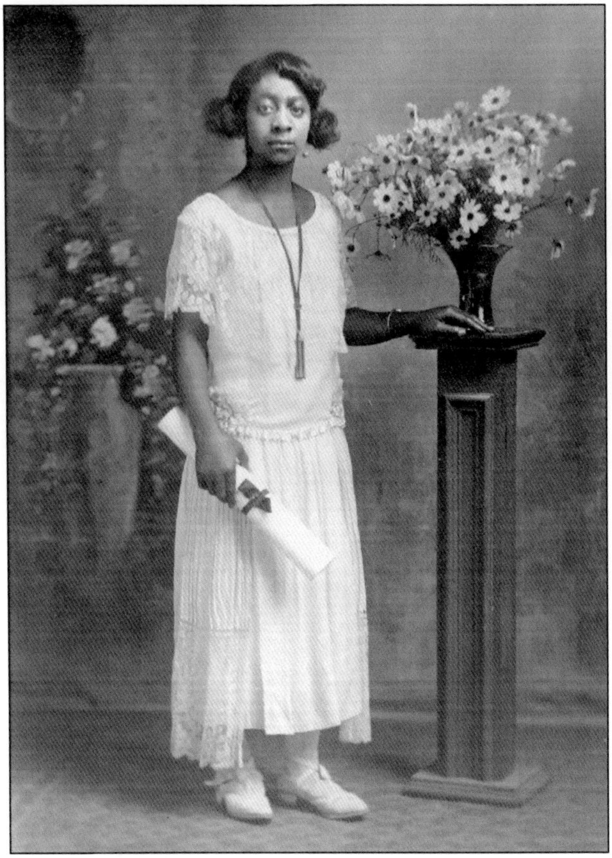

Carrie Lou Haywood Washington was a Hall County educator. She received a B.S. degree from Savannah State College in Savannah, Georgia, and is pictured here with her diploma in hand. (Courtesy of Wilbur and Dixie Ramsey.)

Ella J. Rucker was a renowned community musician and music teacher. Born on March 15, 1892, she taught piano to more than 500 Hall County children during her lifetime. Ella Rucker was a faithful member of St. John Baptist Church, where she served as the church pianist for over 50 years. She also served the community as a librarian at the McCrary Branch of the Hall County Library. (Courtesy of Shirley Lipscomb.)

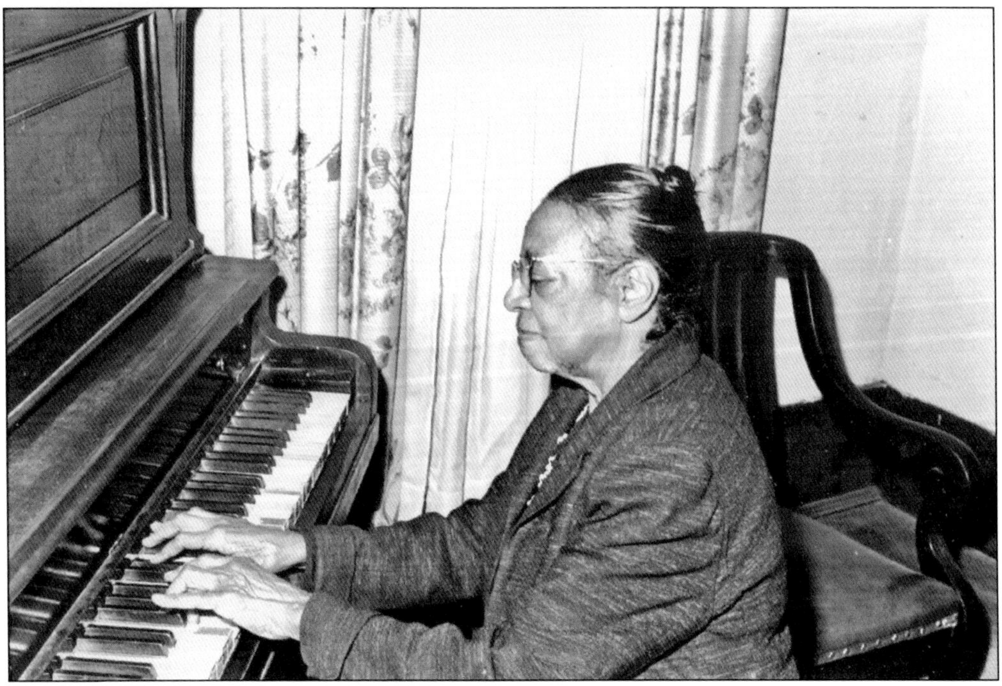

G.S. (General Sherman) Moon was a pioneer educator and prominent citizen of Hall County. He was born on November 24, 1865 and was elected principal of Gainesville's Public Colored School (Summer Hill) by the Gainesville City Council on August 15, 1895. He was the second principal of Gainesville's Public Colored School. The first principal was Prof. D.H. Sampson. (Courtesy of the Fair Street/ Butler Alumni Association.)

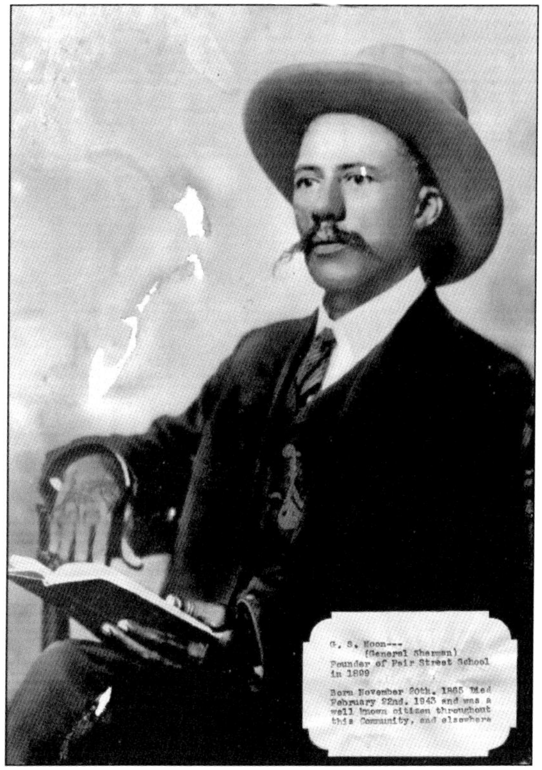

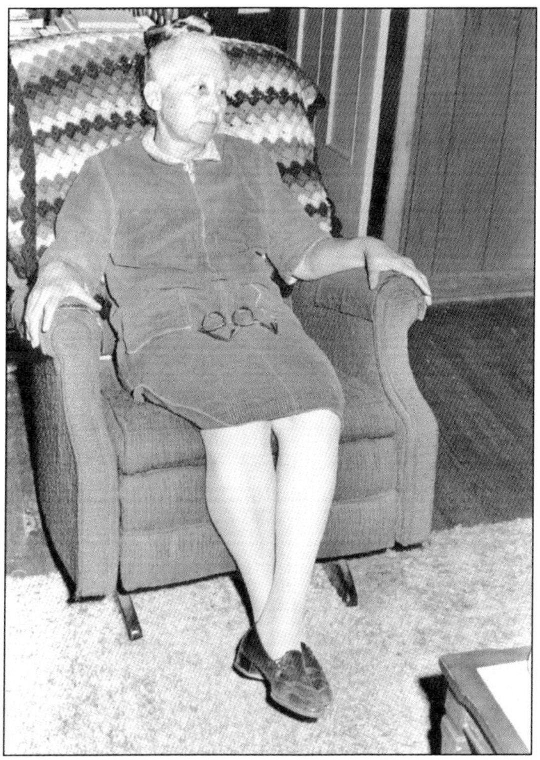

Mattie Moon was a prominent Gainesville educator and community leader. The daughter of G.S. and Carrie Garrison Moon, she was a graduate of Fort Valley State College in Fort Valley, Georgia, and received her masters degree from Atlanta University. Mattie Moon was inducted into the Georgia Association of Educators' Hall of Fame. She belonged to several organizations and served on countless committees and boards. She was honored by the community at a "Mattie Moon Appreciation Day" in March of 1985. Following her death in 1985, a scholarship was established in her name at Gainesville College. (Courtesy of the Hall County Black History Society.)

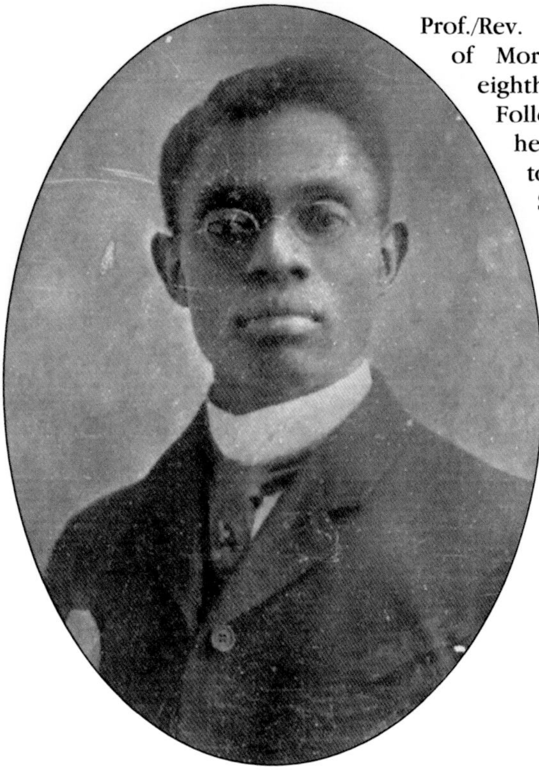

Prof./Rev. Eugene J. Thompson, a graduate of Morehouse College in Atlanta, was the eighth pastor of St. John Baptist Church. Following his tenure as pastor of St. John, he was asked to return to Gainesville to serve as the principal of Northwestern School. A talented choir director, he is remembered for the beautiful anthems he taught to the choruses at Northwestern School. His wife, Florence, was a pianist and she accompanied the choruses and choirs. Professor Thompson served as the principal of Northwestern School until his death in 1941. (Courtesy of Cathy McCrary Kimbro.)

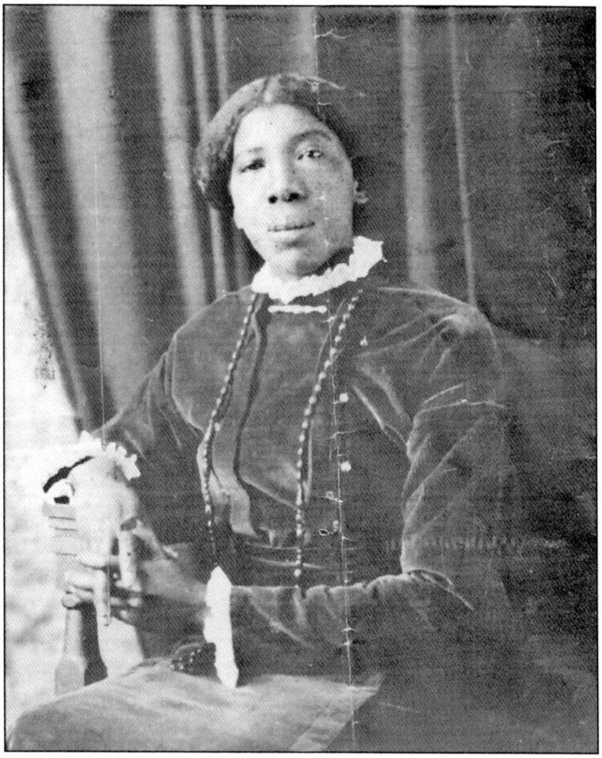

Beulah Rucker Oliver was a pioneer educator in Hall County. She founded the Beulah Rucker Oliver Industrial School on Athens Highway in Gainesville for African-American students. She graduated from Knox Institute, with honors, in 1909 and completed her college education at Savannah State College in Savannah, Georgia, in 1944. She studied thesis writing at Atlanta University in Atlanta, Georgia. (Courtesy of Fair Street/Butler Alumni Association.)

Lillie Belcher was an early Hall County educator. She taught school on the Whelchel farm off of the old Dawsonville Highway *c*. 1916. The New Bethel Church located on property owned by Mr. Marion Whelchel served as a one-room school for African-American children living in the area. Mrs. Belcher also taught in Gainesville and Auburn, Georgia. (Courtesy of Gladystine Burt Green)

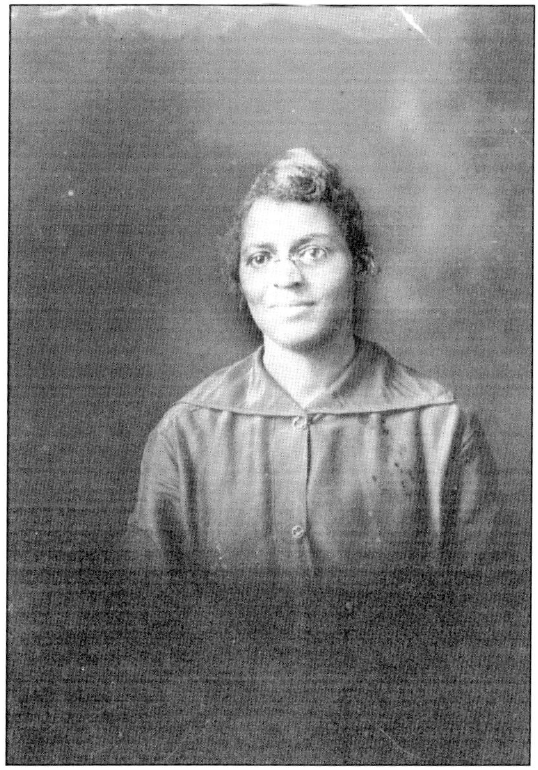

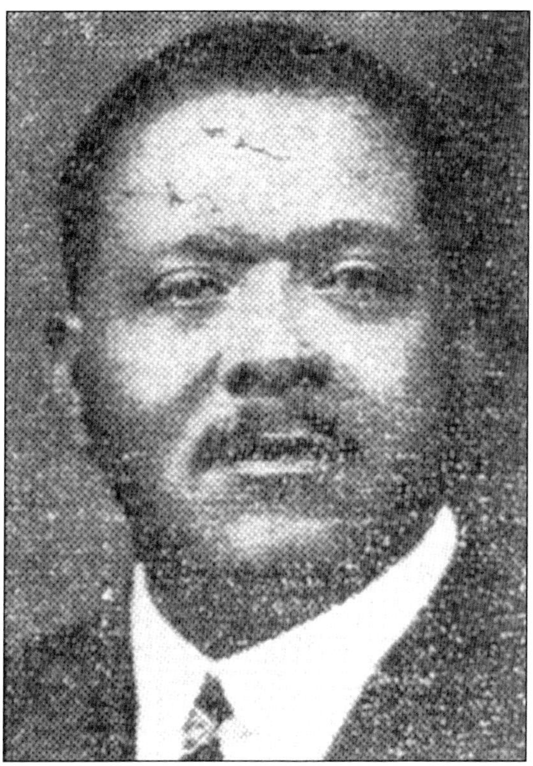

Prof. W.H. Harper was the principal of Summer Hill and Fair Street Schools in Gainesville from 1916 until 1941. He was an active member of St. Paul Methodist Church. (Courtesy of Gladystine Green.)

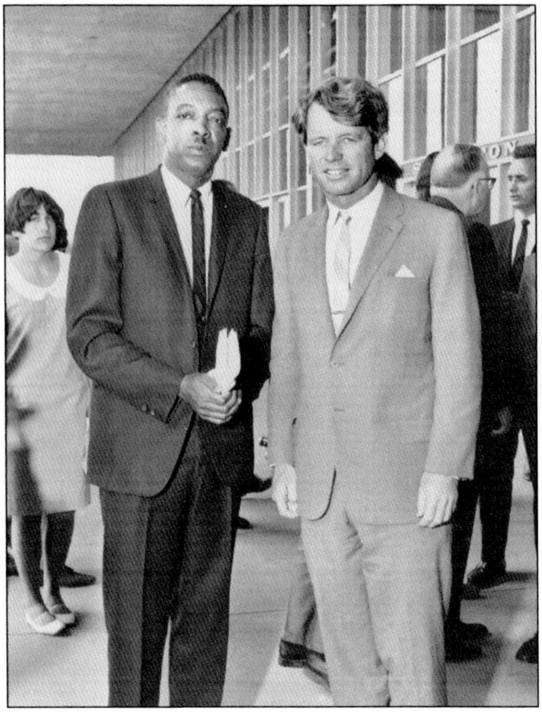

Dr. Bronell Whelchel, a native Gainesvillian, was a computer science specialist. He was a graduate of Morehouse College and Atlanta University and received a masters degree and Ph.D. from Stanford University in Palo Alto, California. Dr. Whelchel taught for a short time at both Brenau and Gainesville College in Gainesville, Georgia. He worked as a statistician for the OPEC oil nation of Nigeria and was later employed as a civilian by the United States Defense Department. Dr. Whelchel is pictured here with Sen. Robert "Bobby" Kennedy in the 1960s. (Courtesy of Margaret Whelchel Osborne.)

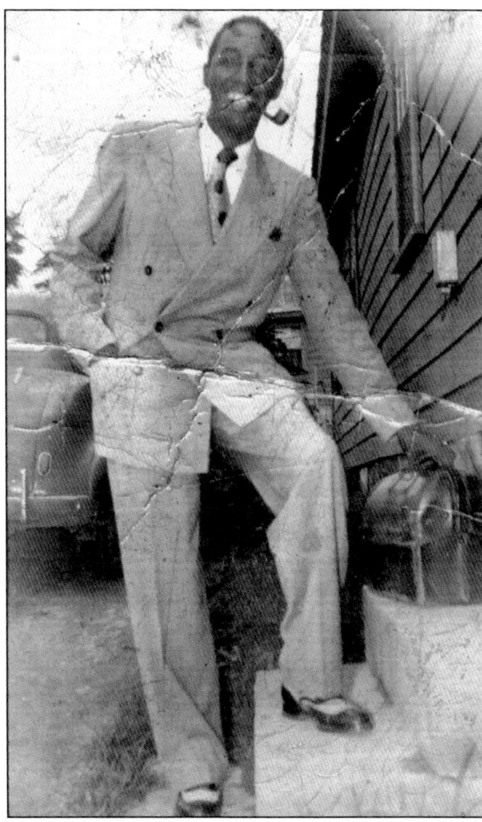

Dr. Emmett Etheridge Butler was a prominent Gainesville physician and community leader. He completed his high school and college education at Morehouse College in Atlanta. He graduated from Meharry Medical College in Nashville, Tennessee in 1934. Dr. Butler began practicing medicine in Hall County in 1936. He organized the Men's Progressive Club and later served as its president. He was the first black member of the Gainesville Board of Education and a deacon of the St. John Baptist Church. Dr. Butler was also a member of Omega Psi Phi Fraternity and the Fair Street Athletic Association. E.E. Butler School and E.E. Butler Parkway in Gainesville are named in his honor. (Courtesy of Evelyn Ware Glasper.)

Dr. Henry B. Wright was one of the two first African-American doctors in Gainesville. The son of a founder of St. Paul Methodist Church, he graduated from Meharry Medical College. He was extremely active in the church. Dr. Wright played the trumpet for the senior choir and organized a "Mozart Club" for the youth. He died suddenly on May 6, 1932. (Courtesy of Grady Richardson.)

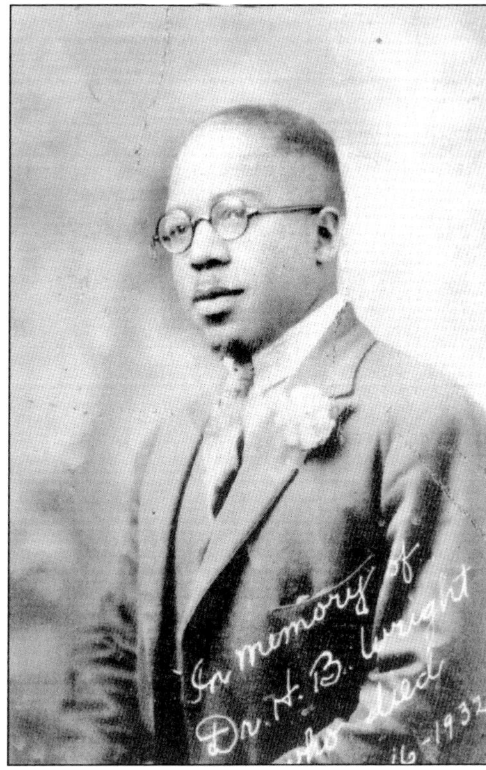

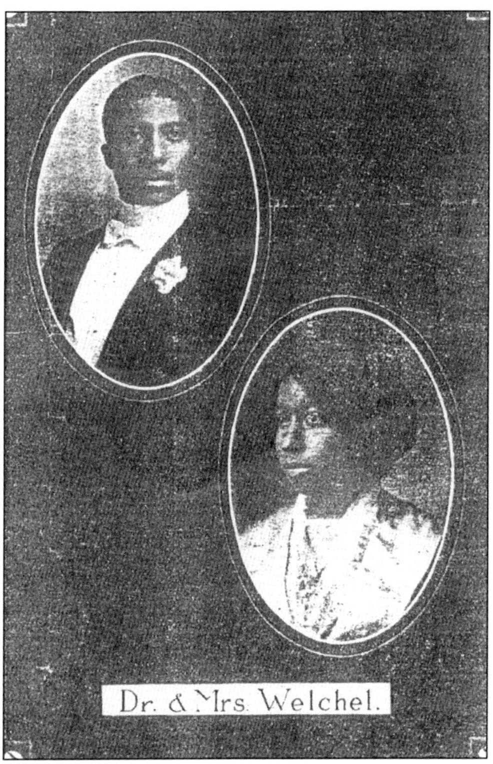

Dr. Elbert Mitchell Whelchel was Hall County's first black dentist. A native of Hall County, he graduated from Meharry Dental College in Nashville, Tennessee in 1914. He practiced in Gainesville for 38 years until his death in 1952. Dr. Whelchel was a member and steward of St. Paul Methodist Church. He and his wife, Julia Bell Whelchel, are pictured here. (Courtesy of the Hall County Black History Society.)

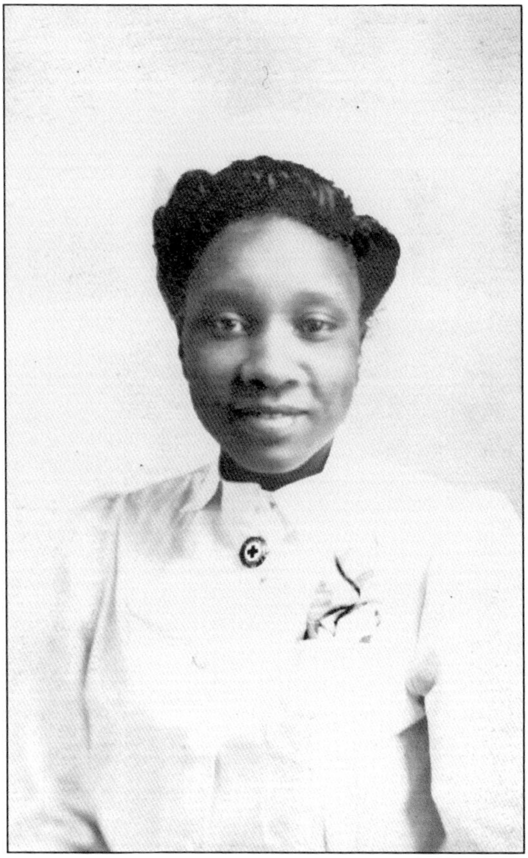

Registered Nurse Ruth Greenlee, daughter of Levi G. Greenlee and sister of T.J. Greenlee, is pictured in her uniform. She graduated from Tuskegee Institute in Tuskegee, Alabama. Nurse Greenlee was employed at Hall County Hospital and later served in the office of Dr. E.E. Butler. (Courtesy of Wilbur and Dixie Ramsey)

Roberta Cifors Morgan was a community leader and the daughter of Cynthia Cifors, one of the founders of St. Paul United Methodist Church. She was an agent for Atlanta Life Insurance Company for many years. (Courtesy of James Brooks.)

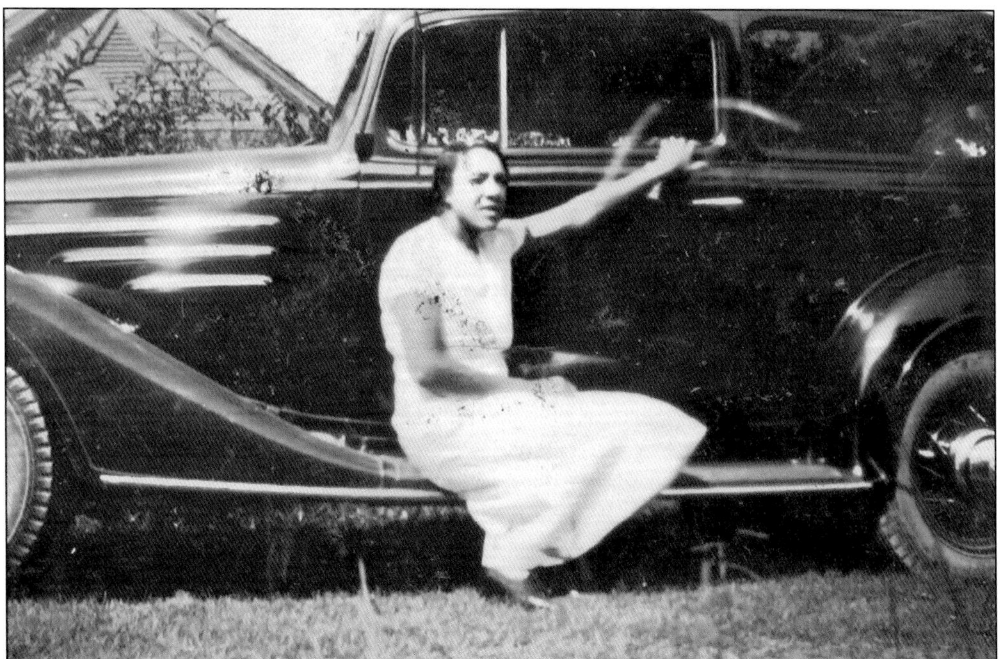

Catherine Florence Brown graduated from the Grady School of Nursing in Atlanta, Georgia. She received her training in Public Health Nursing from the Medical College of Virginia in Richmond. Nurse Brown was unanimously elected Coordinator of Nursing Service by her peers. She was named Coordinator of the Northeast Georgia District Family Planning Program in 1969. Catherine Brown was a faithful member of St. Paul United Methodist Church. (Courtesy of the Fair Street/Butler Alumni Association.)

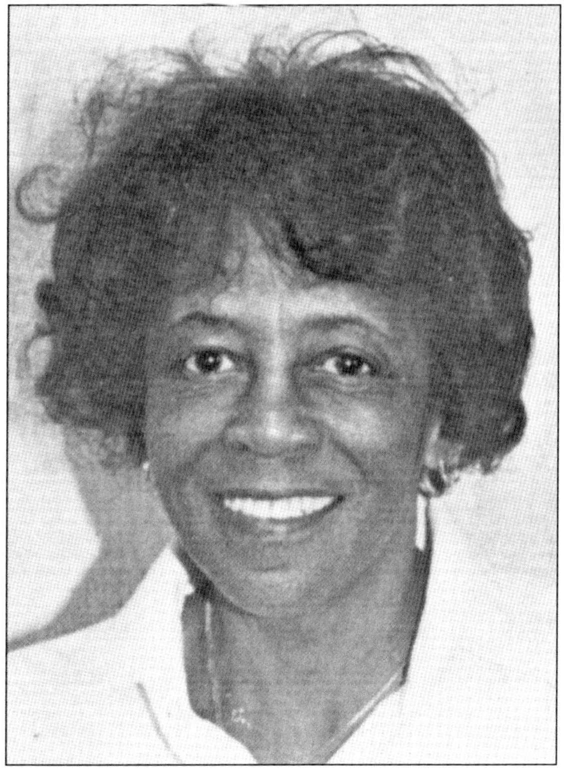

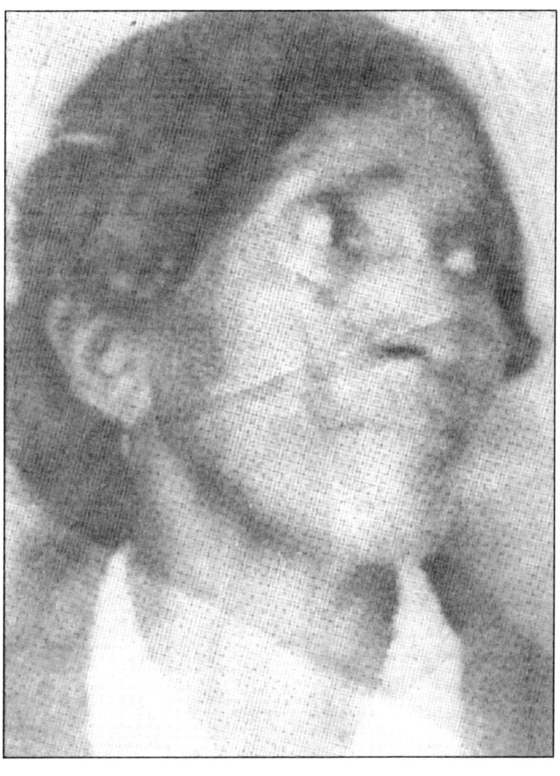

Florence Kesler was a midwife for nearly half a century. She is credited with ushering approximately 500 natives of Hall County—both black and white—into the world. She began her career as a midwife in 1914 at the age of 22. In the early days, she and her husband, William "Bill" Kesler, would travel to the homes of expectant parents in their horse and buggy. Payment for her services often came in the form of chickens, eggs, canned goods, dairy products, or fresh vegetables. (Courtesy of *The Times*.)

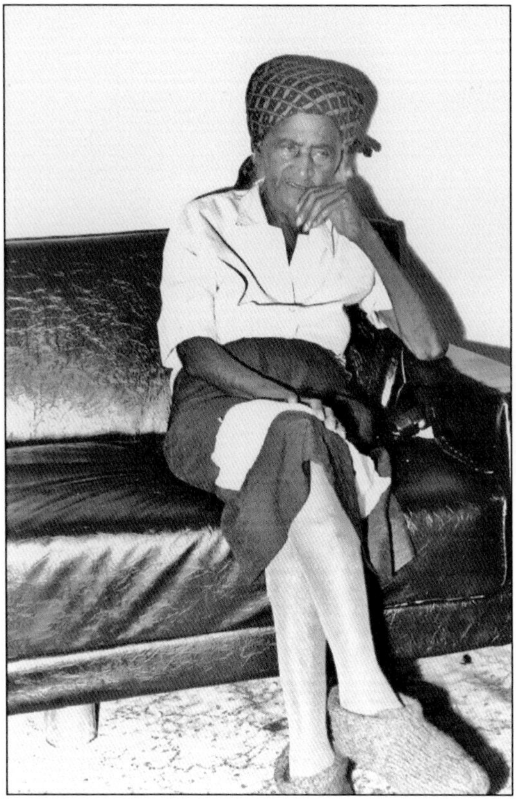

Nina Moon lived in Gainesville for 70 years. She resided on Atlanta Street. Miss Nina was known in the black community as an herbalist and folk doctor. People came to her to heal burns, babies' thrash, worms, and other such ailments. (Courtesy of Hall County Black History Society.)

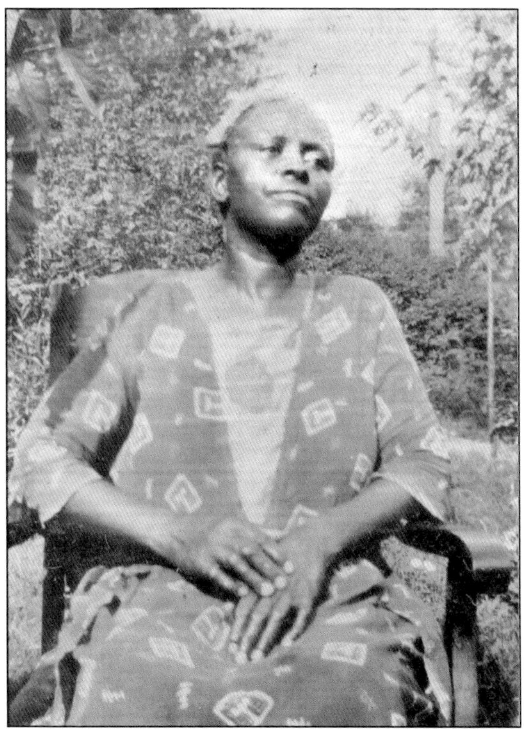

Born in 1867, Mimie Burt Cantrell was well known and respected in Gainesville and Hall County as a skillful midwife, nurse, and herbalist. She was one of the pillars of St. Paul Methodist Church. She was also an important member of a committee headed by George W. Stephens to fight for the installation of running water and a sewer system in Gainesville's Southside neighborhoods. (Courtesy of Gladystine Burt Green.)

Sarah Jane Gowder Moon was a Lula community midwife. "Miss Sarah" was born on November 25, 1870, to Jim and Rebecca Faulkner Gowder in Belton, Georgia. In 1885, she married Jep Moon. She earned her midwife registration certificate from the State of Georgia in 1932. "Miss Sarah" is pictured here with other family members. From left to right are (front row) Mary Moon and Howard Moon; (back row) J.C. Moon, Ione Moon, Sarah Gowder Moon (midwife), and James T. Moon. (Courtesy of Sarah Kidd.)

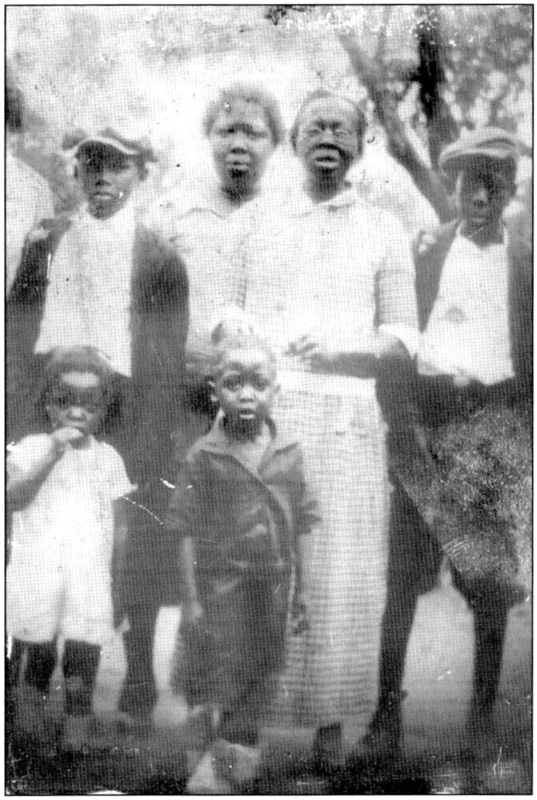

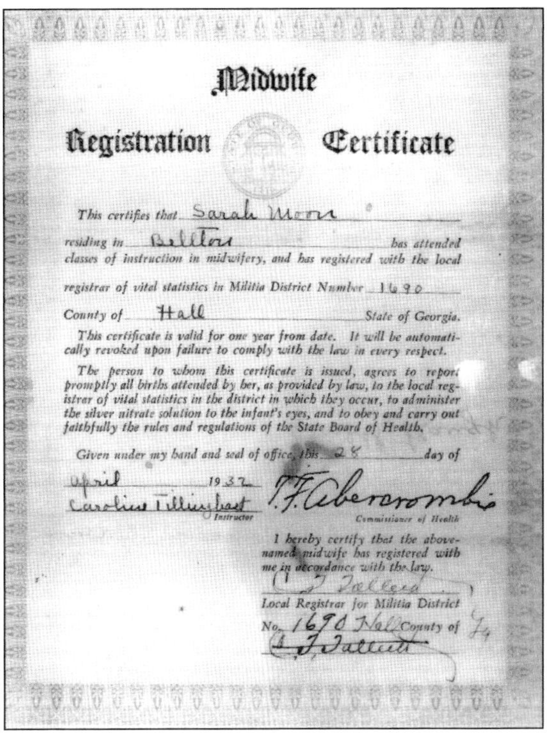

Midwife

Registration Certificate

This certifies that Sarah Moon

residing in Belton *has attended classes of instruction in midwifery, and has registered with the local registrar of vital statistics in Militia District Number* 1690

County of Hall *State of Georgia.*

This certificate is valid for one year from date. It will be automatically revoked upon failure to comply with the law in every respect.

The person to whom this certificate is issued, agrees to report promptly all births attended by her, as provided by law, to the local registrar of vital statistics in the district in which they occur, to administer the silver nitrate solution to the infant's eyes, and to obey and carry out faithfully the rules and regulations of the State Board of Health.

Given under my hand and seal of office, this 28 *day of* April 1932

Caroline Tillinghast, *Instructor*

T.F. Abercrombie, *Commissioner of Health*

I hereby certify that the above-named midwife has registered with me in accordance with the law.

Local Registrar for Militia District No. 1690 Hall *County of*

This is a replica of the original Midwife Registration Certificate issued to Sarah Moon by the Georgia State Commissioner of Health in 1937. (Courtesy of Sarah Kidd.)

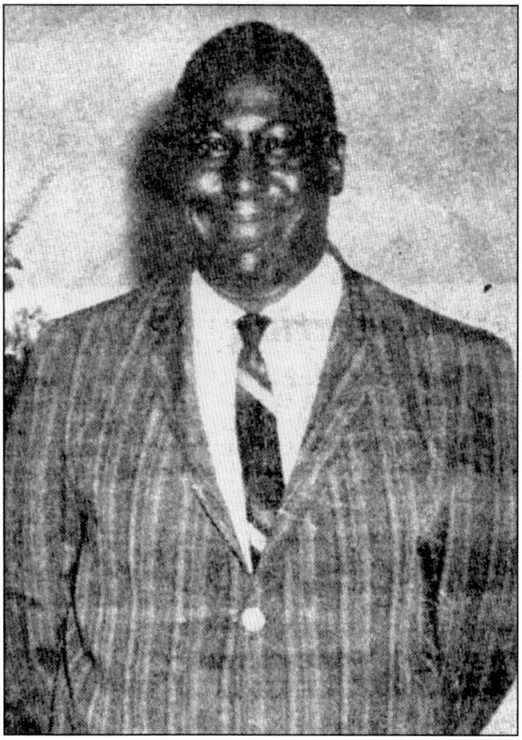

Maynard Brown Sr. was an outstanding Hall County businessman and civic leader. He was the proprietor of Brown's Grocery and Package Store on the Old Athens Highway in Gainesville for 29 years. A community leader, he served on the Northeast Georgia Medical Center Board and the City of Gainesville Planning Commission for several years. He was also a member of the Men's Progressive Club and the Century Club of Gainesville College. (Courtesy of Elizabeth Strickland.)

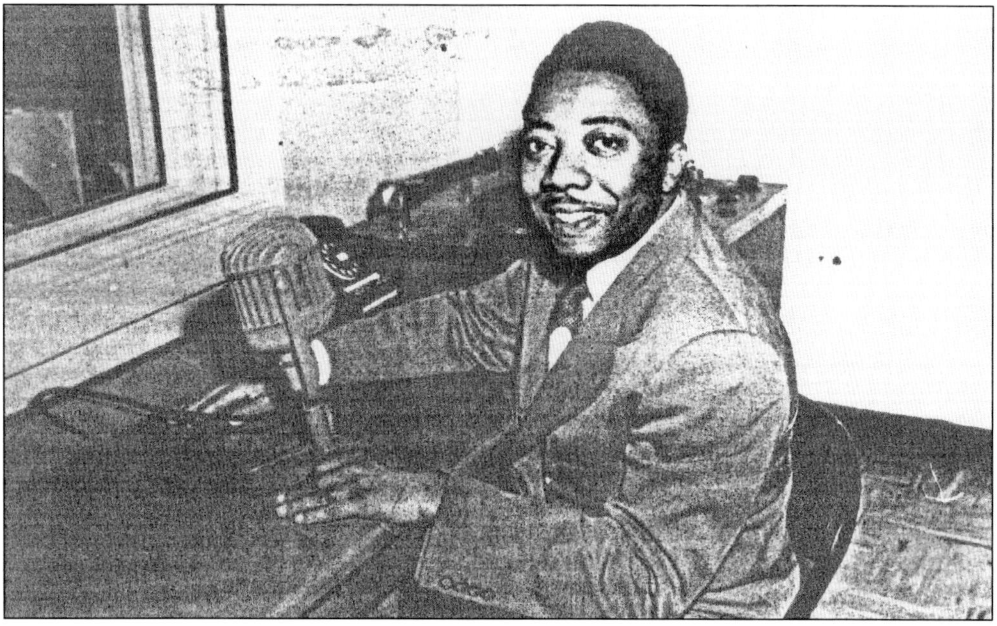

J. Wesley Merritt was the first official disc jockey in Gainesville. His show, called "Athens Street on Revue" and later known as "The Wes Merritt Show," was broadcast live on WDUN. He was also the announcer for the Fair Street Tiger football games. He and his family were featured in a locally produced 1951 film about black family life entitled *Palmour Street*. (Courtesy of James Brooks.)

George Stephens was a successful Gainesville businessman and a prominent community leader. Mr. Stephens was so successful as a tailor and dry cleaner that he was able to lend the City of Gainesville approximately $10,000 when it found itself in a financial tight spot in the 1920s. He was a faithful member of St. Paul Methodist Church and served in every available laity office in the church. He joined the masons on July 1, 1903 and served as worshipful master for 43 years. George Stephens died in 1971 at 102 years of age. (Courtesy of James Brooks and *The Times*.)

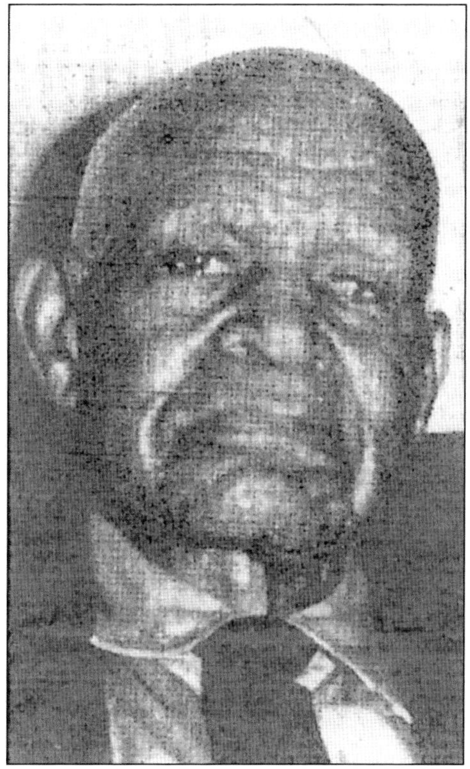

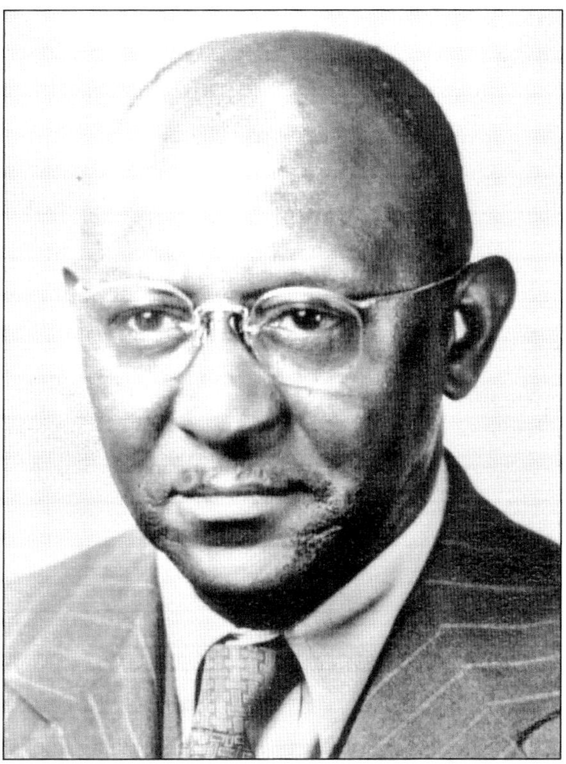

Walter Chamblee was a prominent Gainesville business and civic leader. Although Mr. Chamblee was engaged in the insurance business for a number of years, he is best remembered as the owner and operator of the soda fountain and drugstore, which was located at 761 Athens Street in Gainesville. Walter Chamblee was an active member of St. John Baptist Church, the Southside Chamber of Commerce, and the Men's Progressive Club. (Courtesy of Jennie Harris.)

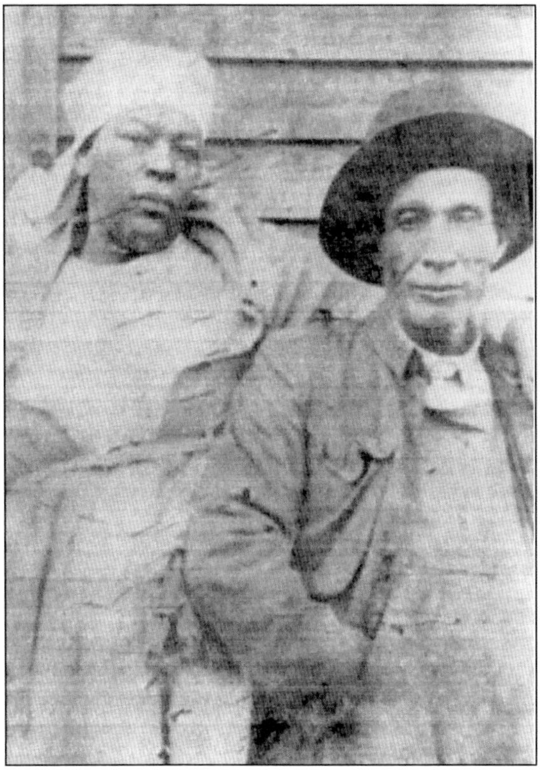

Rev. and Mrs. John Lincoln (Lina Gowder) Brown were residents of Belton (now Lula), Georgia. The parents of 14 children, Reverend and Mrs. Brown were farmers who raised vegetables, cotton, chickens, and pigs. They posed for this picture in 1917. (Courtesy of Ollie Bryson Buffington.)

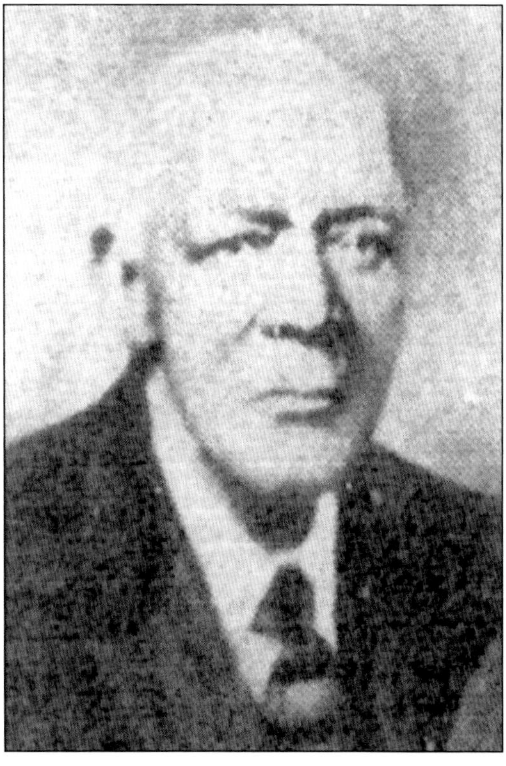

Rev. Green Hunter's estimated date of birth is June 27, 1853. Reverend Hunter organized several of Hall County's black churches, including Pleasant Hill, Cross Plain, Timberidge, St. John, Mount Zion, and Wahoo. He founded and served as the first moderator of the Northwestern Baptist Association and began a private school (Northwestern School) for African-American children. Green Hunter Homes (Atlanta Street projects), and Green Hunter Nursery were named in his honor. (Courtesy of the Fair Street Butler/Alumni Association.)

Perry Swinger was employed as a gravedigger at Alt Vista Cemetery. He was one of the owners of the Oddfellow Building and the grandfather of William Henry Maxey. He is pictured on the right with one of his grandchildren. (Courtesy of William Henry Maxey.)

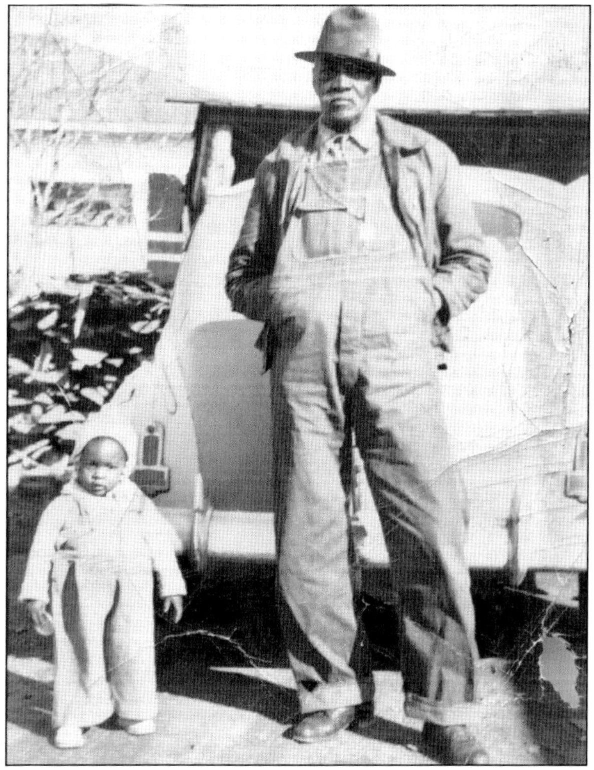

Mr. and Mrs. William (Mary Randolph) Lipscomb were residents of Gillsville, Georgia. The Lipscombs were farmers and owned over 30 acres of land in Gillsville. William and Mary were faithful members of the Pleasant Hill Church and once owned a small community store in the area. They were the parents of 11 children. (Courtesy of Rev. and Mrs. William Lipscomb Jr.)

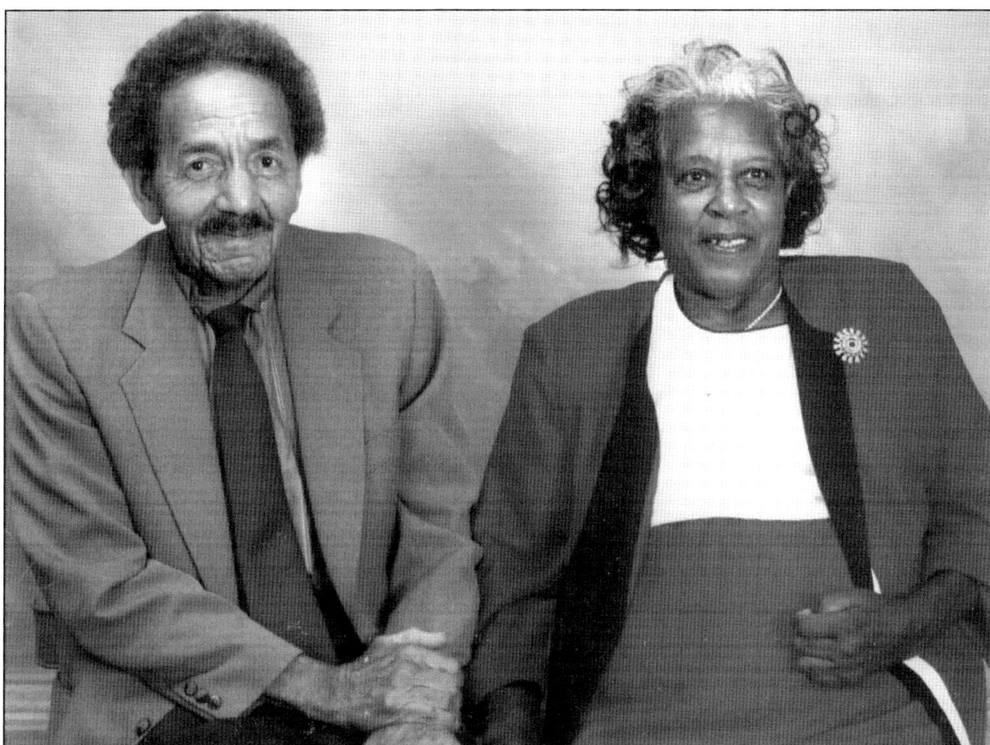

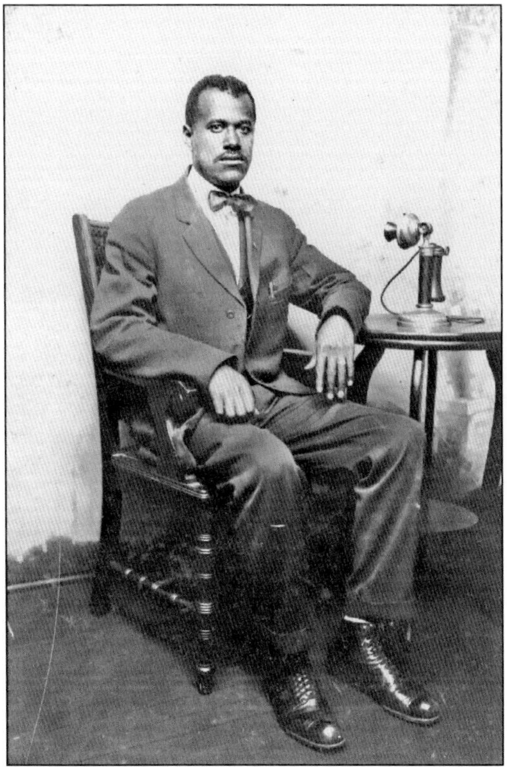

Dock S. Lowe Sr., a 38-year Atlanta Life Insurance employee, was a church and community leader. He was a member of the First Baptist Church and served as president of the J.R. Benevolent Association in Gainesville. Dock Lowe Sr. was the First Baptist Sunday School superintendent for over 50 years. He was a church deacon for 60 years and served as a trustee of the Northwestern Baptist Association for 30 years. (Courtesy of Mattie Lowe.)

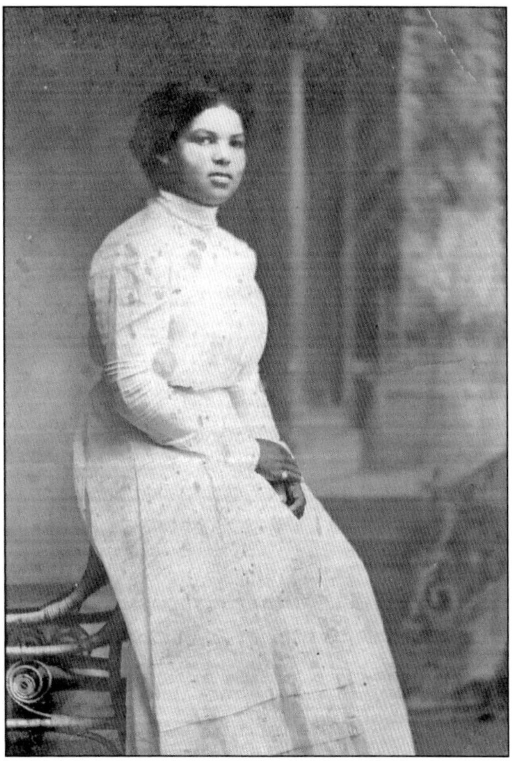

Lillian Canady Lowe, wife of Dock Lowe Sr., was born February 16, 1892. She was a homemaker and the mother of Georgia Irene Lowe, Robert Lowe, John Emory Lowe, Harold Lowe, Dock S. Lowe Jr., Mattie Lowe, and Annie Maude Lowe. She died August 16, 1931. (Courtesy of Mattie Lowe.)

Joe Watson Moon, a citizen of Lula, Georgia, was a Pullman porter for the Southern Railroad Company. Lula was once considered a booming railroad town. Joe is shown here wearing his porter's uniform. (Courtesy of Linda Rucker Hutchens.)

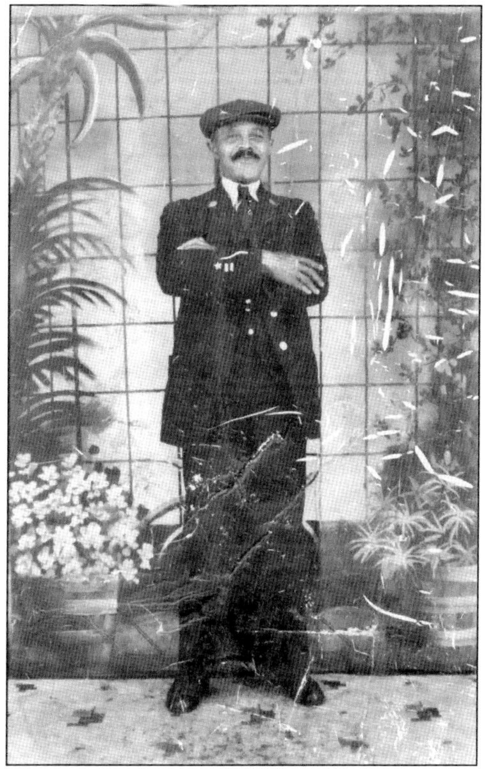

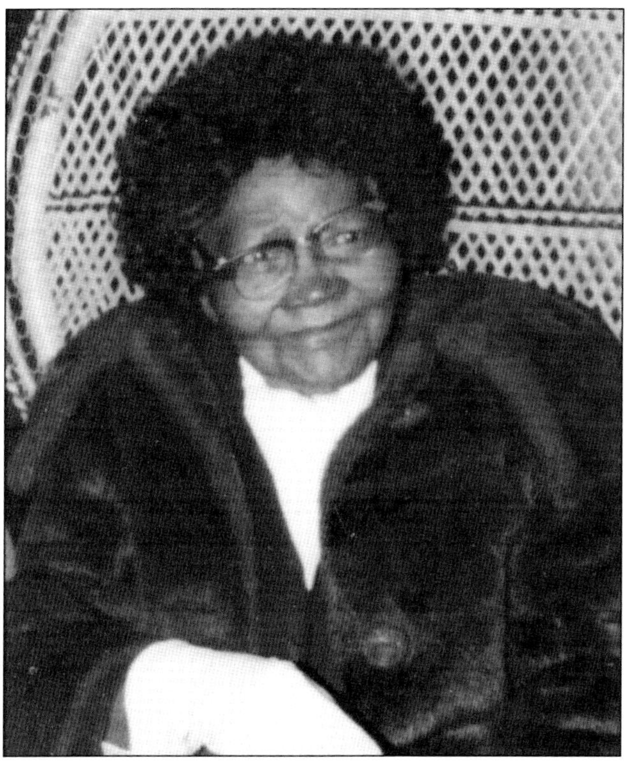

Mrs. Ruby Wilkins was a pioneer Hall County community activist. She was an advocate for progressive change in the Newtown and Southside areas of Gainesville. Much of Ruby Wilkins's work was accomplished through the Newtown Florist Club, which she helped to establish. Under Ruby Wilkins's leadership, the Newtown Florist Club played a key role in securing the funding for Desota Park and the development of the Butler Recreation Center. (Courtesy of Clyde Wilkins.)

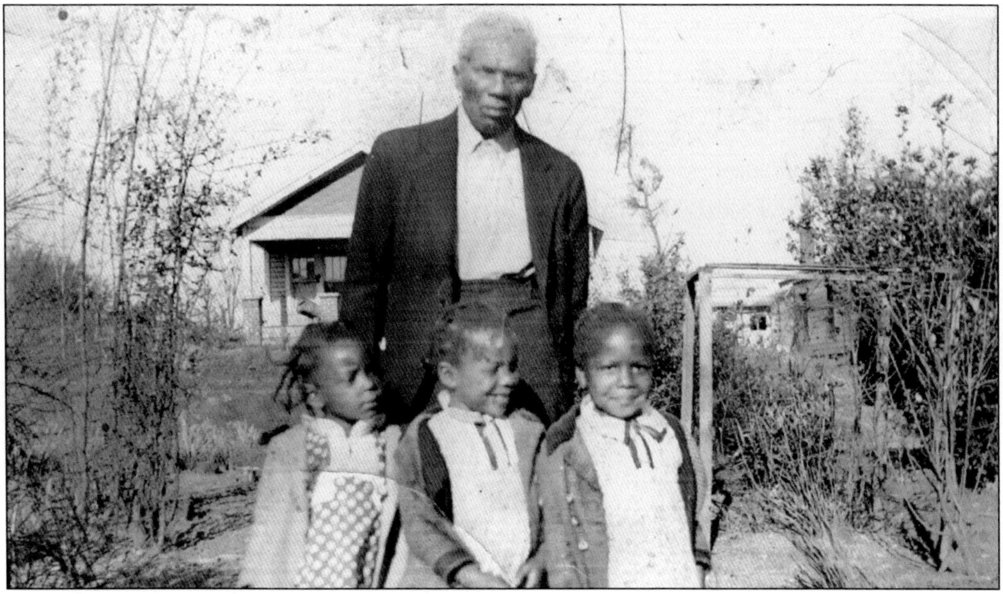

Warren Butler was an employee of the Street Department of the City of Gainesville for 59 years. He also served as chairman of the board of deacons at First Baptist Church for more than 40 years. He is pictured here on his 78 birthday. The girls pictured with him, from left to right, are Lula Borders, Gertrude Brown Carey, and Martha Marshall Mize. (Courtesy of Jennie Harris.)

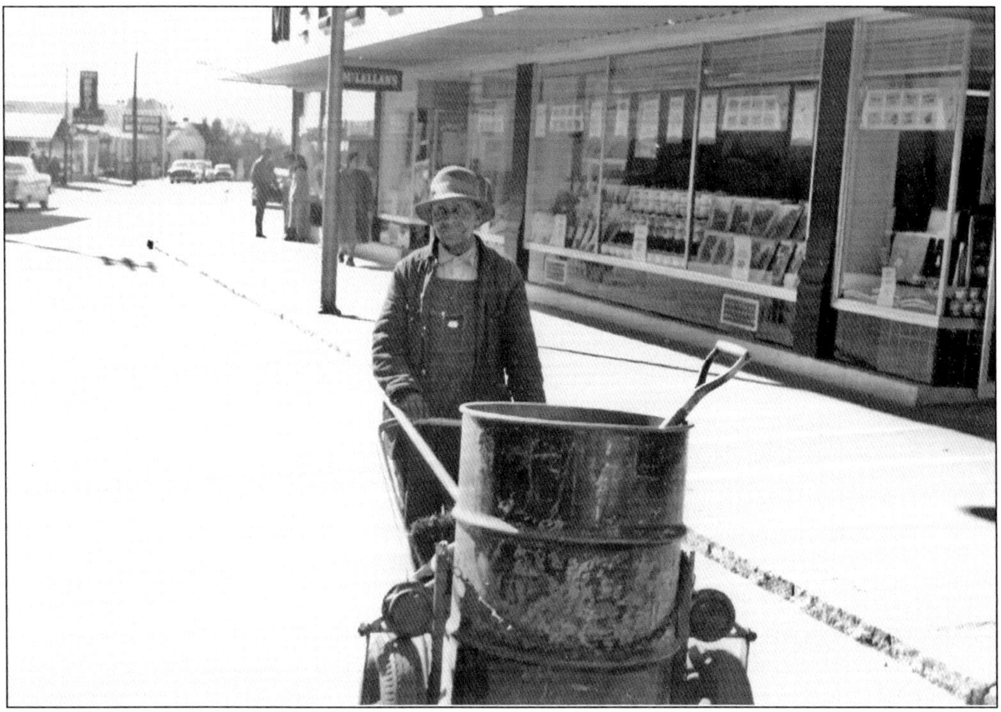

Howard "Possum" Bailey was employed by the Street Department of the City of Gainesville. He cleaned the streets of Gainesville's for many years. (Courtesy of the Hall County Library.)

Labuoy Blake, a native of Gainesville, began singing with the original 1950s group, The Platters, in 1979. The group performed at the Georgia Mountain Center in Gainesville on June 9, 1980. (Courtesy of Jeanine Blake.)

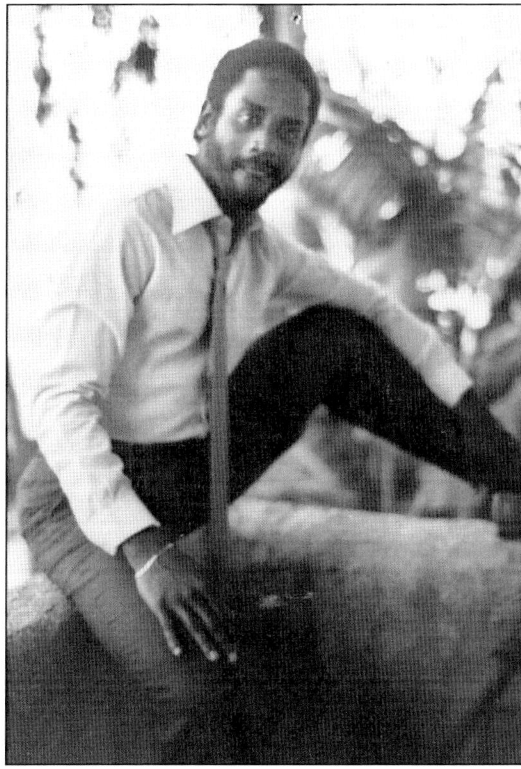

The Soules of Calvary, a gospel singing group, included, from left to right, (front row) Amos Welch, Edward Glenn, and Chester Willis Sr.; (back row) Bonnie Riley and Newell Wilson. Bonnie Riley was the first elected black council member for the City of Flowery Branch, Georgia. (Courtesy of Donna Riley Stringer.)

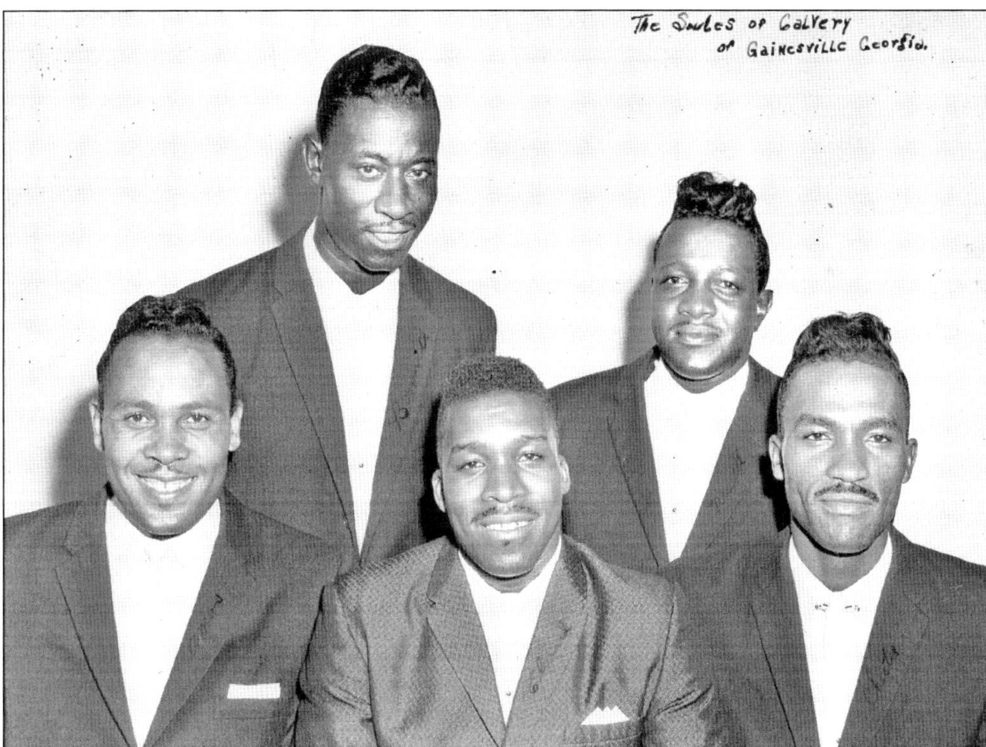

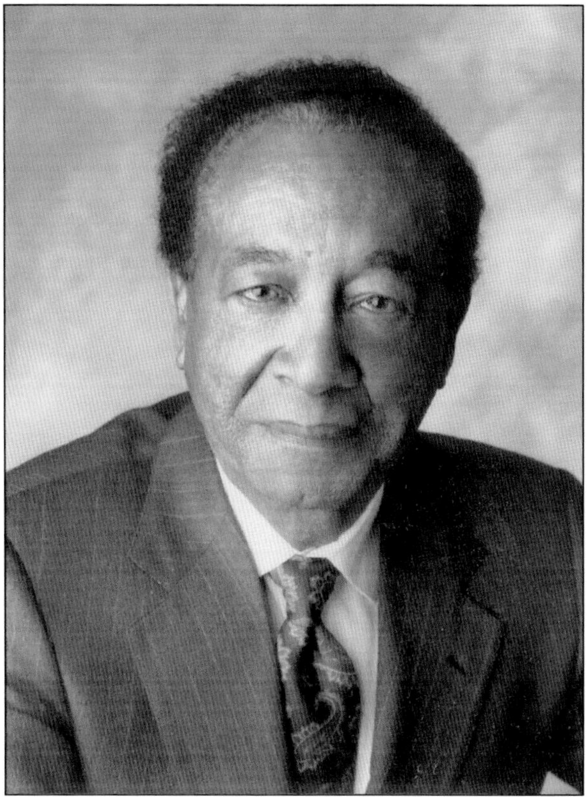

John William Morrow Jr. was born on June 17, 1918 in Hall County to Mr. and Mrs. John William (Gladys Vincent) Morrow Sr. He was one of two black men appointed to the Gainesville City Board of Education in 1957. He became Gainesville's first black councilman in 1979. In 1985, John Morrow became Gainesville's first African-American mayor. John Morrow Parkway in Gainesville is named in his honor. (Courtesy of Emily Force Morrow.)

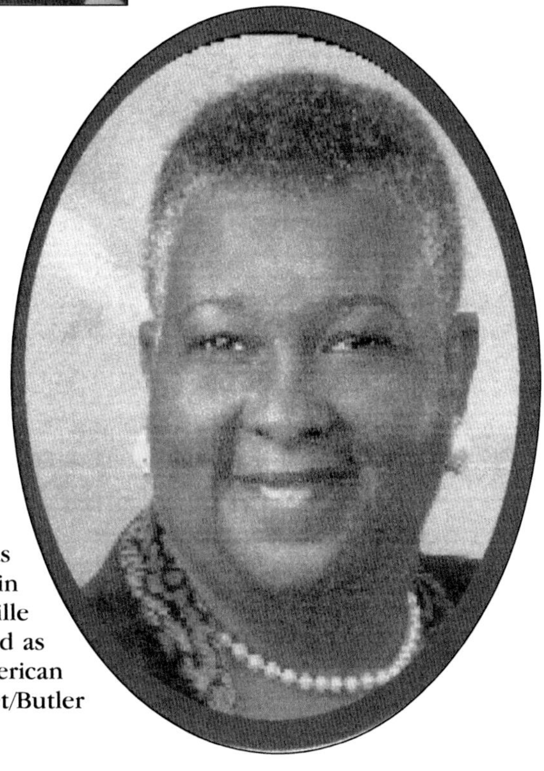

Willie Frances Jenkins Meadows was the first black employee to work in the administrative offices of Gainesville College in 1969. In 1992, she was elected as Hall County's first African-American commissioner. (Courtesy of the Fair Street/Butler Alumni Association)

Nine

They Answered the Call
The Military

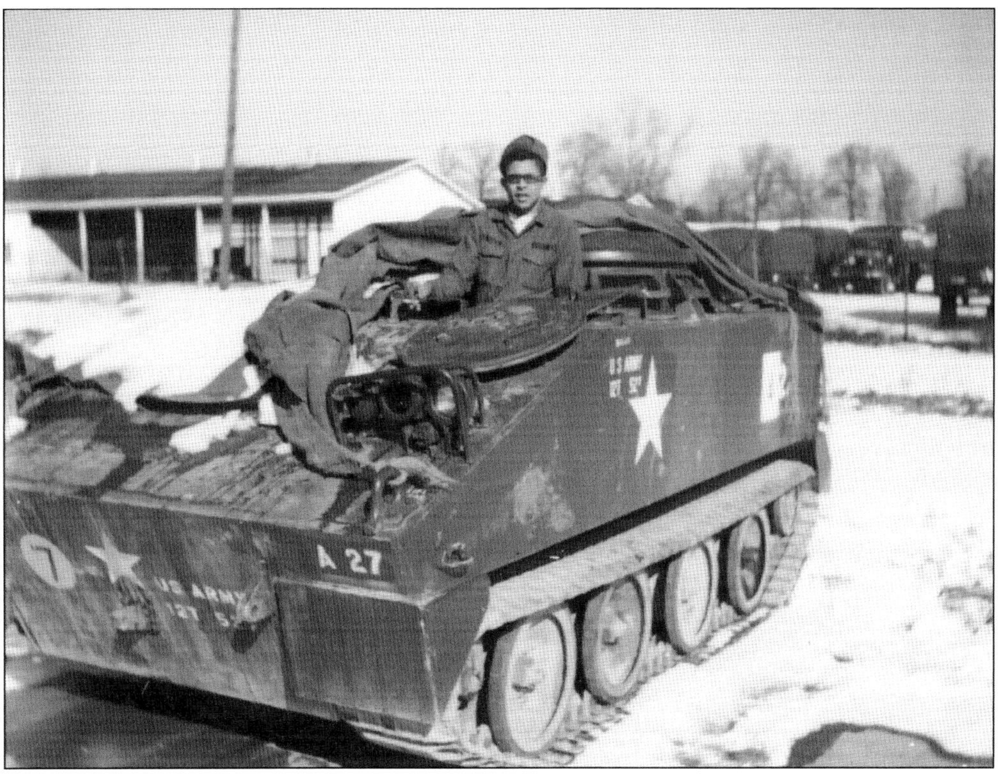

Johnny Millsap served in the U.S. Army in the Vietnam War. He posed for this picture at the army training camp in Fort Knox, Kentucky, in 1970. (Courtesy of Donna Riley Stringer.)

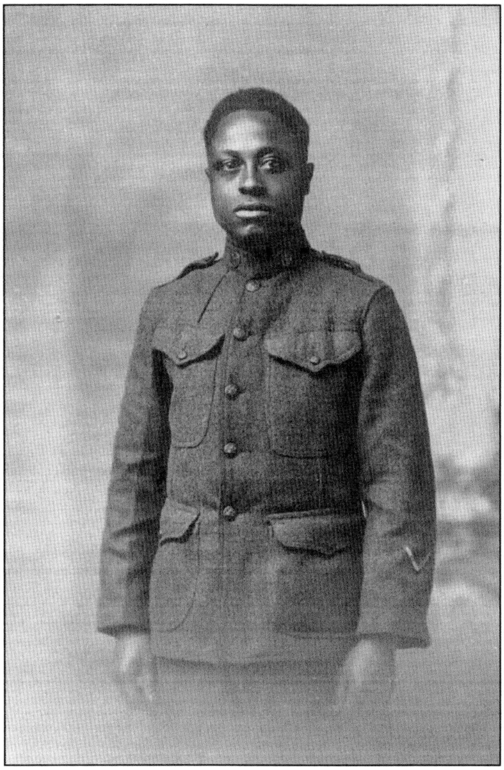

Hall County's African-American citizens made significant contributions to the Armed Services during World War I. Although the majority of African-American troops served in the quartermaster labor units, the segregated 92nd and 93rd divisions played important roles in the overthrow of the Central Powers. Dock Harrison, who is pictured here, served in the Army during World War I. (Courtesy of Katie Earle)

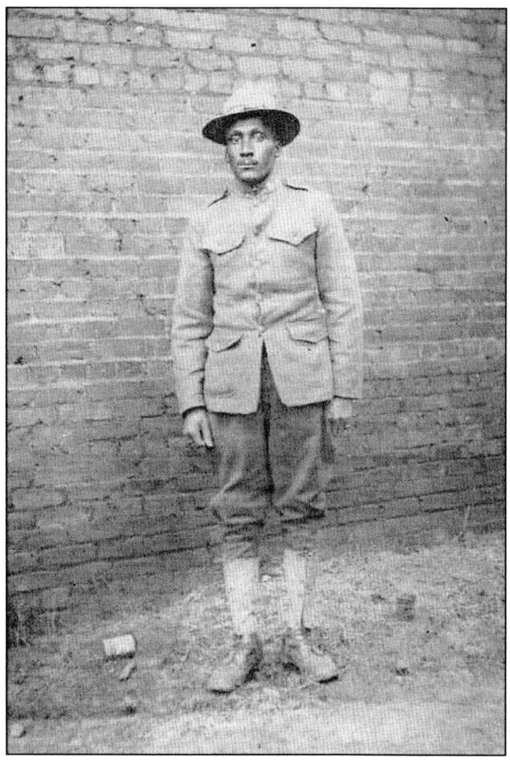

Troops engaged in building roads, digging trenches, and completing other construction tasks were known as pioneer regiments during World War I. These regiments were usually composed almost entirely of African-American troops. Henry Law posed for this picture in his United States Army uniform during World War I. (Courtesy of Emma Law Tutman)

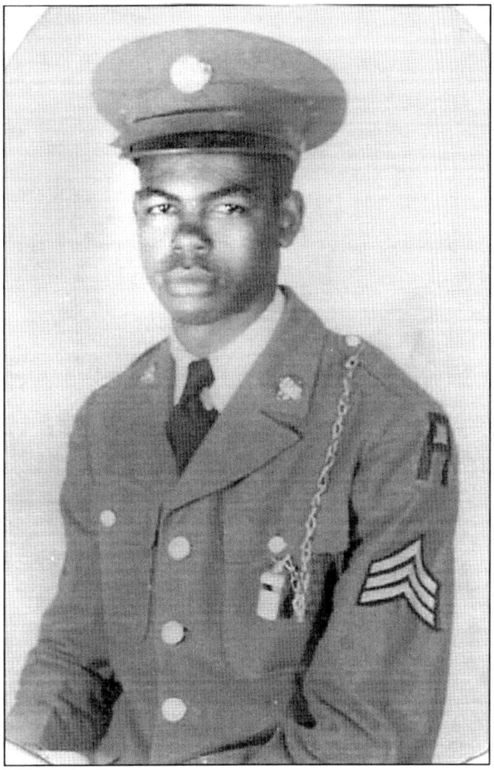

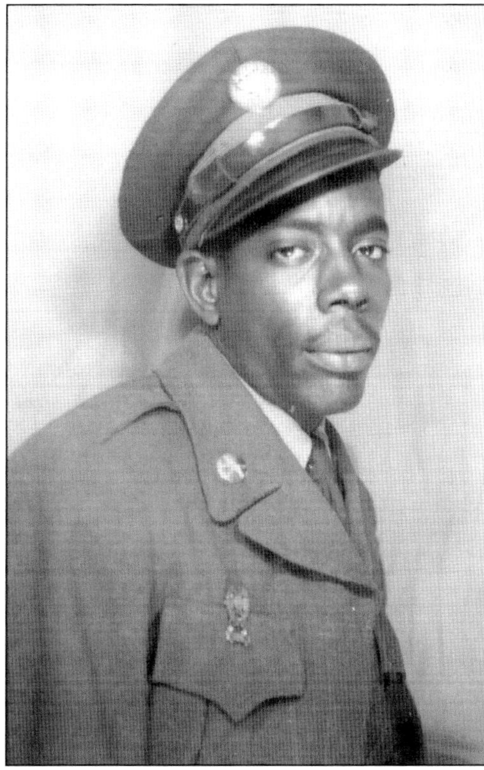

(*above, left*) Benjamin Rucker Sr. received the American Defense Service Medal, the Asiatic Pacific Service Medal with one Bronze Star, the World War II Victory Medal, and the American Service Medal for combat in the Solomon Islands during World War II. (Courtesy of Linda Rucker Hutchens.)
(*above, right*) David Dabney served in the United States Army during World War II. (Courtesy of Annette Cantrell.)

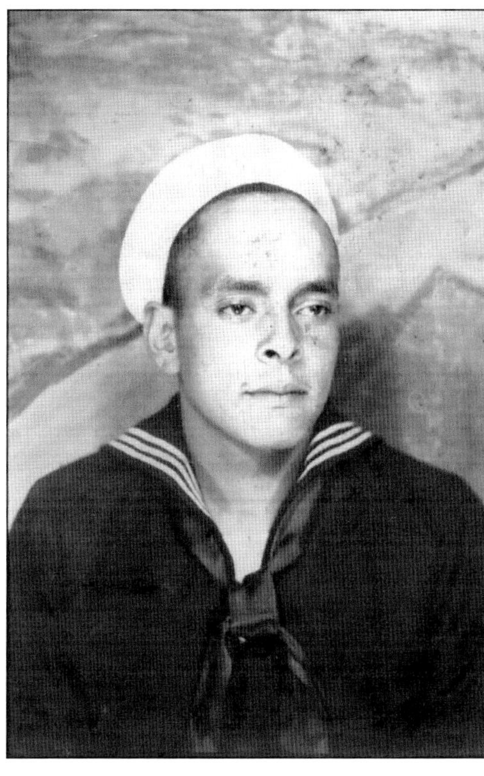

John Henry Edward Cheeks was assigned to hospital duties during World War II. He is seen here in his navy uniform. (Courtesy of Donna Riley Stringer.)

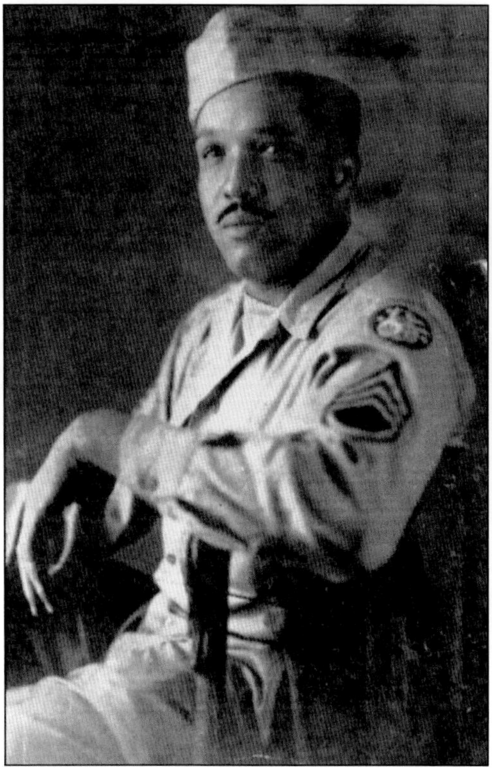

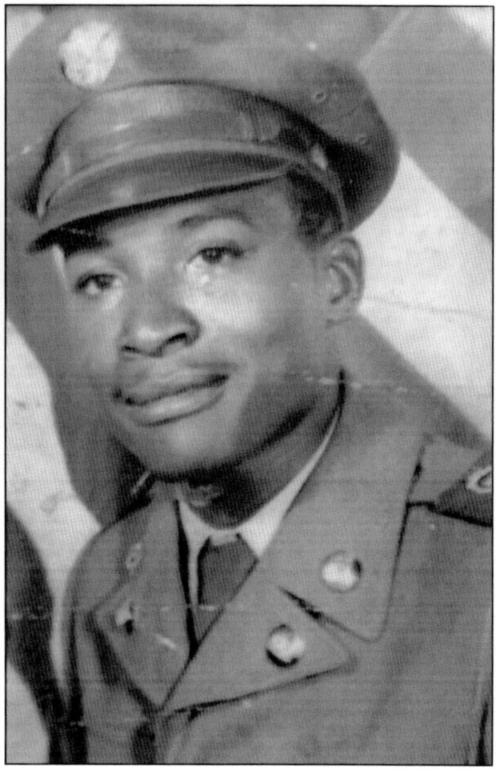

(above, left) Doyce Hughey was one of the first black men from this area to fight in World War II. He was 24 when he joined the United States Air Force and was a staff sergeant when he was discharged. (Courtesy of *The Times*.)
(above, right) PFC James Mattox served in the United States Army during the Korean War from 1951 to 1952. (Courtesy of Gary M. Cox.)

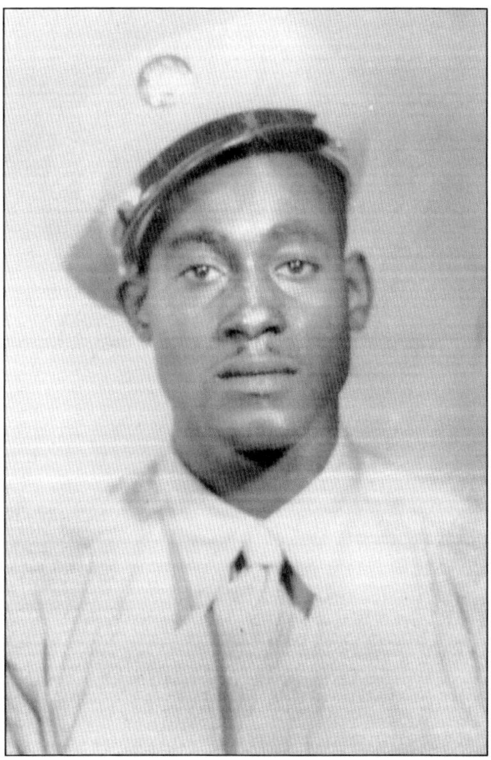

Johnny H. Turner was a veteran of World War II. He served in the United States Army in the 1,318th Engineer General Service Regiment as a demobilization technician. (Courtesy of Rosalyn Turner.)

Dr. Hubert Whelchel (right) served in the United States Army during World War II. Another Hall Countian, PFC Eugene Brown of the United States Army was killed in combat on March 21, 1945 during World War II. The Eugene Brown Post #521 of the American Legion in Gainesville was named in his honor. (Courtesy of Margaret Whelchel Osborne.)

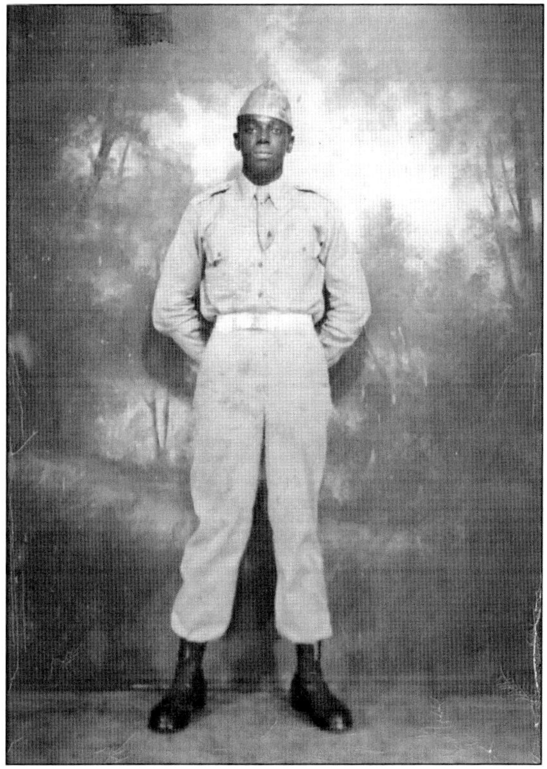

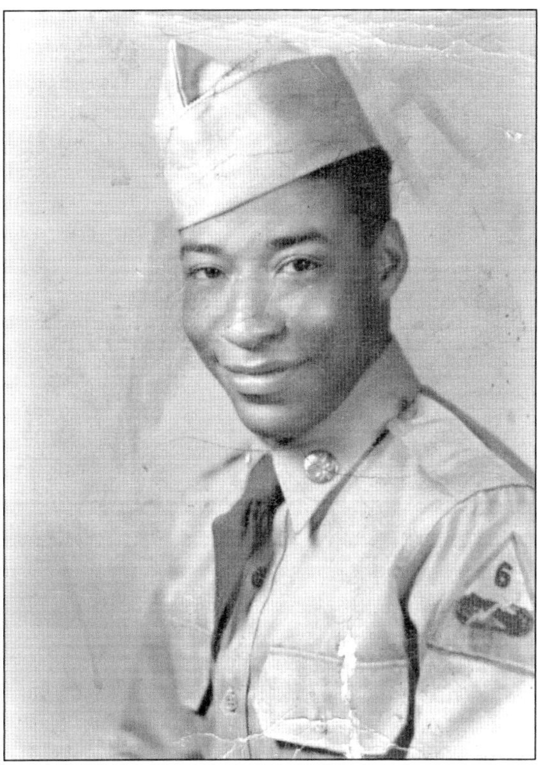

Charles Lipscomb served in the United States Army during the Korean War in the 1950s. At the age of 22, Lipscomb was reported captured by enemy troops during the war. His body was never recovered. (Courtesy of Berlinda Turner Lipscomb.)

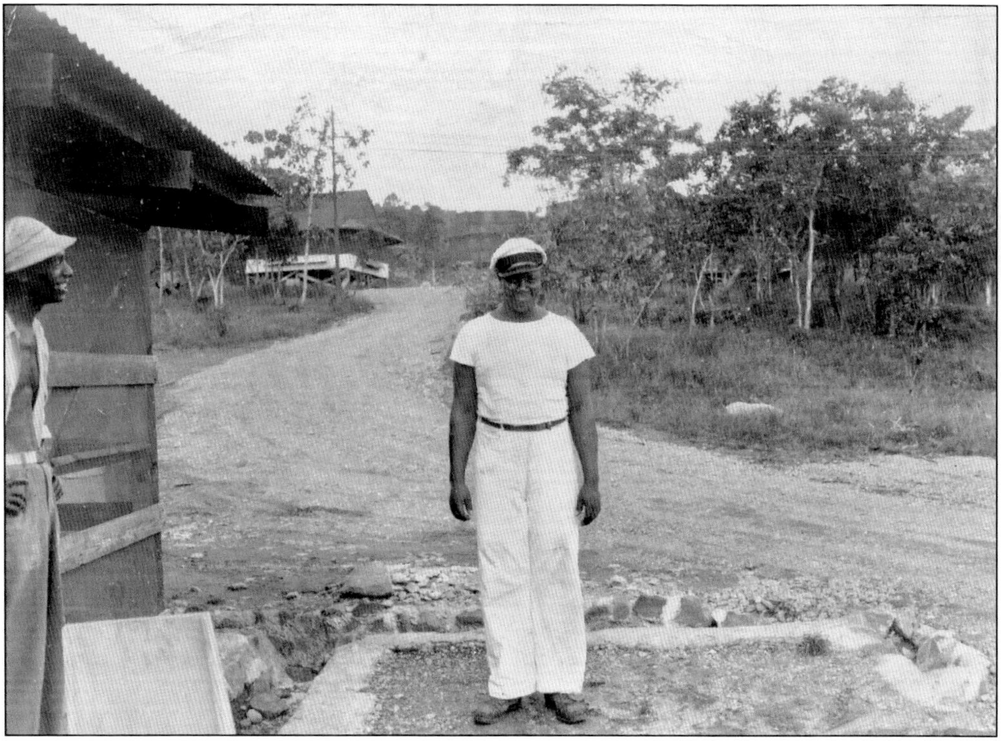

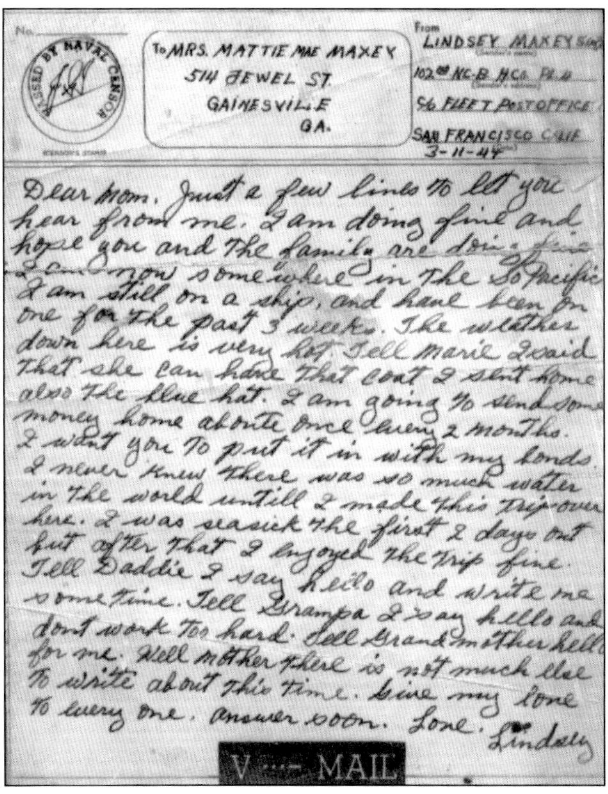

PASSED BY NAVAL CENSOR

To MRS. MATTIE MAE MAXEY
514 JEWEL ST.
GAINESVILLE
GA.

From LINDSEY MAXEY
102nd NC-B
c/o FLEET POST OFFICE
SAN FRANCISCO CALIF
3-11-44

Dear Mom. Just a few lines to let you hear from me. I am doing fine and hope you and the family are doing fine. I am now somewhere in the So Pacific. I am still on a ship, and have been on one for the past 3 weeks. The weather down here is very hot. Tell Marie I said that she can have that coat I sent home also the blue hat. I am going to send some money home aboute once every 2 months. I want you to put it in with my bonds. I never knew there was so much water in the world untill I made this trip over here. I was seasick the first 2 days out but after that I enjoyed the trip fine. Tell Daddie I say hello and write me some time. Tell Grampa I say hello and dont work too hard. Tell Grand mother hello for me. Well mother there is not much else to write about this time. Give my love to every one. answer soon. Love. Lindsey

V-MAIL

Lindsey Maxey served his country in the U.S. Navy. He was a chief petty officer with the Navy Seabees. (Courtesy of William Henry Maxey.)

This V-mail was written by Lindsey Maxey to his mother from the South Pacific during his service in the United States Navy. (Courtesy of William Henry Maxey.)

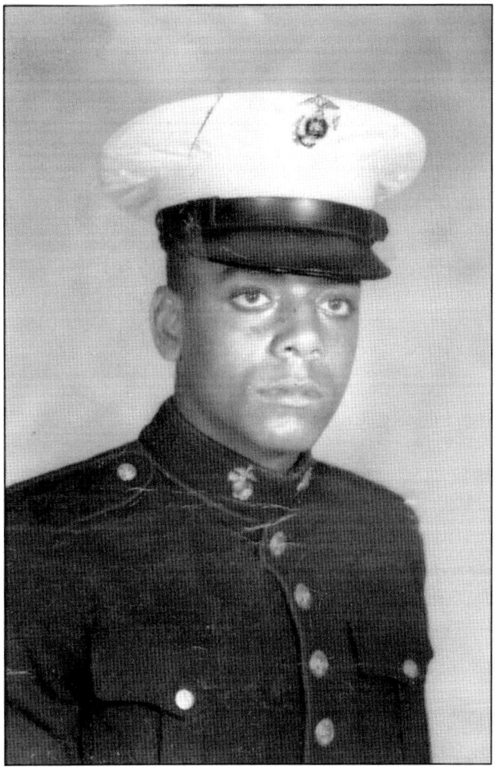

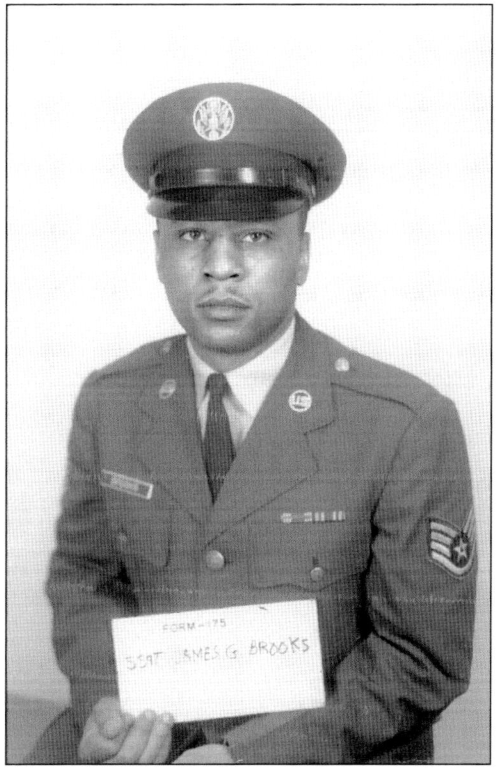

(*above, left*) Harold Williams Jr., a native of Lula, Georgia, served in the United States Marines Corp for 5 years before joining the United States Navy, where he served for over 20 years. He retired from the Navy as a recruiter. (Courtesy of Linda Rucker Hutchens.)

(*above, right*) James G. Brooks joined the United States Air Force in October 1956. He served in the jet aircraft maintenance career field as a flight line mechanic, flight chief, maintenance central supervisor, and quality control supervisor during his more than 22 years of military service. James G. Brooks retired as a Senior Master Sergeant in November 1978. (Courtesy of James Brooks.)

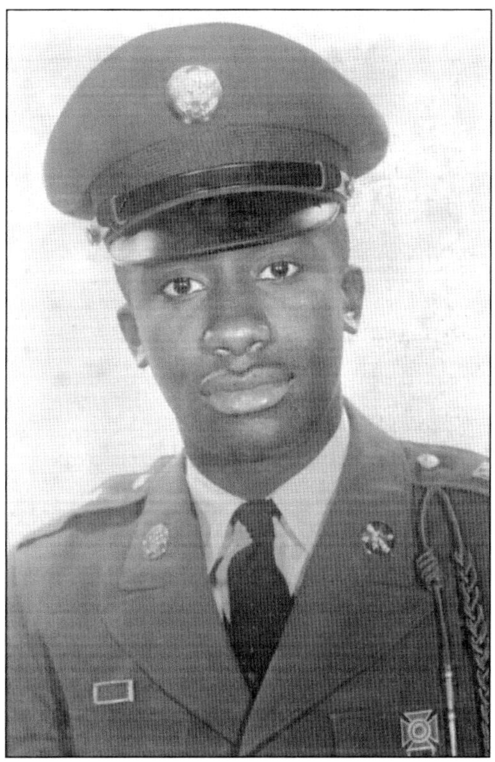

Kenneth Thornton retired as an E-7 after serving 21 years in the United States Army. Thornton received two Purple Hearts and served in Germany, Korea, and Vietnam. He is a native of Lula, Georgia. (Courtesy of Linda Rucker Hutchens.)

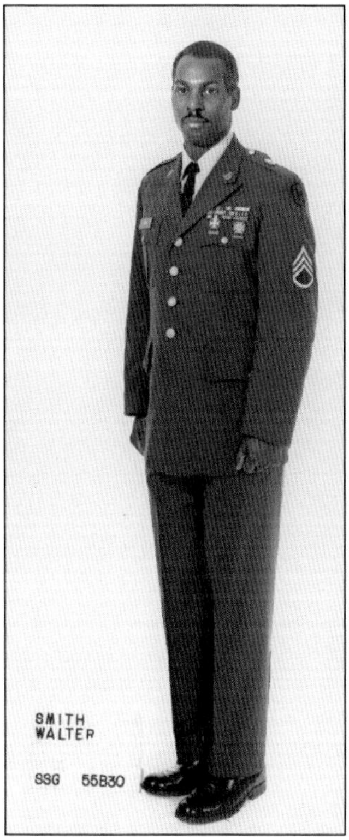

Walter Lee Smith has served in the United States Army for the past 29 years. He has completed tours of duty in Japan, Korea, Germany, and Italy. He is currently an active member of the United States Army Reserves. (Courtesy of Ella Jean Wilmont Smith.)

Sp4 George Hutchens is pictured 12 miles outside of Saigon. He served in the First Battalion, First Brigade, and the First Infantry Division (Big Red One) of the United States Army. Hall County's African-American casualties of the Vietnam era were Sgt. Forrest Goudelock, PFC Wilbur F. Mattox, PFC Johnny Bill Robertson Jr., and Sp4 George Lamar Young. (Courtesy of George and Linda R. Hutchens)

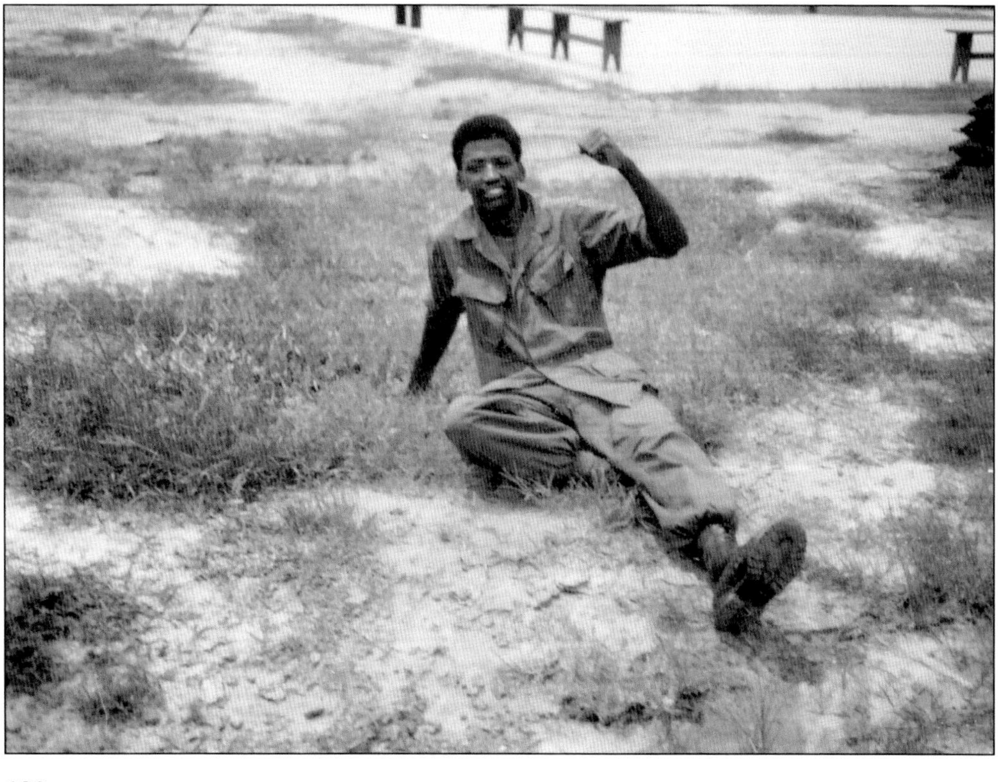

Ten

A BIT OF THIS AND THAT *Miscellaneous*

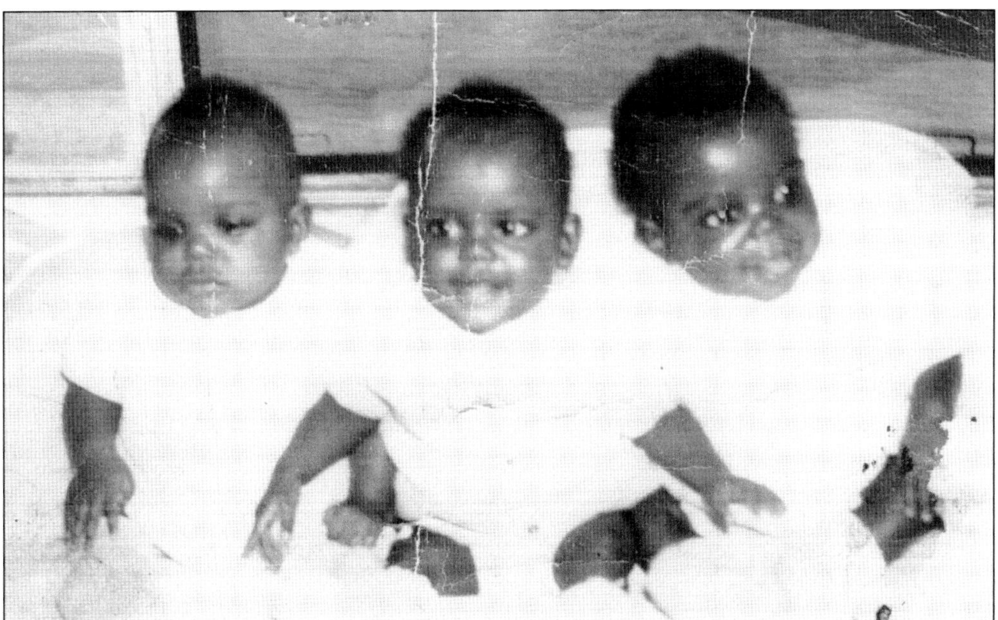

The first documented African-American triplets born in Hall County, from left to right, are Jerry Moon, Mary Moon Glenn, and James Moon. They were born on March 1–2, 1948 in Lula, Georgia. (Courtesy of Ollie Bryson Buffington.)

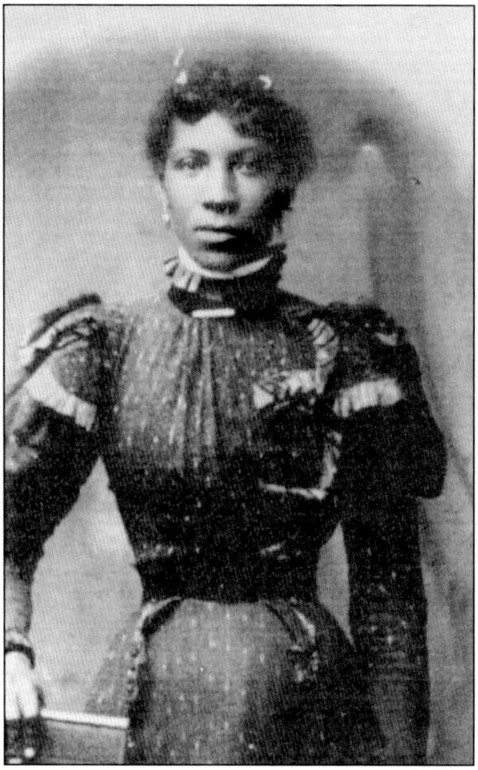

Mary Hamilton Smith was the mother of Ella Smith Turner and the great-grandmother of Ella Jean Wilmont Smith, Hennon Wilmont, Wenell Wilmont, Sandra Wilmont, Sharon Carrington, Johnnie Carrington, and Toni Carrington. (Courtesy of Ella Jean Wilmont Smith)

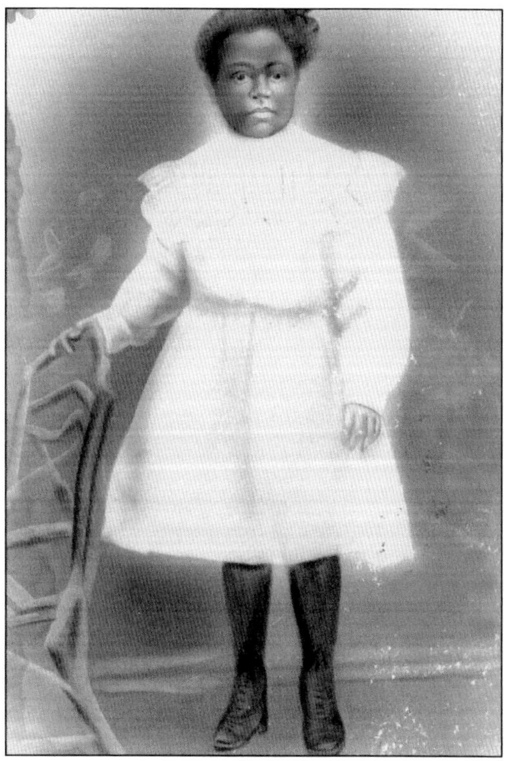

Carrie Lee Victoria Rice Deadwyler posed for this picture in 1903 at the age of five. She was the maternal grandmother of Linda Rucker Hutchens, Bobbie Jean Cox, Dr. Benjamin Rucker Jr., Walter J. Rucker, and Jonathan Rucker. (Courtesy of Linda Rucker Hutchens.)

Eva Mae (Williams) Brooks, mother of James Brooks, is seen standing in front of Hester Patterson's (her grandmother's) home at 726 Carlton Street in Gainesville. "Miss Eva" was a member of the 1936 Class of Summer Hill School. She distinguished herself as a loving, care-giving, nurse's assistant at Northeast Georgia Medical Center in Gainesville, Georgia. (Courtesy of James Brooks)

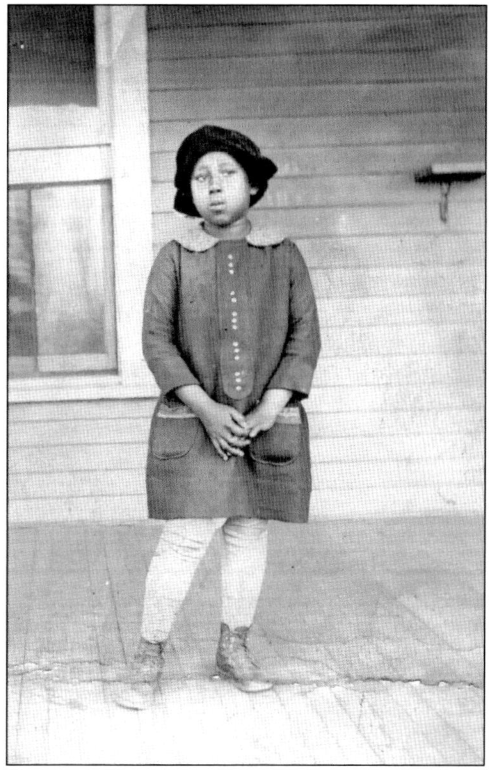

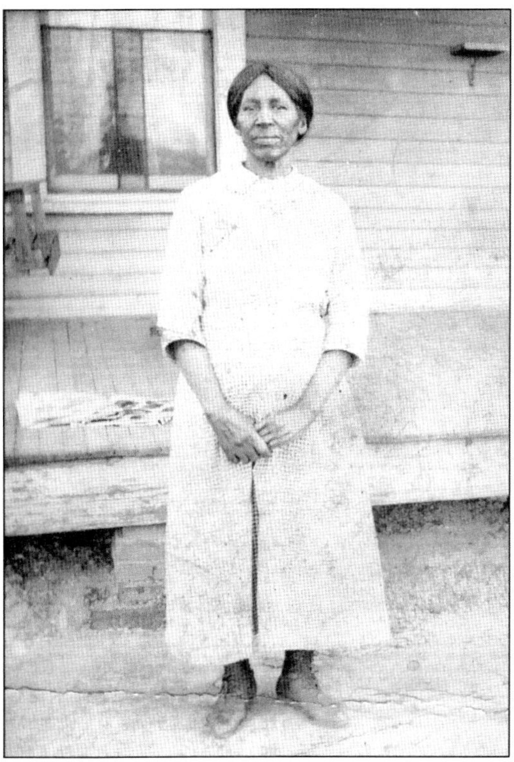

Hester Patterson, great-grandmother of James Brooks, stands in front of her house, located at 726 Carlton Street in Gainesville. She had the house constructed between 1907 and 1909. This house has been continually occupied and was renovated by her descendants. Hester Patterson was employed by Brenau College for 43 years, initially as a nurse and later as a maid. Hester died on February 26, 1937 at the age of 80. (Courtesy of James Brooks.)

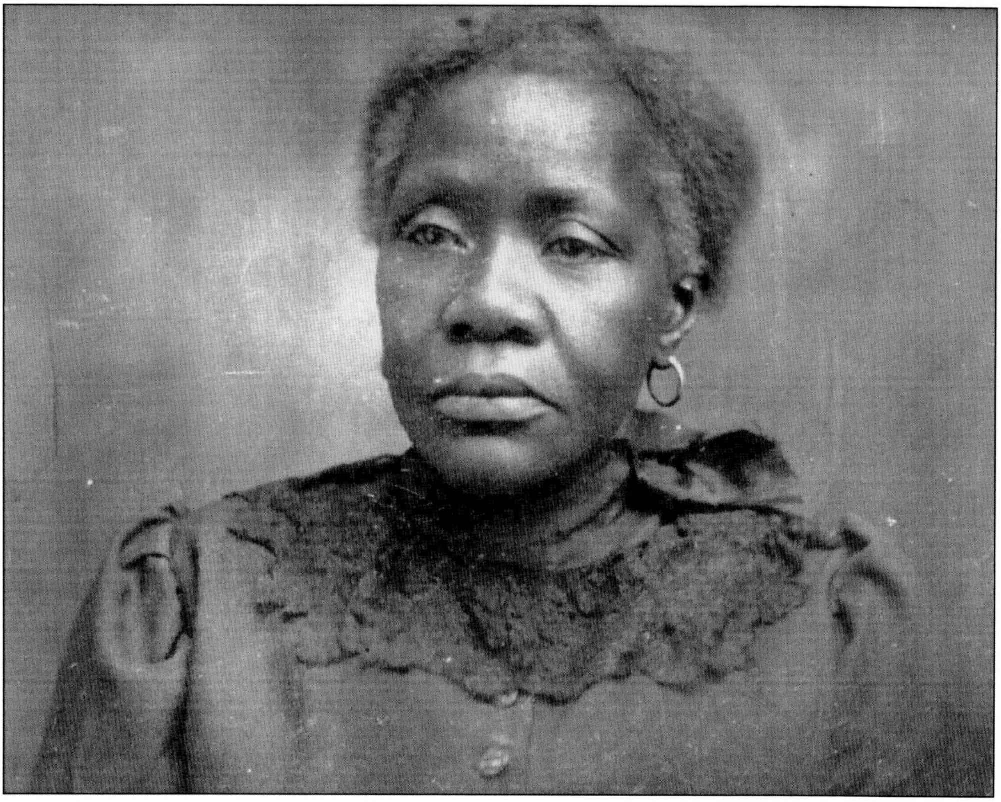

Cornelia Merck was the mother of Richard Carlton Merck, the grandmother of Lydia Merck Barnette, and the great-grandmother of Jennie Porter Harris. (Courtesy of Jennie Harris.)

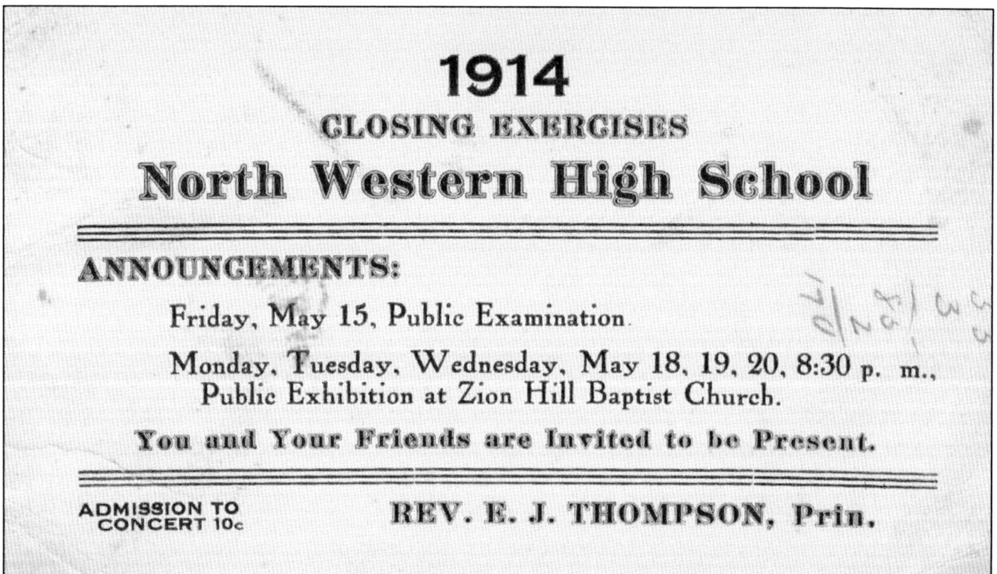

1914

CLOSING EXERCISES

North Western High School

ANNOUNCEMENTS:

Friday, May 15, Public Examination.

Monday, Tuesday, Wednesday, May 18, 19, 20, 8:30 p. m., Public Exhibition at Zion Hill Baptist Church.

You and Your Friends are Invited to be Present.

ADMISSION TO CONCERT 10c

REV. E. J. THOMPSON, Prin.

This invitation was extended to the public to attend the 1914 school term closing exercises for Northwestern High School in Gainesville. (Courtesy of Cathy McCrary Kimbro.)

Gladystine Burt Green is pictured as a first-year high school student in 1927 at Clark College (now Clark Atlanta University) in Atlanta, Georgia. Summer Hill School had only eight grades at this time. African-American students who wanted to continue their high school education had to seek further education elsewhere. The black colleges in Atlanta offered high school educations to students who could somehow manage to pay the tuition. (Courtesy of Gladystine Green.)

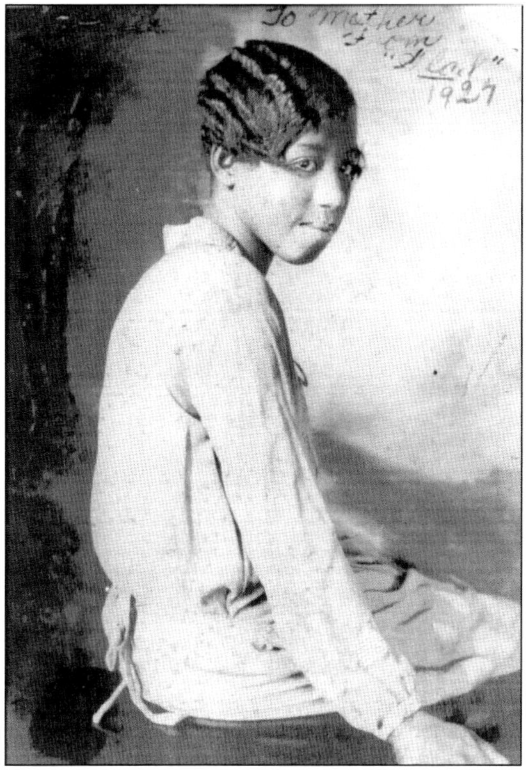

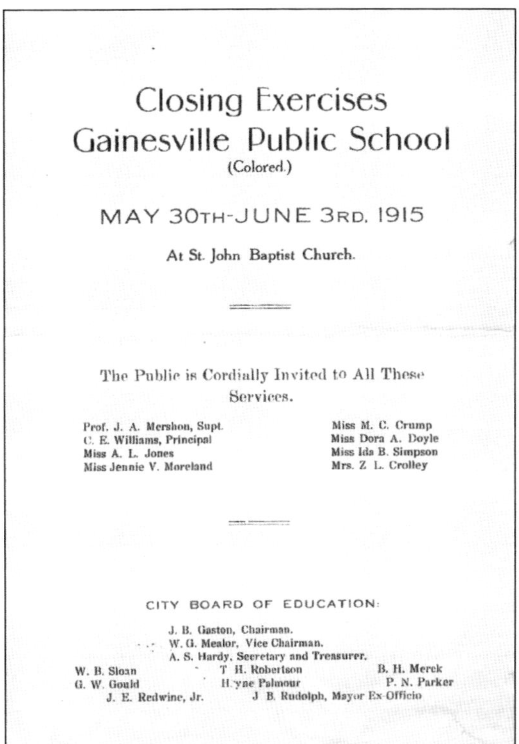

Closing Exercises
Gainesville Public School
(Colored.)

MAY 30TH-JUNE 3RD. 1915

At St. John Baptist Church.

The Public is Cordially Invited to All These Services.

Prof. J. A. Mershon, Supt.
C. E. Williams, Principal
Miss A. L. Jones
Miss Jennie V. Moreland

Miss M. C. Crump
Miss Dora A. Doyle
Miss Ida B. Simpson
Mrs. Z L. Crolley

CITY BOARD OF EDUCATION:

J. B. Gaston, Chairman.
W. G. Mealor, Vice Chairman.
A. S. Hardy, Secretary and Treasurer.
W. B. Sloan T H. Robertson B. H. Merck
G. W. Gould H.yne Palmour P. N. Parker
J. E. Redwine, Jr. J B. Rudolph, Mayor Ex-Officio

In 1915, Gainesville Public Colored School (Summer Hill) held their closing exercises at various neighborhood churches. The closing exercises lasted over a period of five days. This program lists the closing activities scheduled for Summer Hill School. (Courtesy of James Brooks.)

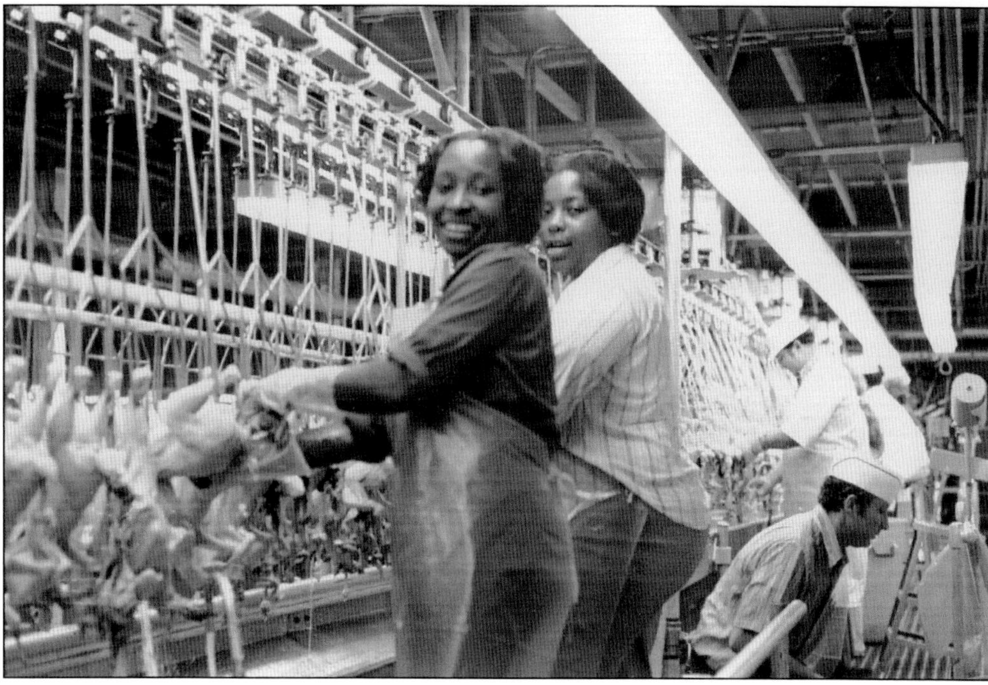

Many African Americans were employed by the poultry industry in the Gainesville area. Linda Harbin Randolph (left), Linda Jones Sheats (right), and two employees of J.D. Jewell Inc. are shown processing chickens in this 1973 photograph. (Courtesy of the Hall County Black History Society.)

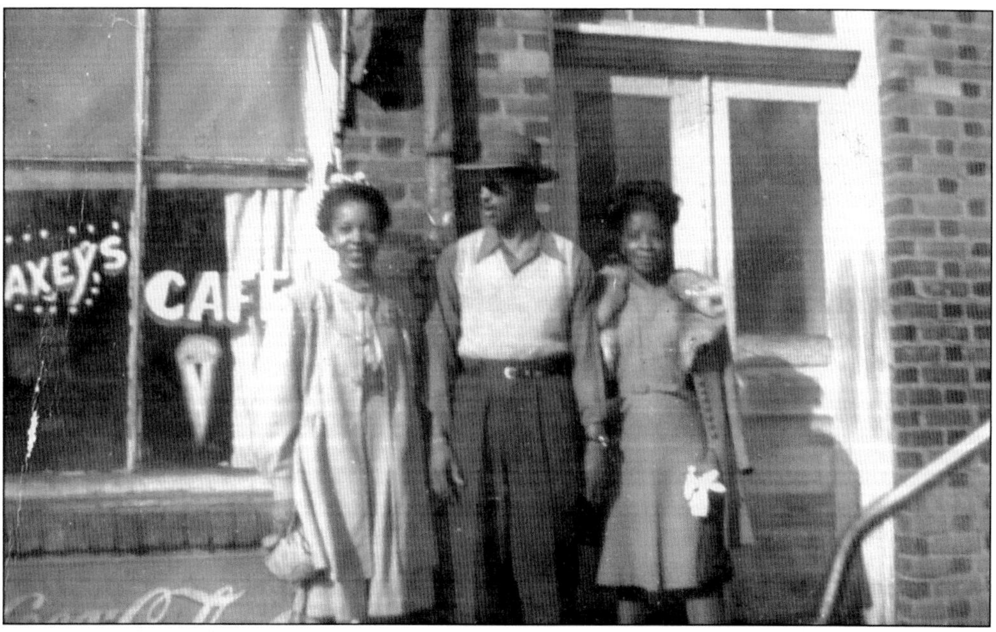

Standing in front of Maxey's Café from left to right are Hilda Hunter, an unidentified man, and Eloise Price. Maxey's Café was located on Athens Street in Gainesville. (Courtesy of Jennie Harris)